HARVARD BUSINESS STUDIES

VOLUME II

AN APPROACH
TO BUSINESS PROBLEMS

BY

ARCH WILKINSON SHAW, A.M.

LECTURER ON BUSINESS POLICY IN
HARVARD UNIVERSITY

EDITOR OF "SYSTEM"

CAMBRIDGE
HARVARD UNIVERSITY PRESS
LONDON : HUMPHREY MILFORD
OXFORD UNIVERSITY PRESS
1916

PREFACE

BEFORE a science of business can take shape, there must first be built up a system of business practice. The methods, plans, and rules of the most efficient organizations must be brought together, tested, and compared, and the most effective must be selected and coördinated. Some of this work has been done. Trade associations, universities, periodicals, and various governmental agencies have been studying the details of production and distribution.

But up to the present, no plan for the guidance of the student in the maze of business practice has been offered. To supply this deficiency, to discover a classification molded on the living activities of business, to supply a uniform method of approach to business problems in whatever form they may arise, and to illustrate the application of this method to typical problems, including those involving the relations of business to society — these are the purposes of this book. I need hardly say that in all this the book makes no claim to finality. If the classification and the uniform method should do no more than suggest improvements upon themselves, the work, I feel, would have been worth while. But I venture to hope also that they will be of some practical value in their present form: that they will make it easier for business men and all thinking men to see each activity of business in its relations to others and to visualize and weigh all the significant factors bearing on any business problem.

PREFACE

The book is a development and rearrangement of materials used in a course of lectures begun by the writer six years ago in the Graduate School of Business Administration at Harvard University. It would be difficult to list all the individuals to whom I am indebted for help with the lectures and the book — colleagues at Harvard, members of the staffs of the magazines *System* and *Factory*, and scores of business men with whom I have debated the problems and policies here discussed. In reorganizing and elaborating the lectures and in preparing the present text, I have been aided particularly by Mr. Daniel V. Casey, Dr. Selden O. Martin, Mr. R. E. Coulson, Prof. Homer B. Vanderblue, and Mr. F. M. Feiker. I can conceive no form of acknowledgment, however, which would properly express my obligation to Dean Edwin Francis Gay of the Graduate School of Business Administration at Harvard. Without his inspiration and help, neither the lectures nor the book could have the forms they have taken.

What have been the materials on which we have had to draw for the lectures and the book? To begin with, there were the rules and guiding policies of practical business men — the accumulated knowledge of years of experience and observation. No man ever reaches a position of power and responsibility without formulating certain general truths which he believes fundamental in the conduct of his enterprise. Let a new situation come up, a fresh problem present itself, and he can usually marshal this fund of information to an effective settlement. Yet ordinarily he can contribute little that is positive and general in application, outside his own factory, office, or store. Men of

PREFACE

larger mold, to be sure, have viewed things nearer their real proportions and have enunciated rules of action more broadly true and applicable. But many of these precepts even, like that of Marshall Field, "The customer is always right," must be accepted with reservations, although they have profoundly influenced merchandising ideals.

So with many business proverbs and maxims. One frequently hears, for example, that "Goods well bought are half sold." Yet this is misleading unless good buying comprehends a knowledge of all the complex conditions which govern the market. Cheapness alone is not a final test of good buying, for the loss from overstocking in order to secure price concessions may more than counterbalance a price advantage. Applying the proverb in a mere mechanical way, therefore, might bring loss, if not disaster.

Of broader usefulness for our purpose have been the generalizations contributed by economic theory, which, as one of their greatest services, give a sense of direction to business thought. The important law of diminishing returns, for example, declares that beyond a certain fixed point increased expenditure secures less than a proportional increase in product. Cultivating a market, that is to say, is much like cultivating a field. Two "doses" of capital and labor may not bring twice the returns of a single adequate "dose"; there is a point at which the rate of return falls behind the rate of increase in expense. Applying this principle to the field of business, we find, for instance, that the larger the number of salesmen in a given territory, the larger ordinarily will be the total number of orders. At some points, however, the orders per salesman fall,

PREFACE

although the expense per salesman holds relatively constant. In time, the point is reached where the return falls below the point of profitable expenditure. Other such generalizations have been drawn upon, and still others proposed, in the body of the book.

But, after all, it is by observing the complex and multiform activities of business itself that we can best discover and verify the reactions and relations of all these activities, and check and organize the knowledge we already possess.

CONTENTS

INTRODUCTION

CHAPTER I

Every activity of business represents the application of motion to materials. When we inquire the *purpose* of each motion, we find it identifying itself with one of three groups of activities, production, distribution, or administration. The classification as an aid to finding useless motions, that they may be eliminated, and determining others that may be usefully added. Because production is concerned more with tangible factors and is better understood and systematized than either distribution or administration, this book will develop and demonstrate a systematic approach to problems in the first group and then apply it to those in the last two. Operating through all departments of any business, however, will be found the fundamental principles of interdependence and balance, giving rise to the manager's need of a strategic position overlooking and controlling all departments but free from routine concern with the details of any. Not only larger profit but also a larger measure of individual and social freedom the reasonable effect of the observance of these and other principles.

CHAPTER II

The activities of production divide according to their purpose into plant and operating activities, the former concerned respectively with location, construction, and equipment of the plant, and the latter with materials, agencies, and the organization of factory processes. In administration and in each of the two larger divisions of distribution, namely, demand creation and physical supply, corresponding sub-groups of activities are found. This, then, is a detail outline, a diagram, if you please, of business activities, at every point of which practical problems arise. Qualities of thought which help or hinder in the solution of these problems. Distinctive success largely a matter of small advantages consistently cultivated and conserved. The principle of cumulative differentials. The four steps in the systematic approach to business problems: (1) elimination — or at least recognition — of the personal factor; (2) separation of the problem into its constituent problems; (3) listing the factors; and (4) taking a fresh point of view. Illustrations of each.

CONTENTS

PART I

THE PROBLEMS OF PRODUCTION

CHAPTER III

The systematic approach is applied to the problem of selecting a site for a factory. A number of factors bearing on the suitability of any factory location are indicated, including: accessibility of raw material sources and of markets; control and cost of the more conveniently situated raw materials; labor supply and current wages in the locality; peculiar financial advantages, if any; adaptability of the type of building to the business needs, to the site; lighting conditions; water supply; drainage facilities; accessibility of a suitable residence district for employees; factory laws; taxes; insurance rates; fire protection, etc. Analysis and listing of factors illustrated from the experience of a silverware factory and a drain tile plant. Relative advantages of locations at and away from trade centers.

CHAPTER IV

The same approach is applied to the problems of choosing the best kind of building and of selecting the most suitable equipment for it. Among the considerations involved in the former are: the relative advantages of single-story, multi-story, hollow square, oblong, and other styles of buildings, and of brick, steel, concrete, mill, and other kinds of construction, taking into account the funds available, the types of machinery to be installed, and the site adopted. The availability of any type of building and of any kind of building material will be influenced by the weights of raw materials and manufactured parts to be moved, the cost of moving them from floor to floor as compared with that of horizontal movement, the need of daylight illumination, the exigencies of assembling, the probable growth of the building, its salability, and other indicated factors. Illustrations from a New England weaving mill, a Detroit stove foundry, and other plants. Factors bearing on the choice of equipment, in turn, include: initial cost and cost of upkeep, output, patent rights, safety, etc.

CHAPTER V

A factory's policy as to materials must be determined by analysis of conditions having to do with (1) the kind of material to be used, (2) the quality of material, (3) possible sources, (4) control, and (5) utilization in the factory. The kind selected should depend on future as well as present

CONTENTS

conditions, on the probability of continued supplies of raw materials at reasonable prices, and the possibility of introducing a satisfactory substitute in case of shortage as well as on present salability and service. In determining the quality, the management must be governed largely by financial and marketing considerations — the selling price and the profit per unit of output. By control is meant, particularly, the maintaining of proper quantities and balance of raw stock on hand. The carrying of excessive raw stocks, according to efficiency engineers, is a common fault in American factories. The problem of utilization, in turn, is finally solved only when the last by-product is used to the best advantage. The value of laboratory standards. The systematic approach as an aid in solving each of the five phases of the problem

CHAPTER VI

The management's problem as to its factory workers is to overcome whatever indifference, suspicion, or antagonism they may entertain toward it and to make clear that loyalty to the company is compatible with loyalty to themselves and to labor organizations, where such organizations exist. The most effective appeal is pay scientifically proportioned to individual effort. In working out such a wage system the management must hold to its established ratio of cost, quality, and service, cutting down cost where it consistently can. The great defect of the traditional day rate is that it offers no direct incentive to the individual to exert himself to his full capacity. The ordinary piece rate, without at least an approximation to scientific standards, gives too much play to the personal factor in fixing rates. Among the improvements on these methods the chapter discusses the Franklin, Towne, Rowan, Halsey, Emerson, and Taylor systems. Industrial training as a further incentive to the workman and as a policy profitable to the plant. New outlook and opportunities opened to workmen by the training incidental to scientific management. Various systems of instruction supplied by individual plants alone and in coöperation with schools and universities. Eliminating the personal factor is nowhere more desirable than in dealing with unions. Thrift clubs, "welfare work," variation of employment, and other means for reducing labor turnover.

CHAPTER VII

This chapter considers the various methods of delegating authority in a factory, the management's broad problem here being to distribute authority and supervision effectively and at the same time retain control. Three distinct types of shop organization are found in practice: (1) the line, (2) the functional, and, midway between the two, (3) the line-and-staff. In line organization, which is the traditional form, each department and sub-department head is held responsible for everything within his jurisdiction. His functions are thus of many kinds: hiring the men, placing them, planning and apportioning the work, fixing the payment, watching the machines,

CONTENTS

and so on. The functional type, on the contrary, is the strict application of the principal of the division of labor to shop management. First, it separates planning from performance. Then each is subjected to subdivision of responsibility. In a typical functional scheme, the planning is divided among an order-of-work clerk, an instruction-card man, a time-and-cost clerk, and a shop disciplinarian, while the direction of performance is divided among a gang boss, a speed boss, a repair boss, and an inspector. A line-and-staff organization may represent any one of a variety of compromises between the line and functional types. Some one of the three types must be best adapted to each individual business; the systematic approach helps to determine which.

PART II

THE PROBLEMS OF DISTRIBUTION

CHAPTER VIII

Since the time when barter and sale by bulk ceased to be the universal rule, distribution has embraced the two distinct functions of demand creation and physical supply. The former is the process of communicating to prospective consumers ideas about the goods that will arouse desire for them and the latter is that of transferring the goods to the consumer. The close relation of the two functions again illustrates the principles of interdependence and balance. To find markets rather than to supply those already active is in general the more difficult problem of business today. Until within recent years, the reverse was true. The long period during which the pressure was upon production rather than distribution accounts in part for the fact that distribution is now less systematized. The factors in distribution, including the agencies of demand creation and physical supply, being more imperfectly understood than those in production, it follows that the management must give them more of its attention. The history of barter, sale by bulk, sale by sample, and sale by description sketched. Improved machinery, education, and means of communication among the factors in the development. Broadly, the problem of distribution is to arouse the desired maximum of demand at a minimum of expense, and to supply this demand with the least possible leakage.

SECTION I — DEMAND CREATION

CHAPTER IX

The method of approach to the problems of locating, building, and equipping a plant, developed in the production section of this book, is here applied to the corresponding problems of demand creation. Shall the

CONTENTS

selling plant be located at the factory, at the largest neighboring city, at the largest trade market, or at the chief city of the country? What type and size of quarters shall it occupy? How shall they be equipped? All these questions are considered from the standpoints of the production, administrative, and distributive departments of the business. Illustrations from the furniture and other trades. Construction and equipment problems, in particular, are governed by considerations similar to those applicable to factory construction. Advertising value as a factor.

CHAPTER X

Following the order of the classification, this chapter takes up the first of the operating activities of demand creation, those having to do with materials. The materials of demand creation are ideas which, when put into circulation by certain available agencies, will cause consumers to want the goods — the agencies being middlemen, salesmen, and direct and general advertising. The ideas can be handled as definite, almost tangible things. The effect they may be expected to produce can be determined with a degree of accuracy not yet generally realized. Moreover, they can be classified, indexed, and filed for future use. Like the materials of production, the ideas must be considered from the standpoints of their (1) kind, (2) quality, (3) sources, (4) control, and (5) utilization. Certain elements of good and bad practice in these various phases of the problem are discussed. The problem is further concerned, as in production, with the adoption and development of laboratory standards. Practical methods of testing ideas by direct advertising and the law of averages are described and illustrated. Results of tests uphold these methods. Similar laboratory tests through salesmen and other agencies are practicable.

CHAPTER XI

Beyond obtaining the most effective ideas for demand creation, the manager's problem is to determine which of the available agencies — middlemen, exclusive salesmen, and direct and general advertising — are adapted to transmit the ideas most effectively to possible purchasers. One, two, or even all of the agencies may be used by a business. The tendency of many producers to go around the middleman is considered in the light of the development of the middleman system. The necessary functions the middleman performs: sharing the risks; transporting the goods; financing the operations; selling or creating demand; and assembling, resorting, and shipping the goods. The rise of other agencies for performing these functions: insurance companies, express companies and the parcel post, commercial banking, direct salesmen, advertising mediums and agencies, factory warehouses and branches, etc. The middleman's reluctance to reduce his percentage of profit as certain of his functions have been assumed by other agencies — the function of demand creation by producer advertising, for

CONTENTS

example — is one cause of the growth of direct selling. His aversion (in many instances) to new brands, based often on what from his point of view are sound enough reasons, is another. The most effective answers of middlemen to the tendency have been combinations for buying, the adoption of house brands, controlling factories, and manufacturing on their own account. Summed up, the movement as a whole is one of consolidation, on the part of trade as well as of industry, its natural effect being the reduction of distributive wastes.

CHAPTER XII

Where the character, quality, or use of an article is not evident but requires the demonstration or development of ideas unfamiliar to the trade and the consumer, the work of transmitting its selling points to the final user through two or more middlemen becomes difficult and uncertain. Hence, for an increasing variety of non-staple articles, the direct salesman is recognized as an essential agent in demand creation. The producer's initial problem as to a direct sales force is to determine whether such a force is necessary to create a maximum demand for his goods with a minimum outlay of money. Once he has decided to use direct salesmen, he finds that his problems with them, as with factory workmen, center about four chief points of contact with the men: (1) hiring, (2) training, (3) paying, and (4) directing. Psychologists and business men are not as yet agreed on anything approaching scientific tests for salesmen, and so the average employer still depends on personal "sizing up," together with records of past performances. While the saying, "A salesman is born, not made," reflects a certain truth, it is more significant that the effectiveness of salesmen can be multiplied by intelligent training. Methods of training described. The value of standardized selling points and processes reëmphasized. The broad problem of paying and handling is to keep the salesman exerting his best efforts after he has achieved what he conceives to be his standard. Standards based on close analysis of selling areas are part of the solution. Sales contests are useful in some circumstances and inadvisable in others. To pay a salesman too much or to pay him the right amount in the wrong way may produce as bad results as paying him too little. Relative advantages of salary and commission payment. As with factory labor, again, the best payment is in general that which is most scientifically proportioned to individual effort and results. But the management can never have a satisfactory relation with its salesmen unless back of all its methods is a genuine friendliness for the men.

CHAPTER XIII

Advertising is an outgrowth of sale by description. It may be employed either as a substitute for middlemen and salesmen, for purposes of demand creation, or as an auxiliary to aid them in their exercise of the selling function. It tends to displace these other agencies, in whole or in part, whenever it is a less expensive or more effective means of communicating ideas to the

CONTENTS

consumer. Illustrations showing how it justifies itself from the social as well as the business point of view. When waste occurs in advertising, it is generally due to one of five things: lack in the product of those elements of quality and service which appeal to the consuming public's need or desire, ignorance of the true function of advertising, blundering application of recognized principles, failure to develop laboratory standards for ideas, or neglect to keep in operating balance the other essential agencies of distribution. The characteristics which peculiarly commend advertising are its expansive reach, its economy, and the complete control it allows the management over the presentation of ideas to prospective buyers. Factors bearing on the formulation of a policy as to advertising.

CHAPTER XIV

The problems incident to organizing for demand creation fall into three groups, which are concerned respectively with analysis of the market, fixing a price for the goods, and the combination and coördination of agencies, each of the three groups being an important factor in the others. The business man's broad problem in analyzing his market is to find where his product can be marketed profitably, and in approximately what quantities. In approaching the problem, he finds an indefinite body of possible purchasers, widely distributed geographically, living under the various conditions of town and country, and exhibiting various degrees of purchasing power and intelligence, various tastes and beliefs and both conscious and unconscious demand. Every locality in which it is proposed to distribute his product should be examined with respect to these and still other conditions. The method of examination illustrated. Tests of typical localities give typical reactions, and thus show, at relatively small cost, the desirability or undesirability of using the same policy in a larger field. How a market analysis made it possible to equalize the seasons of a department store. A suggestive list of factors to be considered in analyzing a market.

CHAPTER XV

Not the cost of production but the requirements of the market are the primary consideration in fixing prices. The manager has the choice of three general price policies: (1) selling at the market minus, (2) selling at the market par, and (3) selling at the market plus. The first policy aims to increase volume of sales by reducing price. Ordinarily, it does not involve differentiation from other stock products of like nature. Selling at the market minus is the easy method of securing distribution, although other than economic motives govern sales in many instances and the middleman's indifference becomes an obstacle unless it is turned into active interest by the prospect of larger profit on the new article. Subject to certain restrictions, the policy tends not only to draw purchasers away from competitive

CONTENTS

goods but to bring new purchasers into the market. To sell at the market par, the merchant must, in general, differentiate his product from those of his competitors and build up a particular demand for it. Under this policy, new purchasers may be drawn into the market by giving the product an added importance in their eyes. Selling at the market plus is perhaps the most characteristic feature of modern distribution. It makes the severest demands on the ability of the distributer and offers correspondingly great rewards for success. Usually the product is more effectively differentiated, more closely adapted to human needs or desires, and the large profits it sometimes brings — not infrequently out of all proportion to the added cost of manufacturing the article — may be regarded as the price society pays for this special service.

CHAPTER XVI

The agency that is most effective for demand creation in one geographic or economic or social division of the market may not be so in another. The manager's problem in this field, therefore, is to determine not merely which agency is most effective in any single section or which will serve passably for all sections, but what combination of agencies is most effective for the entire market. The method of sale — by bulk, sample, or description — as a factor in the choice of agencies. Facilities and difficulties offered by middle men. In directly assuming the burden of demand creation, the manufacturer has the choice of two agencies, an exclusive sales force and direct or general advertising. Combination of the two is often desirable, because, while advertising has the broader reach, the direct salesman can adapt himself more precisely to individual cases. And while advertising usually allows the more careful arrangement of ideas, the salesman has the advantage of spontaneity and personal presence. The salesman's function is often to follow up "leads" that result from advertising. Salesmen and direct advertising may also be used separately or together in combination with middlemen. When all are used, it may be preferable for the middleman to devote himself altogether to physical supply or to coöperate with the others in demand creation. The interest of each agency no less than of the purchasing public is served best when each agency assumes the functions which it can most efficiently perform.

SECTION II — PHYSICAL SUPPLY

CHAPTER XVII

The broad problem of physical supply is to satisfy the maximum of aroused demand with minimum demand leakage and expense, present and future sales both being considered. If minimum leakage of demand is to be attained — and it is extremely important — the principles of inter-

CONTENTS

dependence and balance must be observed consistently as between production, physical supply, and demand creation, that the first two may keep pace with the last. The activities of physical supply, like those of production and demand creation, break up into plant and operating activities, and these, in turn, into corresponding sub-groups. Warehouses and their attendant shipping facilities are the plant. The goods themselves are the materials. And the agencies may be: (1) functional middlemen in the transportation field, including railroads, express companies, and the parcel post; (2) areal middlemen, including wholesalers and retailers; or (3) agencies of direct supply, including branch houses and exclusive agencies or retail stores. The organization sub-group embraces those persons and arrangements through which physical supply is immediately directed and supervised. The systematic approach indicated for each sub-group, and characteristic factors suggested.

PART III

THE PROBLEMS OF ADMINISTRATION

CHAPTER XVIII

The facilitating operations of business, including those having to do with finance, purchasing, employment, credits, collections, accounting and auditing, suggest unit handling under a common executive, with authority corresponding to that of the factory superintendent and sales manager within their fields, or at least recognition of their equality as a group with the other two major divisions of business. This view simplifies the maintenance of interdepartmental balance and contributes to efficiency. The activities of the administrative group break up in accordance with the general classification and yield themselves to the systematic approach. The nature and conditions of the various sub-groups of activities considered. The character and scale of the business help to define their scope. The manager's position, aloof from routine concern with facilitating activities as well as those of the other departments, leaves him free to sense and solve the larger activities of his business.

CONCLUSION

CHAPTER XIX

The business executive of today is not the autocrat of a private undertaking, able to base his policies on personal whim or desire or an entirely selfish conception of business. Society is asking more seriously than ever before, what besides the market minimum of value and service at the price he is going to supply as *its* profit on *its* investment of community machinery and opportunity. Besides the internal problems of business, therefore, the

CONTENTS

manager has also a pressing set of external problems to solve. These problems have to do not merely with the shaping of legislation, but with public opinion, upon which the laws are formed. His task is not only to influence public opinion, but to be influenced by it in the formulation of his policies, whenever justice and prudence dictates that course. Recent business legislation considered. Mutual understanding between business and society and cooperation in behalf of the common interest is the great solution.

INTRODUCTION

AN APPROACH TO BUSINESS PROBLEMS

CHAPTER I

THE ACTIVITIES OF BUSINESS

WHEN a workman in a factory directs the cut of a planer in a malleable steel casting, he is operating on a piece of raw material for the purpose of changing its form.

When a clerk in a store passes over the counter to the consumer a package of factory-cooked food, his operation is one that results in change of place.

When a typist at his desk makes out an invoice covering a shipment of merchandise, he is operating, not to change the form of matter or the place of commodities, but to facilitate these changes.

Isolate any phase of business, strike into it anywhere, and the invariable essential element will be found to be the application of motion to materials. This may be stated, if you will, as the simplest general concept to which all the activities of manufacturing, selling, finance, and management can ultimately be reduced.

Starting with this simple concept, then, it becomes evident that we have an easy and obvious basis for the classification of business activities. With the philo-

1

sophical aspects of the concept itself I am not here concerned. Sufficient that it gives us a simplifying, unifying principle from which to proceed, instead of a mere arrangement by kind or characteristic, of the materials, men, operations, and processes which we see in the various departments of a business enterprise.

The nature of the motion does not of itself supply the key to a usable classification. For while the action may be characteristic of one part of a business and not duplicated elsewhere, like the pouring of molten metal in a foundry or the making up of a payroll, it may, on the contrary, be common to all the departments into which the organization is divided, like the requisition of a dozen lead pencils or a box of paper clips. It is not until we single out the common fundamental element and inquire "What is the *purpose* of this motion?" that we find the key.

I do not wish to exaggerate the importance of this simple and apparently obvious idea; but for me it has opened a way to locate the activities of business and disclose their relations to one another and to their common object, and so has proved a thing of daily use. For the final function of the classification, as it is the practical problem of all business, is to find those motions which are purposeless, so that they may be eliminated, and to discover new motions of sound purpose, that they may be introduced.

If you study an individual motion or operation in itself and in relation to the other activities surrounding it and no satisfactory answer can be found to the question, "What is its purpose?" you have strong grounds for assuming that it is a non-essential and useless motion. It may have the sanction of house tradition or trade custom, but its superfluous character persists and the wisdom of eliminating it becomes plain. Conversely, a motion proposed for adoption may never before have been tried in the trade, but that alone is not an argument against it. Purpose again is the decisive test. From the social standpoint, any motion which has no valid purpose is economically useless and wrong. The effect of such a motion in business, like the effect of omitting a useful motion, is to keep down profits when they might reasonably rise.

From the manager's point of view, then, the purpose of the analysis is not alone to place the activities of business and trace out their relations, but to order his thought so that he can more readily see what activities he should discontinue and what others he should add.

This does not always mean a reduction in the total number of motions. In our roundabout system of production,[1] with its minute subdivision of labor, it is possible to make a greater number and variety of motions and distribute them over a longer period of time, yet increase the eventual output or decrease the cost through the group effectiveness of all the motions.

In the three operations mentioned above — those of the factory workman, the retail clerk, and the office typist — each application of motion was for an economically valid purpose and each instance was typical of one of the three great groups of business activities:

1. The activities of *production*, which change the form of materials.

2. The activities of *distribution*, which change the place and ownership of the commodities thus produced.

3. The *facilitating* activities, which aid and supple-

[1] See E. V. Bohm-Bawerk, "Positive Theory of Capital," pp. 17–20.

ment the operations of production and distribution. No adequate descriptive term suggests itself; *facilitation* is awkward, *administration* is inexact because it suggests all the relations of the management to a business rather than a separate group of functions toward which the manager should maintain the same sort of relations as with those of production and distribution. I shall, however, for convenience use the term administration in this narrower sense.

Whatever the nature or kind of any business activity, its final effect is one of the three just indicated. Such a categorical grouping is necessary in any schematic approach to the problems of business; for out of the relations of these activities, each with the others and with the materials affected, emerge those problems with which this book is concerned.

Before we take up the study of the individual problems, it may be well to make a brief general survey of the three groups and note certain likenesses and differences that characterize these groups of activities.

Production is relatively well standardized. In any scrutiny of practical business, it becomes clear that the manager concerns himself less with the activities of production than with those of distribution and administration. The problems of the factory as a rule demand, on his part, less of analysis and synthesis, less of study and experiment and constructive thought because production has been brought much nearer to standardization in its operations and policies.

For upwards of a century economic conditions directed the attention of the ablest business minds to the perfection of manufacturing processes rather than the development of sales methods. The market expanded

4

fast enough to absorb the increased offerings: the big prizes went to the men who could speed up production without adding to the expense of a unit of product. Improvement of factory methods and processes, too, was the manifest way to economy and profit. The factors involved — machines, materials, the actions of men — were all concrete, visible things which daily thrust themselves on the attention of the manager. Short cuts almost suggested themselves. Lost motions and other inefficient applications of human or mechanical energy made themselves apparent to men of open minds and demanded study until the wastes were reduced and better methods inaugurated. Because every operation was easily distinguishable from every other one, the advantages attending the division of labor were discovered and the application of the principle extended. This took place, however, without affecting the processes of distribution in any marked degree.

As a consequence of this century of invention, development, and refinement, production is, in point of systematized economy, far more advanced than distribution. Moreover, there have developed, on the factory side, recognized classes of specialists — technically trained superintendents, engineers, chemists, designers, foremen — who are capable of assuming, and frequently do assume, all the responsibilities of production.

In distribution and administration there enters a different set of factors, more largely psychological. Men meet not only as units in a business organization — as colleagues, subordinates, and superiors — but also in the delicate personal relations of seller and buyer. Production problems are usually problems involving the cost of materials, of labor, of equipment, and so on. In distribution, on the contrary, the factor of cost is over-shadowed by that of price, and the latter is determined largely, at times, by changing conditions over which the seller has very little control. Competition, encountered to some extent in the field of production, in the hiring of men, the buying of materials and the like, is in the field of distribution almost ever-present and frequently acute.

Finally, there are few trained experts in distribution and administration, and few absolute standards of practice, except perhaps in the special field of accounting. The approach to the problems of these groups, therefore, as contrasted with those of production, is still largely empirical.

It would seem, then, the logical plan to consider first the activities of production, since here conditions, reactions, and results have been reduced to something like accepted standards; then, after developing and demonstrating in this known and charted field a method of analysis, a standard classification and a systematic approach to business problems, to apply this approach and analysis to distribution and administration, about which so much less is known and the factors of which are all less tangible, less understood, and more variable.

The function of the general manager of a business is to coördinate and direct these three groups of activities. Therefore it is practical as well as convenient that we should approach them from his point of view, the course of our approach itself indicating what that point of view should be. This will bring out and establish the permanent strategic position he should occupy toward all three. Further, in treating general policies involving coördination of the problems arising under each, a uniform method of approach will be outlined and applied.

Every manager maintains and must maintain certain definite policies toward production, distribution, and administration. In determining what these policies shall be, there are at least two basic principles of which he must never lose sight. The first of these is the interdependence of all business activities. Each has relations more or less direct with all other activities. No problem can be solved, therefore, without making allowances for the connection the solution may have with other problems.

In their broader aspects, this mutual interdependence extends to all the activities of production, distribution, and administration. No business problems are strictly intradepartmental. They all have implications reaching out and affecting activities in other departments. The extent and importance of these is unobserved by many managers at present; hence, most businesses are out of adjustment.

Every man of experience will recognize this interdependence, I think, as a fundamental principle in business. Likewise the corollary principle, that a balance must be maintained in these relations. The ratio of cost, quality, and service observed in the actual manufacture of a product, for example, must be the same as that put forward by the sales force. Otherwise customers will be dissatisfied, internal friction will develop, and efficiency, good will, and profits will suffer. If, on a scale of 100, the stress on quality stands at 60 in the production department, it must stand at 60 in the distribution and the administration departments. The credit policy must balance with the production policy, the purchasing with

7

the selling, and the selling, again, with the production; and so on. If production is under pressure to manufacture at low cost with relative indifference to quality, while distribution bases its appeals upon quality and service, the business is clearly out of adjustment. The production force is not delivering the kind of thing that the distribution force is trying to sell.

The lack of proper adjustment and balance in many businesses is not surprising when we remember that the average business exists because the man behind it is a specialist. He has capitalized his buyer's instinct for values, his salesman's tact and enthusiasm, or his ability and patience as a shop organizer. He has built on this special talent and comes to depend on it too exclusively. This departmental bias, if permitted to run its course, carries the grave consequences of a failure in efficiency. The department on which the manager concentrates must carry the burden of those he neglects; as a consequence, the growth of the business is impaired.

Perhaps the worst effect of departmental bias is seen in what might be called the tangential development that takes place in certain cases of joint or composite management, where, for instance, a man strong in selling takes for a partner a man strong in production, and the two proceed to manage the business together, each stressing his specialty without regard for the principle of interdependence. Instead of a straight parallel pull toward a common goal, such as observance of the principle of interdependence would insure, their pull becomes more and more tangential, their angles with the business become wider and wider, until finally each is pulling squarely against the other, and the business comes to a standstill.

THE ACTIVITIES OF BUSINESS

I once heard a production engineer in New York speak of selling as a "necessary evil." The owner of a great business who was present disagreed with him and said quite as emphatically that selling was the one vital function. Knowing that the sales enthusiast had built up a remarkable business from a small beginning, I took the trouble to check his statements about his company's experience. What I found was this. The owner personally concentrated on selling and honestly believed that selling was the function which contributed most to the success of a business. But he had instinctively gotten hold of the principle of interdependence, and had surrounded himself with men in other departments who were strong in their lines and who supplemented his own specialty without straying into tangential development. Thus the activities of production and administration were properly coördinated with those of distribution. The business was a success because the owner had unconsciously observed the principle of interdependence without formulating it or perhaps without being aware that it was something to be formulated.

A very commonplace illustration will show how intimately the principles of interdependence and balance apply in the mere routine detail of department policy, and also show how rapidly the manager's thought must pass from considerations involving the one principle to those involving the other. Take the case of a concern proposing to install an automatic conveyor in its factory. Here are some of the questions which a consideration of these principles should bring at once to the mind of the manager:

Is the estimated charge for interest, upkeep, and depreciation more than the present cost for trucking? If

9

so, of how much importance is this factor of added expense? To what degree does the additional tax on capital operate against the change? If speedier work can be done in the shop, quicker delivery and a more rapid turnover may cut the overhead to counterbalance the added expense. How important, then, is quicker delivery as a factor in distribution?

What will be the effect on the rest of the production process? Will the automatic conveyor facilitate or retard the progress of parts or partly finished goods from machine to machine or department to department? Will a fixed rate of progress for work lead to carelessness and hurry in any section and the possible sacrifice of quality? Or will the conveyor, by reason of the more even flow of work in process, contribute to both quality and service? Will there, finally, be an advertising advantage in the use of the conveyor, like the "untouched-by-human-hands" argument which in the case of a food product might be a distinct factor in the popular estimate of its desirability?

Here we may plainly see to what extent an apparently intra-departmental problem spreads out and becomes inter-departmental; and also how the constituent factors should be judged with due regard for a balance between cost, quality, and service.

Since so much depends on strict conformity to these two principles, the manager should be placed where he can observe them impartially. He should occupy a detached, supervisory position over all departments, free from routine concern with the details of any. Or, if the business is small and it is necessary for him to serve also as a department official, he should cultivate the habit of withdrawing mentally to the position here indicated when performing his managerial functions. I was careful to say that the manager should be free from *routine* concern with departmental details, because he will probably spend the greater part of his time dealing with symptomatic details whose importance is not to be measured by their size or the amount involved. A customer's complaint involving thirty-five cents may in itself be a trifle. If it points the way to a weak link in distribution, however, and this in turn shows a corresponding lack of coördination in production or administration, it becomes significant and presents a problem for the manager.

In the position described, aloof from the various groups of his business activities, the manager can more readily free himself of the tendency toward bias, which is exceedingly strong when he keeps a routine connection with any one department, or involves himself anywhere in non-symptomatic detail. He can keep a clear vision and true perspective of the whole field. He can coördinate the functions of the three departments, shaping them all in accordance with the relations which he wishes to maintain between his business and the public. It is only from such a detached position, indeed, that he can see clearly what these relations should be; can take from the public the suggestions and incentives which he needs, and can gain a broad and comprehensive view of the workings of his own organization and the possibilities of the markets that it serves.

I have said of the principles of interdependence and balance that at least these two should be observed by every manager. Are there not other principles just as simple and profitable as these, some already known to business practice but others yet to be detected and defined? Is it too much to hope that the movement of analytical business thought may in time distinguish a whole body of business principles — principles now operating unnoticed wherever there is a factory, a store, or an office? Not, it seems to me, until we gain by some such process a clearer understanding of the forces with which we are dealing can we realize the fullness of individual and social freedom into which industry is capable of bringing us.

CHAPTER II

A METHOD OF APPROACH TO BUSINESS PROBLEMS

WE have seen that every activity of business, whatever its nature, will find itself in one of three great groups of business activities, — production, distribution, or administration. On closer examination, it is seen that the activities of each group yield themselves to a further classification, and that this classification is almost identical for each group.

Thus the activities of production split according to their purpose into those having to do with the preparation of a ready-to-run factory, which for convenience we may call plant activities, and those having to do with the operation of the factory, which will be termed operating activities. Plant activities divide into those concerned with (1) location, (2) construction, and (3) equipment of the plant. Operating activities are those relating directly to (1) materials, (2) the agencies processing the materials, with labor as the first to be considered, and (3) the coördination and direction of factory processes.

In distribution, two distinct functions dictate a broad preliminary division. One of these, demand creation, is concerned with the making of a market for the goods, through the transmission of ideas about them to possible purchasers. The other function, that of physical supply, consists of the operations necessary to put the buyer in possession of the goods. But the activities of each of these groups break up into two sub-groups like those of production: plant activities, which are occupied with location, construction, and equipment, and operating activities, which relate to materials, agencies, and organization. The materials of demand creation are ideas about the goods; in physical supply they are the actual merchandise delivered.

Again, in the third major division of business, the activities of administration group themselves along the same lines as in production and distribution. On the plant side, they closely parallel those of demand creation, because of the physical likeness of the functions performed. Operating policies, however, although they have to do with the usual three groups of activities — materials, agencies, and organization — are governed in part by factors which do not appear elsewhere. So far as its chief function goes, each administrative department has direct relations with the manufacturing or selling department whose work it facilitates, as well as with the other units of its organization group. In addition, the materials to which motion is applied are paper representations of the activities facilitated.

Here, then, are the three great general groups of business activities, with numerous subordinate groupings under each. All along the lines of the classification, at this point and at that, arise the practical problems of business. Above and outside the groups stands the manager. Keeping constantly in mind the vital principles of interdependence and of balance, his task is to solve these problems.

Before developing a definite method of approach to their solution, however, something may be said about the qualifications and general state of mind of the successful business man. Calm, deliberate analysis is an important factor; imagination, judgment, courage, and executive ability are others. To quote Professor Taussig: "Executive ability is probably less rare than the combination of judgment with imagination. But it is by no means common. It calls, on the one hand, for intelligence in organization; on the other hand, for knowledge of men. The work must be planned, and the right man assigned to each sort of work." [1]

How does the able manager differ from the ordinary business man? Or the conspicuously successful concern from that whose margin of profit is never very wide or safe?

I am inclined to think that the difference between moderate and distinctive success in business is in the main just a sum of individually small advantages. The average employer, for instance, contents himself with the run of the labor market, and pays approximately the market price. The able manager, on the contrary, recognizes that there are many grades of executives, salesmen, mechanics, and clerks, and that the difference in productive capacity between competent and mediocre workers is almost always greater than the difference in the cost of their labor. He makes it his business, therefore, to pick out and hire the best individuals available for each type of service required, going beyond the local market if that supply is unsatisfactory.

From this careful selection of help, he gets his first differential of profit on labor. But it is only the first in a series. He has learned that even skilled and industrious men are capable of much greater effort than, of themselves, they are likely to put forth. His part, then,

[1] F. W. Taussig, "Principles of Economics," Vol. II, page 164.

AN APPROACH TO BUSINESS PROBLEMS

is to supply the conditions and the stimulus which will tap these reserve powers and bring them to bear on the day's work. All along the line, such further differentials come to him: from his control of operations, the quality of the training and supervision he gives his men, the class and condition of his equipment, the convenience and certainty of his system of work-supply, his method of paying for work accomplished, and a host of indirect factors like the lighting, heating, cleaning, and ventilation of his workrooms and offices.

Moreover, all these advantages tend to augment and multiply one another. Greater output is not the only effect of the able manager's discriminating labor policy. He gets also a more even, if not a superior, product. This builds up his "good will" and facilitates sales. Increasing sales and growing prestige in turn invite favors from raw material supply houses, banks, and transportation companies; and these favors tend progressively to greater volume of business, smaller unit costs, and larger profits. So the small advantages, if consistently cultivated and conserved throughout a business, make in the long run an enormous difference.

Here is indicated a further principle, that of cumulative differentials, which no manager can well ignore. For who will say that even the notable innovators, men like McCormick, Field, Henry Ford, the Butlers, and Montgomery Ward, could have developed great ideas into mighty businesses without constant observance of this principle.

But how characterize the unsuccessful? Broadly speaking, there are at least two classes of business men whose inefficiency is due to faults of temper. There is the excitedly busy man who attempts to know every detail, and so loses what is significant in the mass of what is not. His desk is piled with papers. He always insists that no step, however trivial, be taken without his immediate supervision. It is of this kind of inefficiency that Bagehot[1] was thinking when he wrote that if the head of a large business "is very busy, it is a sign of something wrong." Another class of inefficients is composed of the trouble borrowers. Here the typical man anticipates his problems. He expends his energies in worrying about questions which never arise, or when they do arise, solve themselves almost automatically.

As Dean Bailey of Cornell once said in a talk to his students: "Many problems solve themselves if left alone. I suggest that each man give himself lessons in the gentle art of keeping cool." When the crucial time comes, the solution can be worked out in the light of actual conditions rather than of probabilities. Business changes too quickly for the solution of to-day to be of much service to-morrow. Styles, the market, labor conditions may shift. Indeed, the example of Napoleon, who is said to have filed his letters thirty days ahead before answering them, has its moral for many business men. Not that such a policy could be taken over bodily into business. The illustration is extreme. But it serves to emphasize my point. The business man should not go out to meet problems which are not yet due and may never arise. "The great art is to be governed by time," the Corsican genius declared; "that which ought not to be done until 1810 cannot be done in 1801." The energy of the executive must be conserved for the big problems actually before him, which demand the concentration of his best efforts.

[1] Walter Bagehot, "Lombard Street," Chapter VIII.

AN APPROACH TO BUSINESS PROBLEMS

The trouble with a great many men in business is that they have no definite and ordered way of going at their problems. When a new situation or emergency arises, they take counsel with this man and that, waver from one viewpoint to another, and allow themselves to be influenced in one direction or another by the opinions and snap judgments of advisers who have, perhaps, an entirely erroneous conception of the issue involved. Instead of analyzing the problem and locating all the activities which affect and are affected by its solution, they see it only from what appears to be the principal function involved. Lacking a systematic method of approach, they come to a conclusion which sacrifices more advantages, perhaps, than it conserves.

The first step in this approach is the elimination — at least, the recognition — of the personal equation. Immediately a new proposition is brought up, this question almost always intrudes: "How will this affect me personally?" The first reaction is almost sure to be based on personal convenience. Will extra time or extra effort be required? Yet if the business man is to solve his problems scientifically, he must look at them as a scientist looks at his — objectively. This may at first thought seem simple. It is in fact very difficult. Most men cannot detach themselves. Sometimes it requires a determined, conscious effort.

Then the problem must be resolved into its constituent problems, for nearly every problem which arises in business is, as it were, a bundle of distinct minor problems, which together make up the whole. But if the composite problem is analyzed, and the individual units in the bundle are put into their proper places, the broad policy can be seen in its true proportions. Many of the minor problems can be solved, sometimes almost at a glance. And the solution of the big problem will become more and more simple as these individual solutions cancel off. So it is true that a problem thus analyzed often solves itself.

Take such a simple case as that of inaugurating a system of approval shipment. Some of the sub-problems are indicated in the following questions: What will be the effect on collections and on the cost of shipment? What is to be the credit policy? Will the stock in transit or in the hands of customers reduce the number of turnovers per year? Will the risk of damage to returned goods be great enough to jeopardize the regular profit? Will the increase in sales more than offset any added cost in the administration departments? Yet no consideration of this broad problem would be complete without taking into account the psychological factors in selling, such as customers' curiosity and caution.

After a problem has been separated into its constituent problems, the factors entering into the solution of each should be assembled, perhaps listed, especially where a large number of varying elements is to be considered. The advantage of listing the factors is clear. It is always simpler to deal with a situation if you have all its elements before you in black and white. Proper weighing and cancellation can be done more accurately and deliberately than if the attempt is made mentally to keep track of the factors and at the same time determine their values. In fact, when all the elements are set down in logical order, it may be possible to reduce them to something approaching a mathematical basis of values. The measure of each factor must be more or less an approximation, but usually each can be expressed in terms of percentages.

The last step is to take a fresh point of view — to look at the problem as a new problem, one never solved before. It is impossible to overemphasize the importance of the fresh point of view. I do not mean that experience is of no value, but that it is not to be relied upon to the exclusion of experiment and initiative. The value of this open-mindedness is well expressed in a letter from a firm of efficiency engineers to a manufacturer of national reputation. It is well, they said, "to put your business under the microscope of the production engineer for these reasons: We analyze your business from a new viewpoint. We are not swayed by sentiment. We are untrammeled by routine or the customs of your particular line."

The last point is probably the most important. Business has long been hampered by tradition. This is to be expected from the nature of its development. Even when a new idea is established in one branch of industry, the man in another almost invariably says: "My business is different; that idea would not work under our conditions." Between buggies and men's collars, for example, there is no apparent analogy. Yet the manager of a vehicle works found in the cutting room of a collar factory a refinement in method which saved him thousands of dollars when applied to the shaping of his leather trimmings.

His cutters, working on narrow tables, were accustomed to "size up" each hide as they unrolled it, then apply their patterns to a section of it and slice out the pieces needed. Five minutes' study of the collar cutters led the manager to substitute at home tables wide

enough and long enough to accommodate a full hide
flat. On this each cutter was taught to shift his patterns about until every possible inch of leather was utilized before touching knife to it. The time required to
cut up a hide was doubled and new cutters had to be
employed; but more than half the saving of ten thousand dollars in costly raw material remained to be
added to the company's net profit. All because a manager with an open mind recognized in an alien industry
an operation fundamentally identical with one of his
own processes and forthwith readjusted his viewpoint
on this process.

Other instances might be cited of the value of a new
angle of vision in a business. The rearrangement of an
office, suggested by a subordinate, saved daily for his
superior half a mile of unnecessary walking. And a
casual visitor at a large mail-order house, where it was
thought every unnecessary motion had been eliminated,
pointed out wasted effort in the order department. In
filling out the blanks, the notation "P. O." was used
for post-office money orders, "E. O." for express orders,
and so on. Since ninety per cent of the 30,000 remittances received every day were by post-office order,
there was a waste represented by the time used in
27,000 unnecessary notations. By tagging only the
3,000 orders on which remittances were made in some
other manner, postal orders could be distinguished
without further effort.

The adoption of a new point of view was the starting-
place in the development of the Taylor system of shop
management. If scientific management means anything, it means an entire divorce from tradition. Old
methods of work must be tested, and, if found lack-

ing, must be replaced by a standardized operation determined upon after analysis and time-study of all the motions involved. Scientific management may be nothing but applied common sense, as some of its critics have declared. It is important, however, because it is common sense applied in a new way.

This systematic method of approach:
(1) Elimination of the personal equation,
(2) Separation of the problem into its constituent problems,
(3) Listing of the factors involved,
(4) Taking of a new point of view,
is not intended to be a conscious process. Only when it has become habitual to the user is it most effective. A man should not pause in the process of thought to consider the method of his thinking. But when a problem is complex and many factors are involved, the formal use of this method may be of benefit. The assembling in written form of the constituent questions and their chief factors, with the value and importance of each approximated, should at least clarify the situation and increase the chances of a satisfactory solution.

PART I

THE PROBLEMS OF PRODUCTION

CHAPTER III

LOCATION OF THE PLANT

THE activities of production, we have seen, are concerned either with the providing of a ready-to-run factory, its location, construction, and equipment; or with its subsequent operation, the processing of materials through the agency of labor, and the organization of these processes. Before taking up the first group of plant activities, those having to do with location, let me explain that what follows here is to be an illustration of a definite and systematic approach to business problems rather than a complete analysis of the conditions. It would not be in accord with the plan of this book, indeed, to attempt anything like comprehensive treatment of a subject susceptible of so many combinations of varying influences.

According to one engineer, there are twenty-six factors to be taken into account in selecting a location for a factory. He includes with major items like access to markets, sources of materials, and supplies of labor, indirect factors which contribute to the satisfaction of the working force, like climate and water, schools and churches, housing and local transportation, parks, theaters, and other community attractions. This view may seem extreme, almost finical. Contrasted with the usual method of choosing a location, however, it emphasizes the importance of the first step in the suggested method of approach — the elimination, or at least the recognition, of the personal equation in considering your problem.

One of the notable large factories of the United States supplies a negative case in point. In plan, arrangement, construction, equipment, and working conditions this plant could hardly be improved upon. It employs several thousand men and consumes merchant steel and iron, lumber, coal, and other supplies by the train load. For many years, this great bulk of materials had to be trucked nearly two miles from the city freight yards to the factory and the product in turn hauled back to the freight houses for shipment. Recently, after a long campaign for an enabling ordinance, the company secured direct railroad connections which allow delivery of its heavier materials in the factory yards. But it is still obliged to maintain a fleet of nearly forty motor trucks to supplement the limited railroad service which its isolated situation permits.

Going back to the origins of the plant, you find that the personal equation entered largely into its location. Outgrowing his first small shop, the owner — whose commercial foresight in many other respects has been remarkable — permitted sentiment and convenience to guide his selection of a new site. The second factory was erected on his father's farm, remote from the railroads and because of its topographical surroundings difficult to reach with a connecting line. Possession of the land was one reason for this choice; but family pride and fondness for the neighborhood were admittedly the compelling motives. Twenty-five years ago, of course, a switch track was not considered essential to a factory; while the most active imagination might have failed to conceive the need, in time, of forty motor trucks as traffic attendants on the little new plant in the corn-field.

Convenience and sentiment still control in the placing of countless industries. In starting a business, a man ordinarily selects his home town for its headquarters. From the viewpoint of finance, his first market and the labor supply, choice of the city in which he is known and commands friendly interest is, perhaps, the part of wisdom. Under certain conditions — limited capital, for instance — any other action might be impossible; but here the personal equation would not actually influence the decision. Convenience and sentiment, indeed, have more to do with the location of plants in particular sections of the city, which the owners prefer because they are easy to reach from their residences or because they want to be associated in the public mind with the districts chosen. To indulge such groundless preferences is to handicap the success of the undertaking, just as mistaken loyalty to his native town or a desire to live in a certain city blinds many a capable business man to the advantages of other more strategic centers.

The surest way to overcome the personal equation is to take the second step in the approach already outlined and resolve the main problem into its constituent problems. Thus the suitability of any factory site breaks up into a number of unit questions: How near and how accessible is the market for your product? What are the transportation facilities and rates, and the chances of alternative service during car shortages? What sources of materials are at hand? Under what control? What will materials cost, compared with costs at competing points? Is there an adequate supply of labor

27

of the kind required at the prices you can pay? Are local conditions such as will help or hinder in the securing, retaining, and handling of the working force? Will any financial advantages accrue from location at this particular point, either in the saving of capital invested or the securing of outside money needed? What will an adequate and satisfactory site cost?

Will the type of construction best suited to the present and future requirements of the business comply with physical and legal conditions? Will the necessary outlay for buildings be greater or less than at other available locations? Will the tax rate be lower or higher? Will the situation of the factory add to the fire hazard and the insurance rate? Will lighting conditions be satisfactory? The water supply adequate? The drainage and other facilities for disposal of wastes sufficient? Are the surroundings likely to affect manufacturing processes or the comfort or health of employees at work? Will the plant be within walking distance or at least not difficult to reach from the homes of employees? Will the location contribute any selling or advertising value to the product? Will it involve any excessive legal limitations on the activities of the business? Unusual circumstances or local conditions may give special importance to certain factors in these problems. The drastic provisions of employers' liability laws in New York state, for instance, have trebled the former cost of casualty insurance. Compared with a New Jersey or Connecticut site, the other advantages of which were approximately equal, a New York location at present might be a poor investment. Yet in the long run it might provide a higher type of laboring force.

The splitting up of the main problem and the listing

of the factors in this way not only prevents the giving of undue weight to any single factor, but also reduces the analysis of competing sites to something like a mathematical operation, in which the advantages and disadvantages of each are compared with those of the others.

The removal of a silverware plant from New York City to a Connecticut factory town several years ago presented a typical problem in location, and the company's method of approach is an excellent illustration of just such an analysis and assembling of the significant factors as are indicated above.

As in so many successful industries, the original factory had been outgrown. Looking about for a new location, the directors found that all available New York sites had one drawback in common. The high cost of land would make it necessary to limit the ground floor area of the new building to the space requirements of the power plant, the shipping rooms, and the general offices. Three additional floors would be needed for current manufacturing operations; further expansion of the business must be taken care of by superimposing other stories. This would mean the probable division of one important department between two floors and would certainly not conduce to economical production. Elevator service for the transfer of stock in process and workmen from floor to floor would increase overhead expense; inquiry showed that in some cases the cost of such service, including repairs, power, operators, and the time of foremen and mechanics using it, amounted to about two per cent of the total pay roll.

Outside New York, in any one of several industrial towns, the same investment would secure a site large enough to permit all heavy manufacturing processes to be concentrated on the ground floor, in the most effective sequence and with the minimum of trucking for stock and of movement for employees. Construction, too, could be of a much cheaper and more flexible type in a two-story detached factory in the country than in a four, six, or eight story structure wedged in between buildings in a city district where the fire hazard was great, insurance rates correspondingly high, and the city building ordinances most exacting. Cheapness and flexibility in construction were vital considerations, for the reason that invention of new machines or new processes might, at any time, necessitate the complete rearrangement of one or many departments. Safety and a low insurance rate were matters of account; so also were daylight illumination of workrooms and freedom from dust and soot. On all these items, the small town site was greatly to be preferred.

Certain advantages were inherent, however, in a metropolitan location. New York offered the best market for raw materials and supplies. It was the sales center of the silverware trade; during the seasons when customers came in to buy, quick and easy access to the plant and the general offices had a definite selling influence on visitors. Direct trucking communication between factory and salesrooms allowed of closer cooperation in filling orders and considerable economies in the handling and refinishing of goods. As a shipping center, also, New York was beyond comparison. Ninety per cent of the company's forwarding was done by express. New York offered a choice of several carriers and direct, immediate dispatch in the case of rush orders; while service in the smaller town might be limited to a single express company and be delayed by the necessity of transfer at New York. Still, the almost prohibitive cost of a city site or the alternative drawbacks in construction, arrangement, and operation determined the directors to canvass the small towns thoroughly before settling the question.

The problem finally narrowed down to choice between a New York location and one in a particular industrial center in Connecticut. Half a dozen other cities in Connecticut, New York, and New Jersey — all within a radius of fifty miles — were considered. Sites at a greater distance were eliminated because nothing they had to offer would compensate for the added difficulty in reaching them. Customer-visits to the plants, it was decided, could not be jeopardized by making the journey long and tiresome. For analogous reasons, various smaller towns were dismissed because hotel accommodations were lacking and train service, both for passengers and express shipments, not so good. In addition to the railroad facilities of the town finally selected, three steamboat lines to New York City provided certain assurance against delays and made a complete tie-up of communication practically impossible. This last consideration illustrates the interdependence of production problems and problems of distribution (already discussed in the first chapter) and the necessity of foreseeing the influence of each upon the other.

Besides the typical small-city advantages as an industrial site, the chosen town possessed other attractive features. The prices of gas and water were below the average. There would be a substantial saving in taxes for two reasons, the rate was lower and the real estate investment would be much less than in New York.

Power could be produced more cheaply than in New York. The water freight on steam coal from the West Virginia fields was nine cents higher than to New York, but this excess would be more than made up by the saving in trucking charges from dock side to boiler room and in disposal of the ashes. The saving, in fact, would amount to nearly seventy-five cents a ton on all. coal burned, in itself a considerable economy.

Conditions were favorable also to the easy handling of labor. The company wanted to carry with it to the new factory all its skilled men and many of its unskilled. City-bred mechanics, however, frequently have a distaste for life in a small town. The employees of one large manufacturer recently voted against removal of the plant from a city noted for its parks, beaches, and public institutions, insisting that they could get more pleasure and relaxation for nothing where they were than they could buy with a week's wages in the other town. The silverware company, on the contrary, was able to present its new site as a better place in which to live and bring up families. Its nearness to New York would enable them quickly and cheaply to run into the city whenever they desired, thus maintaining such connections and associations as they valued. The available sites for the new plant were within walking distance of districts where desirable homes could be bought or rented at figures much below the New York levels for corresponding environments. The saving in time spent in crowded street cars would be at least an hour daily for each workman, to say nothing of the carfare. As for schools, churches, parks, bathing beaches, and other accessible community utilities, New York offered nothing more. Even working conditions would be bettered by the removal to a place where daylight and fresh air were abundant.

Thus, item by item, the company assembled all the factors bearing on its location problems. Certain of these, of possible prime importance to a young business with limited resources, could be disregarded. For example, no question of capital or finance had to be considered. The company was able to pay any reasonable sum for a site, could erect and equip a factory without outside aid. Banking facilities were a minor item, since New York connections could be maintained. Sources and prices of raw materials would not be affected. And so with other factors not analyzed above and ranged as favoring or discouraging removal, they could practically be ignored. And having brought together all the elements that counted, *pro* or *con*, and balanced them in accord with their relative values, the Connecticut town was decided upon as the place for its new factory.

In coming to this decision, the company consciously or unconsciously illustrated the final step in the method I have suggested for approaching business problems — the taking of a fresh point of view. It has been made clear, I think, that they attacked the question of location as a new problem, surveying all the conditions and circumstances without bias of any sort, either personal prejudice or regard for trade customs or traditions. It is the usual thing, for example, to locate new mills in districts where successful mills of the same class or character are in operation. In a particular case, it is quite possible that this customary procedure is the right one to follow; again there may be found reasons for an opposite course. These reasons, however, can be developed only by assuming a viewpoint independent of traditions. As in the case of this silverware company, all the conditions which make for failure or success should be observed and carefully analyzed from the standpoint of a new enterprise. Nothing should be taken for granted.

Certain general advantages, to be sure, reside in a location where other factories in the same line or allied lines are concentrated — as shoe making in Lynn, Brockton, and St. Louis; flour milling at Minneapolis and St. Paul, and cotton manufacturing at Fall River and New Bedford. In such centers, each individual industry, because of the importance of its group, commands resources and service, and profits by various external economies which the isolated establishment is likely to miss. At Detroit, for instance, where the production of motor cars is carried on extensively, subsidiary factories have multiplied and now supply economically and without delay the special machinery and tools, the specialized parts, materials, accessories, and supplies which the parent industry requires. The magnitude of the market open for these specialized products tempts initiative and ingenuity to undertake detail manufacturing tasks which the maker of motor cars prefers not to assume himself, and thus brings about a coöperative effort profitable to everybody.

For like reasons, purchasing conditions are more favorable at the focus of an industry; prices are closer, quality of deliveries is more carefully watched, and deliveries themselves are more apt to be on schedule. Bankers, too, have studied underlying conditions more intensively and the sound enterprise is more easily financed. Public opinion is usually more favorable to the basic community industry in which a large number of citizens are interested. And finally, where many minds are directed upon the same technical problems and there is interchange of information, both privately and through trade association channels, advances in production practice are more frequent and more quickly shared.

Where the factories gather, also, labor congregates. Mechanics of the highest skill or specialized training avoid the isolated plant for definite reasons. If a dull selling season brings about a shut-down or half-time production, the chance of employment elsewhere is small; while a disagreement with a foreman nearly always means removal to some other city. So general is this feeling against the factory at a distance from the greater labor markets, that even the most stable of businesses, when situated thus, find it hard to induce skilled labor to join their forces. One specialty company in Ohio, for example, when re-design of its machine tools was determined upon and twenty additional tool-makers were needed, paid an average of $180 each to start the new men at work. Most of these had families, and their moving expenses were paid on the theory that the families would help to anchor them to their new jobs. In line with this belief is the experience of a plant superintendent in central Illinois who is content if he can keep unmarried operators of screw machines three months before they make their next jump to St. Louis or Chicago. In an isolated plant like this, the loss of a few skilled workmen in a processing department might cripple production until they could be replaced.

Unskilled labor — no less a necessity of large-scale production — has a similar tendency to concentrate in the big communities, particularly since so many of our pick-and-shovel men have been recruited from southern and eastern Europe. As a result of this common drift on the part of both skilled and unskilled, our cities have become huge labor markets from which any number of extra workers of well nigh any class can be drawn when needed. So long as an industry is given to decided fluctuations in sales and output, it needs such a dependable labor pool. Hence we witness the building up of manufacturing districts like that surrounding the Baldwin locomotive works in Philadelphia, whose scores of machinery houses have taken care of business expansion by adding upper stories to their plants, and sacrificed a certain amount of everyday efficiency in order to insure a flexible labor supply.

These are all general advantages, however, and should not be emphasized to the exclusion of possible special benefits which, in a particular case, might balance or outweigh them. Nearness to supplies of raw materials and cheap labor, for instance, have made it possible for southern cotton mills to compete favorably with New England establishments, especially on the coarser fabrics. This, despite New England's better transportation, lower freight rates, cheaper power, highly organized markets, and notable concentration of the industry, with its attendant advantages. It must also be taken into account that in industrial centers, skilled and common labor are both likely to carry organized effort to limit production and enforce relatively high wage scales much further than in communities where class consciousness has not been fostered.

For the sake of showing how definite, almost arithmetical, the approach to a business problem can be made, the steps in the location of a drain tile factory in the middle west some years ago may be recounted here. The owners made nearness to market their first consideration, though the other salient factors were not overlooked. Their product would be bulky and of low value relative to weight; the plant with the shortest haul would enjoy a real selling advantage in its lower freight rates. The plant was located, therefore, near the center of a district where land levels were low and drain tile in constant demand; the extra cost and added risk in processing the inferior raw materials found there were accepted for the sake of the advantage in transportation. As the customer paid the freight, the saving appealed directly to his pocket. The new company did not need to cut prices and thus provoke disparagement of its product, while the difference in rates emphasized its character as a "home" industry.

There was also a plentiful supply of native labor, with sufficient intelligence to master quickly all but the most technical processes of manufacture. When the balance was struck, the new location scored on four principal counts — transportation, two points; labor, one point; finance, one point (a free site was offered and additional deposits of raw materials could be purchased cheaply); advertising and selling, one half point. Against these, three disadvantages appeared: banking facilities were limited, subtracting one point; material was inferior, one half point; and sources of fuel were distant, increasing the cost and deducting another half point. The net result was a count of four and one half points to two in favor of the central situation.

The problem of plant location, however, does not stop with the selection of a particular city. The actual placing of the factory to satisfy and make the most of local and internal conditions is a matter which can be settled only by the same process of careful analysis and weighing of essential factors. Where in the general district (the traffic zone surrounding a large city, for instance, its boundaries marked by the area to which the city freight tariffs apply) is the plant to be built? What section of the chosen town is most suitable?

Here enter many of the factors which we found important in determining the main problem: transportation (direct railroad connections), power (no neighborhood restrictions on its production), labor (accessibility from residence districts and freedom from objectionable conditions), advertising and selling values, and so on. The physical characteristics of competing sites must also be examined. Can suitable foundations, for example, be secured at average cost? What is the slope of the ground? Can this slope be used in planning the layout of the buildings? How does it affect drainage or the water supply? Will the excavation furnish materials for construction, as gravel or sand in a building of reinforced concrete?

In the local placing of the drain tile plant just mentioned, transportation again governed. The shale beds and free site lay some distance from the village, alongside one railroad but a mile and a half from its junction with another road. To build here would require no investment in a site, while the material could be delivered to the machines at minimum cost. The drawback would be the lack of connections with the other railroad. Many shipments which might secure competitive service and rates if both carriers were accessible would get only routine attention at the maximum rate. Every car shortage might result in serious delays and possible cancellation of contracts. To insure certainty in deliveries, therefore, the management paid fifteen hundred dollars for three acres at the junction and erected its plant there, preferring to pay freight on its material rather than save at the possible expense of sales. Some weight was attached also to proximity to the village; workmen would have a mile less to walk mornings and evenings and could go home to their noonday dinners. The decisive factor, however, was transportation facilities and service in this instance, just as the lower cost of shorter hauls had been the determining cause in locating the plant in its geographical relation to the market.

At the risk of appearing prolix, analysis of the problem of location has been carried out at some length in this chapter, first in order to indicate with quantities having standard and recognized values the scheme of analysis which later will be applied to the less familiar activities of distribution and administration, and also to illustrate how a systematic approach will facilitate the determination of any business question. In succeeding chapters, the effort will be made to sketch rather than to develop the outlines of each problem and the factors affecting its solution.

CHAPTER IV

CONSTRUCTION AND EQUIPMENT OF THE PLANT

IN the construction of a factory the main consideration, of course, is its efficiency as a producing unit.
Size, type, shape, arrangement, cost, number of stories,
and other physical characteristics are essential factors in achieving this result. The determination of
each, therefore, is a problem to be solved by the unbiased and systematic approach illustrated in the preceding chapter on location. In their broad aspects, indeed,
location and construction, as well as equipment, are
parallel and interdependent problems.

The best site for a plant (within the district which satisfies material, labor, transportation, and other primary
requirements) is that tract of land which lends itself to
the erection of the particular kind of building or group of
buildings in which the processes of manufacture can be
carried on most effectively. Conversely, any plant falls
short of its highest efficiency unless, in its planning and
building, advantage has been taken of every favorable
feature of the site. And neither the location nor the
construction can be intelligently or profitably considered
apart from the equipment which is to be accommodated.
In general, it would be better, from the standpoint of
efficiency, to plan and erect the building around the
equipment than to arrange the machinery after the
building was completed.

Preliminary to the analysis and balancing of factors, merely personal considerations must again be discounted. The owner's preference for a special type of building or a certain kind of construction must be eliminated unless the preference rests on practical engineering or commercial grounds. He may fancy his business housed in one of the imposing ivy-covered buildings which are pictured at intervals in the magazines; but if his product can be turned out more economically in a sprawling, one-story plant with a saw-tooth roof, he will do well to dismiss his day dream. The selection, correlation, and placing of the equipment are the things that count in starting a factory; and the plan, appearance, and construction of the building should all be subordinated to the efficiency of the machines.

This does not mean that the structure should be an eyesore; a pleasing exterior or unusual interior finish may possess considerable publicity value for a product with quality or cleanliness as a sales argument, to say nothing of the effect of clean and cheerful surroundings on the working force. The point to be observed in this connection is that efficiency of operation should not be sacrificed to satisfy a personal whim or prejudice.

When we come to break up the problem of design and construction into its constituent problems, we find ourselves concerned with three primary questions: What type shall our building be — single-story or multi-story, oblong, hollow square, or some other standard shape? What character of construction shall be adopted — fire-resisting or slow-burning, brick and steel, concrete or mill construction? What financial considerations are involved — initial cost and upkeep? As in every related group of business problems, we find the principle of interdependence in control, making it impossible to find

41

the right answer for anyone without taking the influence of the others into consideration.

The type of building to be erected (or purchased, as it is frequently profitable to do) should be dictated first by the character and sequence of the manufacturing processes to be sheltered. Where the parts have great weight and bulk, as in a plant producing heavy-duty steam engines or mining machinery, the single-story building appears to be the most practical type. Where the raw materials can be elevated in the first place to the top floor and the successive operations applied to them as they move onward and downward, as in the making of men's hats, the building of several stories suggests itself as more economical. In such a plant a gravity-conveyor system is often used for the transportation of materials in process.

Where the product is an assembly of many relatively small parts, such as a sewing machine, an electric fan, or a motor car, the type of building is of less importance if the routing of materials can be arranged so that all the processing departments feed without lost motion or interference toward a central assembling room or stock room. A simple rectangular building, of one story or many stories, may prove a satisfactory type. Or when several classes of raw materials, such as lumber, pig iron, sheet steel, and brass enter into the make-up of the final product, a building with projecting wings to allow separate but synchronous processing of these materials may be chosen. The same type is likely to prove best for a business making a line of goods diverse in nature. Or these wings may be developed into unit buildings to accommodate wood-working, foundry, machining, and other special operations. In factories of any size, indeed, the best practice gives the foundry and wood-working departments buildings of their own for much the same reasons that make the power house a separate unit.

Apart from the relative cost of single-story and multiple-story buildings, transportation, arrangement of equipment, and providing of sunlight illumination for the greatest number of operations possible are the chief considerations in determining between the types, except where the heavy character of the parts produced dictates choice of the first. Here transportation is clearly the prohibiting cause; even in factories without this limitation, the high cost of handling parts from floor to floor as compared with horizontal trucking is an impressive item. One production engineer, after time studies of the trucking and elevator service in a table factory, discovered that the horizontal time equivalent of an elevator trip to the second story and return was one hundred feet, with an additional fifty feet on the level for every extra story.

For daylight illumination, the saw-tooth roof gives the one-story building indefinite powers of expansion, subject only to the maximum floor spaces allowed in one inclosure by the rules of the insurance underwriters. In any multi-story structure, on the contrary, the effective widths range from fifty to seventy feet, dependent on the height of the ceilings and the proportional area of windows. There are thousands of factories, it is true, which ignore these standards; and other thousands which accept artificial light as a necessary accompaniment of production, even in country situations. But it is equally true that the most efficient modern plants conform to them and rank perfect daylight illumination of work practically as inflexible a rule in construction as solid foundations or a non-leaking roof. Some of them concentrate on the top floors the operations involving very small parts, even providing saw-tooth roofs with northern exposure as insurance against eye strain for workers and spoiled parts for the scrap bins.

There is another motive for adopting that standard type and size which satisfies your production requirements. Not only is such a building less costly to erect, because it utilizes materials of standard market specifications and because contractors are familiar with such construction, but it will also be more salable in an emergency or in the event that removal proves desirable.

For the same reason, the more closely its layout conforms to standard practice, the simpler will be the task of selling it. To be easily disposed of, a plant of any size must have a railroad siding at its shipping platform. Even though his business is of a kind that has little use for direct rail connections, a prospective buyer will not offer so much for a building without a rail outlet. There are many exceptions to this rule, of course, and any number of cases where a switch track would add to the cost of the site more than its use would justify. The damage a millinery house would suffer in its stock, for instance, would wipe out any saving in trucking its light-weight materials. Any light manufacturing business, unless on an unusual scale, could well avoid the extra investment a switch track would demand and use the money for developing a wider market.

This factor of salability should also be considered in the problem of design and construction. It should not be the major consideration, but rather the corrective measure which brought up or down to recognized standards the specifications which might otherwise result in a building costly beyond any reasonable need, or too light in design for any use except that for which it was erected. Both are extremes to be avoided in fireproof or mill construction; when the structure is of concrete, however, the added value of floors capable of sustaining maximum loads is out of proportion to the slight extra cost. Here, bringing construction up to recognized levels of strength also insures the future of the business. Even in light manufacturing, methods and processes are constantly changing. To keep pace with possible developments in machinery, the factory may require all the margin of safety its floors possess.

More important factors in determining the character of construction are the legal requirements of the community in which the plant is located (particularly as these bear on the degree of fire resistance demanded) and the classes of material available, with the relative market price and the comparative cost of handling each kind. Financial considerations must be taken into account as well, since the initial cost and the upkeep of various classes of buildings vary in inverse ratio.

For the business with large resources and long experience, the problem narrows down to choice between different kinds of substantial fireproof or slow-burning construction. This is not alone to keep down insurance premiums and repairs, but also to provide against possible destruction of factory and machinery at the height of a selling season. The owner or manager of a young business, on the contrary, usually has a minimum capital to work with and must figure plant investment down to the lowest point. Frequently he starts in rented quarters none too well adapted to his purposes and buys his power from an outside source at a higher price to avoid the installation of a power plant. In the main, however, these problems of design, construction, initial cost, and upkeep are technical questions which must be settled in individual cases after consultation with a factory engineer or architect and, perhaps, with a building contractor. There are too many possible combinations of conditions to be analyzed or even enumerated here.

The technical expert should have a part, too, in the next step, the assembling and weighing of all the factors that count in construction of this individual factory. The tendency of the architect or engineer to lay stress on the technical aspects of building must be corrected by the practical viewpoint of the owner or manager. An enthusiasm for some special type of construction, for instance, may cause the architect to overlook the peculiar advantages of another and contrasting type for the particular industry under the special set of conditions which may exist. Here the experience and the broader perspective of the manager come in to reduce each factor, technical and practical, to its relative proportions and to strike a balance between these opposing but interdependent elements.

A good architect and a competent production engineer are quite capable of providing an ideal factory and an ideal layout for almost any given industry. But a going business nearly always has an individuality, organization habits, and special demands which must be considered if the new building is to fit its needs and hamper none of its activities. The owner or executive, therefore, can depend upon his technical advisers or aids for the suggestion and carrying out of technical details; but the relative weight to be given each of the general factors must be determined primarily by the management.

Here the fresh point of view has great value. The fact that certain types of buildings and certain kinds of construction have become standards in your district or your line of industry is not a guarantee that either is the one best suited to your purpose. Conformity to this standard will make for salability, but may at the same time seriously affect the efficiency of production.

The furniture factories at Grand Rapids, for example, usually have been of mill construction, with walls of white brick and only the usual quota of windows for lighting. A seasoned furniture man, if he were erecting a new building, might incline to this traditional type, but a man whose experience had been in a machinery or automobile plant, if he entered the furniture field, would be likely to build a factory with windows as wide and high as his walls would permit, using the steel or concrete construction with which he was familiar to balance the extra fire hazard caused by his raw materials. The furniture man, before he decided what type his new building should be, probably would profit by advising with construction specialists and visiting modern machinery and motor-car factories.

The importance of the fresh point of view in construction is suggested by the experience of a New England weaving mill which replaced a three-story building having a width of seventy feet with a one-story structure one hundred and five feet wide and covered with a sawtooth roof. The improved natural lighting and increased facility in handling materials and product brought about the remarkable reduction of one half in the cost of weaving and two thirds in the cost of artificial light.

The foundry of a Detroit stove works affords another striking illustration. Indifferent lighting and foul air are usually accepted as necessities of foundry operation; working conditions are generally worse than in any other processing department. This stove company, however, determined to erect a foundry which would eliminate discomfort and disorder. Except for a six-foot base of brick, the walls are entirely of steel sash and glass. By opening tilting sections of these walls, it is possible to provide satisfactory ventilation in summer and to clear the building of vitiated air within fifteen minutes after each pouring of metal. In contrast with this departure, which allows resumption of work after a short delay, many foundries plan only two pourings a day and turn their men out when these have been completed, with mutual loss of time and output. As foundry capacity in a stove works sets a limit for the whole plant, the value of the fresh viewpoint is indicated by the effect on production.

Like all other business problems, the problems of construction cannot be solved without taking into account the principle of interdependence and the principle of balance. The geographical location of the plant and the actual site have much to do with choice of building materials and the kind of construction adopted. The type of building, on the other hand, cannot be intelligently determined without keeping always in view the character of the manufacturing processes, the space, power, and safety requirements of the equipment and materials, and the physical necessities or desires of the working forces. And again, the size, type, and class of factory erected or leased may rightly be subordinated to considerations which have to do solely with sales or with finance and other administrative activities. No business problem is a simple equation to be settled off-hand without regard for other activities which may be advanced or jeopardized by the decision.

Closely bound up with construction, as we have already seen, is the problem of equipment. Having determined what type, size, and shape your building shall be and what class of construction is best adapted to the necessities and possibilities of your business, the broad outlines of your machinery scheme are already clear, since the general sequence of your manufacturing operations was a factor in your construction planning. For this reason and for the additional reason that knowledge of the development and standardization of equipment is so general, it will be enough here to make the briefest possible application of our method of approach to the problem.

This fact of standardization gives, in the first place, very little play to the personal factor. Assuming that the owner or manager has a reasonable acquaintance with current practice in his field and a competent superintendent or production engineer to advise him, his choice of basic equipment will probably lie between machines designed by rival manufacturers to achieve approximately the same result. Patent control of special machinery held by his competitors may limit this choice and challenge his initiative and ingenuity to find other efficient and economical methods of manufacturing. It is only in his decision on such general questions as that of the type of drive he will use (whether he will have individual electric motors or a belt-driven plant), and in his choice of auxiliary equipment for heating, ventilation, sanitation, and lighting (still in the experimental stage, though of extreme importance because of the legislation which is being brought to bear upon them), that the personal prejudices or prepossessions of the owner, if arbitrarily indulged, may run him into mechanical difficulties or saddle the business with disproportionate expense.

In breaking up the problem of equipment into its constituent problems, the concrete character of the various factors helps to define them for the management. Financial considerations come first, initial investment needing to be balanced against upkeep costs, though both are subordinate, of course, to the prime question of how much money can be devoted to the purchase of machinery. Next in order are the quantity and quality of output required, balanced against the kind and class of raw materials to be used; then safety against both fire and accident; finally, the matter of design. This sub-problem of design will be influenced by all the factors just named and by the additional factor of the capacity of the labor available.

In the end, within the limits set by capital, output, and labor considerations, the manager's problem will narrow down to picking out the particular model of punch press or turret lathe, milling machine or drill press, which will handle the materials he must use or the parts he must process to the best advantage. This is only an outline suggestion of the manner in which one equipment problem might shape itself; it does not offer an ironclad analysis generally applicable. In some cases, one or more of the factors listed above might settle the question out of hand and make the others negligible; in other instances new factors might arise and dominate. But in every case analysis of the main problem into its constituent parts will go far toward suggesting the right solution.

In listing and weighing the factors in equipment, the advice of the production specialist is valuable. The owner or executive, unless he happens to be factory-trained, is not necessarily familiar with technical details, like the most effective speed of screw machines on various classes of work or the formulæ of power transmission. For such information he should call on his superintendent or production engineer. His own function is to assemble and balance all the factors bearing on the general problem, including those furnished by his expert counsel, and to determine the relative weight each is to have in the final decision.

An open mind, a fresh point of view, is nowhere more essential than in determining equipment policies. Changes and improvements are of almost daily occurrence; usage and tradition, therefore, must never be allowed to block the installation of the most efficient types of machinery. It is generally believed, for example, that the economies brought about in other industries by the use of automatic machinery are not equally profitable in the wood-working groups. As a matter of fact, automatic machines have been successfully employed in a number of wood-working operations. Their further development and application will depend largely on the initiative and open-mindedness of the men engaged in the industry, or on the invasion, perhaps, of the wood-working field by men from the metal-working groups who think about any manufacturing problem in terms of automatic machinery.

AN APPROACH TO BUSINESS PROBLEMS

This completes our outline and analysis of the plant activities — the policies which govern the location, construction, and equipment of the factory. As the purpose was chiefly to illustrate the application of a systematic method of approach to any specific set of business problems, no attempt has been made at an exhaustive survey. It was enough to indicate the importance of a definite method of approach and to make clear the steps of that approach in anticipation of its use later in the analysis of problems whose factors are less tangible.

CHAPTER V

MATERIALS

OVER against the plant activities of production — the placing, building, and equipping of the factory — is balanced the group of activities concerned with operation. Their importance hinges on the fact that when the wheels begin to turn the business ceases to concentrate on itself and deals with factors which in many instances are difficult to control, unless control has been considered and provided for in the location and equipment of the works. These outside relations have to do first with materials, their kind, quality, and the freedom with which they can be secured; and second with labor, the extent and character of the market for men. Together with the organization of manufacturing processes, these make up the operating activities of production. As another demonstration of the principle of interdependence which runs through the whole structure of business, their essential relations can be briefly and graphically illustrated in the experience of a group of business men in a small city in middle Illinois.

The first adventure in production made by this group was the manufacture of barbed-wire fencing in the later nineties, before the regulation of big business had been undertaken by the federal government. Standard-gauge wire, the material used by the factory, was bought from the nearest mill of a big rival, which presently adopted a policy of purchase and consolidation of smaller competitors whenever these became annoying factors in sales. After running three or four years with satisfactory returns, the smaller plant suddenly was confronted with advances in the price of wire which wiped out its margin of profit. The manager had foreseen such a possibility and had urged the stockholders to appropriate for a wire-drawing mill. They had refused, however, and when the last advance in materials destroyed the profit margin, there was no time to erect and equip a wire department. Surrender on fairly generous terms was the outcome; the stockholders banked their money and watched the removal of the equipment to another plant. The factory itself was offered for sale.

The manager had learned a drastic lesson in production policy — that you must make sure of the source and price of your raw materials. When the creative instinct stirred in him again, therefore, his systematic approach to his new venture differed only in form from that which has been set forth in previous chapters — recognition of the personal equation, analysis of the general problem, the listing of the factors, and the taking of a fresh point of view.

He concentrated on materials, on the building of an industry which could not be crippled by failing supplies, since his location, construction, and labor problems were already solved if only he could bring his material and equipment problems into accord with them. A factory and power house could be had cheaply, with outlets on three railroads and advantageous freight rates to several merchandising centers. Labor, after a long season of unemployment, could be hired reasonably and could be depended upon for energetic and intelligent coöperation. The men were machine-tenders, "handy men," who could not easily be developed into mechanics. Their capacities had to be considered in deciding what to make and how to make it. Repeat operations by semi-automatic machinery on some uncontrolled raw material were the essentials of success in production.

Three raw materials stood out as possibilities. Plastic shales were abundant locally for the manufacture of sewer pipe, fire brick, and fireproofing ware. Merchant steel was offered by independent sources at fair prices. Lumber and timber were to be had cheaply and in any quantity, particularly soft woods from the great markets on the Mississippi River.

Checking the advantages and disadvantages of each material against the others, the manager chose to enter wood-working. There was a local clay industry whose moderate dividends would stand in the way of interesting capital in another competing plant; besides, the available factory was ill adapted to the making of clay products. Steel-working offered no special advantages such as did the presence of the low-priced timber supply. Wood-working, therefore, was the logical field: but what kind of product? In turn, the manager took up and dismissed the manufacture of kitchen furniture, wooden toys, cheap trunks, incubators, variety store goods, and a number of similar lines. No one of these would command a ready market or possess imperative selling arguments.

By a process of elimination, the manager finally determined to make matches. Not by the patented automatic process controlled by an organization of national scope, but by the German method which broke match-making up into a dozen or more operations by specialized machines. The speed and cheapness of the American process were partly neutralized by the cost of the cork pine required as material. The German machines, on the contrary, would chew almost any soft wood up into match blanks and turn out an acceptable product. Their operation was simple enough to be learned in a day. The match produced had its own good points, besides the powerful sales argument that it was "not made by a trust." In addition, all the neighboring cities were wholesale grocery centers, which would insure a ready market distribution. To sum up in a sentence, the new business was able to double its original capital out of the profits of the first year because its manager had analyzed his plant problems, coördinated them with his operating activities, and worked out a well-balanced scheme of production and distribution.

In solving his material problem, this match-maker was not influenced in the least by personal preference or prejudice, but based his decision entirely on logical considerations. As a rule, indeed, the personal equation does not enter into the choice of raw materials to anything like the same extent as in the determination of other plant policies. The character, quality, and price of the product fix in a large measure the kind and quality of the materials to be used. Yet this is not always true. One publisher, for instance, has such a strong liking for a certain blue-white paper that he uses it for the printing of his magazine, though he might make a substantial saving by using a cheaper natural-white paper which would meet every printing requirement and which probably would be equally satisfactory to the magazine's readers.

The manager's broad policy on materials must be determined by his analysis of conditions from the standpoint of (1) the kind of material to be used; (2) the quality of material; (3) sources from which material can be drawn; (4) the control of material; (5) the utilization of material in the factory.

Within reasonable limits, it is clear that he must indicate the kind of material to be used. In making filing cabinets, for example, he would at least decide whether wood or metal cabinets were to be produced. He would be governed here by consideration not only of current but of future conditions. Is the present supply of raw materials adequate and reasonable in price? Does it threaten to diminish or run out? In such an event, are other sources available, or can a substitute be found at a cost which the price of the product will allow? In certain of the wood-working industries, for instance, pine lumber, when its cost became prohibitive, was replaced by basswood; in like manner when the hardwoods used for furniture appreciated in value, recourse was had to a veneer construction which allowed combination with various cheaper grades of lumber.

In prescribing the quality of the materials, the manager must be governed largely by financial and marketing considerations, the selling price and the profit per unit of output. When the product is a specialty with a wide margin between the factory cost and the selling price, the definite policy may be established of using only the highest grade of materials even though cheaper grades might be employed without sacrificing any of the service rendered the consumer. This probably has been

AN APPROACH TO BUSINESS PROBLEMS

the policy followed by the manufacturers of the more expensive safety razors. Certainly it is true in general that the making of a "quality" article requires "quality" materials. But the management should never lose sight of the fact that the substitution of cheaper, though not less efficient, materials might enable it to lower the price to a point where a marked increase in sales would result.

An instance of the substitution of materials against trade custom is furnished by a manufacturer of vacuum cleaners. He found that the use of pressed steel instead of aluminum gave him a cheaper, lighter, and stronger product. The first cost of the new dies was a strong argument against the change, but it was outweighed, according to the manufacturer's analysis, by the saving that would follow.

The policies influencing the control of materials are dictated not alone by technical or intra-departmental considerations but by those which look to the general good of the business. By control is meant, particularly, the disposition of materials after they have been placed in stock, rather than the insurance of adequate sources of supply. The strategic position of the manager, sufficiently withdrawn from departmental affairs to see them all in their right proportions, enables him to determine policies which will make the most of his resources and result in the greatest general efficiency of the business as a whole. In his control of materials, for example, he must strike a balance between an excessive inventory, representing idle capital, and a possible shortage of materials which would mean a loss due to idle machinery. In order to establish a balance between these two factors, his supply of materials must be brought

58

into equilibrium with the needs of his production departments.

It is here that the assumption of a fresh point of view and the discarding of traditions to make way for decisions based on actual conditions demonstrate their value. According to the records of efficiency engineers, overinvestment in materials, the carrying of excessive raw stocks, is a common fault in American factories. The inventory is usually the first problem they address themselves to, because it is at this point that the quickest and most convincing savings can be developed.

Instances could be cited almost without end: like that of a Massachusetts company which projected a bond issue in order to finance further extensions. Investigation of its assets discovered that at least $200,000 worth of materials were in storage in excess of probable requirements, and the funds needed for expansion were released by reduction of the inventory. Or that of an Indiana manufacturing concern, too young and possessed of too little in the way of tangible assets to attempt a bond issue, which was able to finance a twenty-five per cent increase in sales by strict coördination of its production and purchasing program.

Unbalanced accumulation of stock and supplies is generally the explanation of an excess inventory. One department head is uneasy unless he has materials on hand for six months' requirements; another finds stores for three months entirely adequate. Unless it be more difficult to secure prompt deliveries of the materials used by the first department, or unless other considerations, such as market fluctuations, are involved, it is evident that any stock maintained in excess of three months' needs involves a waste. Use of the capital tied up in the surplus inventory and the space occupied are lost for productive purposes. The importance of maintaining an executive policy of control over stores is obvious; without such general control, overinvestment and unbalanced accumulation are almost inevitable.

The question of utilization also comes up for final decision by the executive, particularly in cases where by-products can be manufactured out of scrap material. The packing industry affords, perhaps, the best known illustration of utilization of raw materials. Even here, however, development has been slow, and the manufacture of by-products as a production policy was enforced by economic necessity rather than adopted deliberately as an essential of constructive business.

In the main, raw materials of every class have been so cheap and abundant in the United States that there has been no such pressure to secure complete utilization as is felt in Germany, France, and England. Effort has been concentrated on manufacturing processes and on the turning out of the finished product rather than on economy of materials.

Solution of these problems of control and utilization, even more than problems of the kind and quality of materials, is facilitated by a fresh point of view on the part of the management. That a business man has prospered, for instance, in the face of incomplete stock records, haphazard buying, and slovenly control of materials in process, is not proof that stock records are negligible or an inflexible system of requisitions for materials unimportant. It may simply mean that leaks in the factory have been covered up by the high profit margin of the business and that these losses, if detected and checked, might have added materially to the net returns or allowed price reductions to the consumer. Too often stock records are regarded merely as insurance against dishonesty, while their larger and more useful function as a stimulus to efficiency is overlooked.

So also with utilization. Modern production standards, it may fairly be said, are based on laboratory studies. Essential in those factories which have to do with highly technical or complex processes, this practice of establishing absolute standards may be overdone or misdirected, but it is normally a most effective application of a new point of view. No progressive manufacturer, for instance, takes chances any longer with his glue, varnish, enamel, paint, wood, or coal.

The day of crude, rule-of-thumb experimentation has passed. Producers now buy their materials on the basis of exact knowledge; they do not buy merely because of somebody's casual recommendation or because the local agent is a friend or because the first cost is low. The furniture maker no longer buys twelve-cent glue if he has found that eighteen-cent glue goes further and holds best. Though higher in first cost, in final cost it may be much the cheaper. Moreover, it saves trouble in the factory and dissatisfaction on the part of customers, the money value of which he can measure only indirectly. To insure that he is getting the best quality of glue available for his money, and that the quality of the adopted brand does not subsequently deteriorate, he often maintains a laboratory or employs a competent chemist on a fee basis, by whom not only glue but all his other materials of manufacture, including his fuel, are systematically tested. This, with an efficient cost system to show him what materials work up to the best advantage and with the least waste, enables him to purchase on a basis of true economy.

Standardization of materials can affect the sizes and shapes in which these materials are bought as well as the quality. A manufacturer of steel folding couches, for instance, was making his products seventy-four and a half inches long. The long pieces in the framework of the couch were made of extra heavy material. The nearest stock length in this weight left nearly two feet of scrap which could not be used for any other purpose. By reducing the length of the couch one and one half inches, however, a slightly lighter angle iron that cut with practically no waste could be utilized, making a double saving of a cheaper material and less waste. Before the change was made, investigation showed that the demand for the seventy-three-inch couch was likely to be just as great as for the longer model.

Somewhat similar was the experience of a large manufacturer of farm implements. At various intervals, as models were added to the line, special designs were made for all the parts, without any attempt at standardization or the establishing of relations with other models. Patterns for certain similar parts varied only an eighth or a quarter of an inch in length; there were literally hundreds of parts which might be made interchangeable with other parts by means of minor changes. The manager, bringing a fresh point of view to bear on a policy which had become traditional, ordered the redesigning of the whole line with a view of standardization and the purchase of raw materials in stock dimensions. Thus the same parts were made available for use in more than one model, and the same lengths and weights of steel rods, bars, and angles became standard for many similar parts. The savings were substantial: buying was simplified and prices were generally lowered; the inventory was reduced; less storage space was required; the number of different sizes of raw stock carried was cut in half; while the standardization of parts lowered production costs and greatly reduced the stock of finished parts in storage.

Such radical departures from routine are likely to be found only when the management has preserved its strategic position, aloof from departmental details and able, therefore, to view problems like this one of materials from the standpoint of general efficiency. Close contact with processes and machinery and familiarity with existing methods breed in foremen and others directly identified with the handling of materials a habit of acceptance. It is by the manager, then, with his unbiased attitude and his ability to analyze conditions that the opportunities for standardization can best be observed and the most effective relations between operations and materials can be established.

CHAPTER VI

LABOR

WHEN the paymaster walks through the factory or office with his box of envelopes, he completes a week's transactions between management and men. The cash or checks are exchanged for labor. How much money for how much labor depends on many conditions. The unit of payment may be the hour or day, with loosely defined minimum and maximum results as the commodity delivered by the worker. Again, it may be a swift repeat operation on a standard part or a complex assembling process requiring many hours to finish. It may be any one of several combinations or variations of time units or result units. But in every case the purpose is the same — to secure for each dollar expended the largest regular day by day and year by year return in productive effort.

To the employee the money is the essential factor in the transaction. How far this pocket appeal can be increased by the method of fixing and paying wages or can be supplemented by cultivating the pride, ambition, latent skill, or unawakened intelligence of the worker depends upon the policy of the management in approaching and handling its labor problems. Low average wages frequently occur in shops where production costs are far above the normal; and thirty-dollar mechanics may predominate in a factory similarly equipped where goods are turned out at bed-rock figures.

The reverse of both statements may also be true; the ratio between wages and efficiency varies widely, though there is a marked tendency toward leveling up and the establishment of standards in certain groups of related industries.

The reason for this variation is plain. In the hiring and directing of labor, the human factor counts for much more than in any other activity of production. Assuming that the manager has been broad and wise enough to minimize his own prejudices and prepossessions (reckoning with trade unionism, for instance, more from the viewpoint of the efficiency of the whole business and less from his personal, social, or sentimental standpoint) he will have to face, and find a way to neutralize, the personal equations of his men. They will concentrate on wages, hours of labor, and, perhaps, recognition of the unions which have exerted so powerful an influence on both wages and hours. His problem is likely to take the form of the query: What more besides wages and hours? These are essential for mere time-serving. Real efficiency must be bought at a higher price and paid for either in added money or applied intelligence of management.

His problem, like all business problems, can be solved more easily and with greater certainty by breaking it up into its constituent parts. Analysis, indeed, will develop two groups of problems. The first has to do with the classification of workers according to their functions, the temperaments and characteristics of the individuals usually exercising those functions, and the motives which appeal most effectively to each group. This classification is basic, for the second group, the process-problems of labor, (hiring, training, paying, and

AN APPROACH TO BUSINESS PROBLEMS

directing), will be found to differ in considerable degree
for each class — factory workers, factory foremen, office
employees, salesmen, and general executives. Because
we are dealing as yet only with production policies
and need not go beyond the factory to illustrate a systematic approach to the general problem of labor, any
reference to the factors which must be considered in
the hiring and managing of men outside the production departments will be only incidental.

Viewed broadly, factory workers have certain class
characteristics which make the problem of managing
them differ materially from the problems which arise
in the managing of salesmen or office help. In common
with all other groups of intelligent workers, they have
ambition; but it is usually ambition tempered by a
certain distrust of the employer's motives and held in
check by what amounts to a class philosophy. It is the
manager's task to overcome this suspicion and to make
clear that loyalty to the company, interest in its progress, and pride in its product are entirely compatible
with loyalty to labor organizations, where such organizations exist. He must keep in mind that the narrow
education of the worker and the constant pressure of
his environment combine in urging him to treat the
employer as an impersonal force whose interests are
selfish and therefore hostile, and to bargain with him
on the basis of giving as little and getting as much in
return as circumstances will allow.

We may as well admit that this is the attitude of
skilled and semi-skilled workmen in every large labor
market. To escape it many firms have chosen to move
to country towns, sacrificing whatever advantages the
large city offered to escape disturbing labor conditions.

LABOR

Other concerns have joined issue on the question, declaring for the open shop on the ground that unionism is the chief factor in antagonizing workers. Still other managers have taken for granted a certain indifference on the part of employees and have directed their efforts toward changing this attitude to one of confidence in the management, comprehension of what it is trying to accomplish both inside the organization and outside, interest in the day's work, however monotonous, pride in the quality or quantity of product, and coöperation for mutual advantage. This is an ambitious program, but it is these latter executives who have made the most important advances in the methods and philosophy of employment, and it is their experience which is drawn upon in the shaping of this chapter.

When a manufacturer analyzes his labor problem into its elements, the question of balanced output comes first and looms largest in his thoughts. How can he secure a reasonable maximum in quantity, the essential accompaniment of low production costs, yet maintain requisite standards of quality and avoid more than a minimum of spoiled parts? Bearing on this, his main objective, are the personal traits of his employees, their honesty and industry, their skill and sense of responsibility, and also their mental attitude toward their work and toward his management. Personal traits and qualities are fundamental considerations in hiring men, though the good ones may be developed by subsequent training and the harmful ones corrected or eliminated. Assuming a factory force of average spirit and caliber, however, its mental attitude is a problem of daily practical concern. How can it be influenced? How can it be brought into accord with the purposes of

67

the management and be made a constructive force, instead of one merely negative or antagonistic?

The broad basis of appeal, he will find, is pay scientifically proportioned to individual effort. Ease, convenience, and safety are convincing arguments. Caution, as to retaining place, service credits, preferred work, or other privileges, is a powerful motive to invoke. Pride in workmanship, in the company's standing, in the perfection and value of its products, is a sentiment which can be stirred only when conditions are generally satisfactory, that is, when the worker is convinced that he is receiving a square deal. Praise of a man's ability or achievement soon loses its savor unless it "gets him something" in the way of increased pay or promotion.

Money and material utilities are the solid foundations on which alone efficiency can be built. The workman's natural tendency is to strike a balance between the advantages the manager offers and those held out by other employers. No appeals less tangible are allowed to outweigh these necessities. Certainty of employment on full time or nearly full time is an essential for men who have families and others who want to get ahead. Self-interest, in fact, is the only compelling motive which can be enlisted to secure coöperation in the betterment of existing methods or the installing of improved systems. If he can adopt the easier or more direct method without losing any of his pay per unit of production, the average factory worker will welcome the change. Unless he gets a share of the profit coming from his increase in output, however, suspicion that he is being "speeded up" is likely to follow. Confidence in the manager and his motives must precede any successful attempt to increase the productive capacity of an organization.

Paying labor, then, is the crucial problem, though training, placing, and directing are vital questions in any efficiency program. Hiring, a preliminary operation, will not be taken up here because, at any rate in the large plants, it is usually an administrative function and will be reserved for discussion with other activities of administration in a later chapter. Any plan of payment, we have seen, should furnish the worker with an incentive to increased production through addition to his income. The best wage system, indeed, is that which makes clear to the worker the exact relation between his effort and the amount which he receives for it. At the same time, it must not add to unit production costs. The manager must hold at least to his established ratio of cost, quality, and service, while the prime object of any change, of course, is to cut down the first element in this business equation. This to the management is no less a test than self-interest to the employee, of any new method of wage payment. Does it actually lower production costs? Personal prejudice, sentiment, or convenience should never be permitted to govern or even cloud the decision.

In his approach to this problem of payment, the manager has for his guidance the experience of other employers, many of whom have conducted extended investigations and long series of experiments to determine the most effective wage plan. He must understand, however, what his real problem is; how it divides; what are the factors that count in the solution of each subproblem; and how he can apply in his own factory the methods which have been more or less successfully demonstrated by other manufacturers and production specialists.

Dividing the problem into its constituents and considering each, the manager finds himself facing a choice among several methods of paying men. There are the systems long in use, the day rate, the piece rate, and the contract system, all relatively simple, but all having the common weakness that the personal factor is large in determining how much productive effort labor shall deliver for each dollar received. Where the straight day wage is maintained, output is often a compromise between customary trade standards plus the man's idea of what is fair and the ability of the management to speed up its machines and workmen without causing revolt. Whether this compromise basis is above or below the average depends chiefly on the personality of the manager, on his sympathy, magnetism, and other qualities of leadership, and in lesser degree on the size and character of the force itself.

The great defect of the traditional day rate is that it offers no direct incentive for the individual employee to exert himself to his full capacity. The piece rate is an advance on this primitive method of measuring energy in terms of time. Where many repeat operations are performed and where time studies or a series of observations and experiments have established trustworthy standards, the piece rate supplies an incentive to higher efficiency and a fuller utilization of the plant. When such standards have not been worked out, however, it gives too much play to the personal equation in setting rates and in the majority of shops leads the men to put a secret but practical limit on individual production. Moreover, without an adequate inspection system, quality may be sacrificed to output. In a word, the interests of manager and men are still tangential instead of parallel. The contract system is simply the piece rate applied to a group or cycle of operations involving a number of workmen, and is subject to the same drawbacks and limitations.

From the simple forms of both day rate and piece rate various systems of payment have been developed to overcome their basic weakness, that is, lack of an imperative incentive for the workman to employ time and equipment to their fullest productiveness. The straight piece rate, which pays one price per unit of work done whether the rate of efficiency be high or low, has been supplemented in many factories by the fixing of a daily or weekly task which the workman must equal in order to hold his place. The graduated or differential piece rate modifies this appeal to caution by offering a high rate for performance of the task in a given time and a lower rate if the workman falls short of this standard efficiency. An interesting variation is the Franklin quality piece rate which puts the emphasis on perfect work by paying the maximum when spoilage is eliminated and reducing the rate paid as the proportion of spoiled parts increases.

The development of the day rate has taken shape in bonus or premium systems, which are based on the idea of rewarding the workman for saving time and cutting costs by sharing with him the money thus saved. The Towne system was one of the earliest of these; it made an annual pro-rated distribution of the saving in labor costs over those of the best preceding year, the company taking its reward in the increased production per factory unit. The Halsey premium plan went a step fur-

ther. It made the workman's reward immediate and
individual by fixing a definite time limit for each operation (based on past performances), paying the worker
his regular hourly rate for the time spent in executing
it, but allowing him a bonus if he finished in less than
the specified time. This premium is usually half the
labor cost thus saved. The Rowan system differs from
the Halsey plan by making the workman's premium
a percentage of the standard labor cost equal to the
percentage of the standard time which his saving
represents.

Both the Towne-Halsey and the Rowan systems
showed flaws in operation — the first by putting the
fixing of the standard times entirely in the hands of the
workmen, the second by cutting the premium paid for
any saving of more than fifty per cent. They are ob-
jected to further because as the workman's production
increases, his earnings per piece decrease. To avoid
these faults, the Emerson system based its standard
times on workmen's performances corrected by expert
motion-and-time studies, demanded two-thirds of this
standard efficiency of every workman, and paid graduated premiums for every increase above the minimum.
When the workman equaled the standard time, his
bonus amounted to twenty per cent of his wages; above
the standard time the permiums increased one per cent
for each per cent of increase in efficiency.

The Taylor differential piece rate puts forward a
final incentive to workmen by providing scientifically
determined standard conditions and times for work,
and offering higher piece rates as the standard time is
approached and passed and lower rates as the workman drops down in the scale of efficiency. The task

and bonus plan evolved by H. L. Gantt in connection with the Taylor system guarantees the regular hourly rate and offers the man a bonus for attaining a previously determined high level of efficiency, each man's bonus increasing as his output above the prescribed standard increases. The ratio of the bonus to the regular hourly rate varies among different trades and occupations, according to the character and difficulty of the work. The regular hourly rate is paid while the man is under instruction.

There is yet another approach to this task of providing an incentive to workers — profit-sharing. In the broader sense, it amounts to any collective payment of bonuses for faithful service, predicated on satisfactory net earnings for the employer. It may take the Henry Ford form of decidedly higher day wages, which divide with the workers every week a predetermined amount of the estimated profits of the company's current operations; though this might be a dangerous proceeding for the average business venture, which is subject to the ups-and-downs of the consuming market. The more familiar form is an arbitrary sum set aside by the directors at the end of every prosperous year for distribution among employees, the size of the lump sum and the amount of the individual dividend depending on the measure of the company's prosperity, thus establishing an incentive for each worker.

The more sagacious plans do not leave the size of the worker's dividend for the management's decision at the end of the year. The amount to be shared is predetermined; or at least the percentage or proportion of the net profits to be shared is announced beforehand. In

fact, in the strict technical usage of the term, profit
sharing means a method of remuneration by which the
employees receive in addition to standard or normal
wages a share of the profits fixed in advance. The
manner of distribution varies. The A. W. Burritt
Company, for instance, after paying six per cent on
capital, divides its net profit between the stockholders
and the workmen in the ratio of capital invested to
wages earned, each workman receiving an amount proportionate to his own wages. The workmen agree
also to share similarly any net losses, up to ten per cent
of their wages. The Farr Alpaca Company pays the
same dividend on a dollar of wages as is paid on a
dollar of capital. The R. F. Simmons Company,
which began by sharing with its workers from eight
to twelve per cent of the dividend voted on its capital,
has gradually increased the amount so as to insure its
representing four or five per cent of the employees'
annual wages. The Simplex Wire and Cable Company determines in January the percentage of profits to be paid at the end of the year to workers who
have been connected with the company for twenty-six
months or more.

This latter emphasis on continuity of service is common to nearly all profit-sharing plans, which fix a minimum period for eligibility and increase the dividend in
proportion to the time of employment. Profit-sharing
programs range widely, indeed, in character and effectiveness; their weakness is that the collective bonuses
they offer fall short of providing the constant, specific,
and measurable incentive to individual workers which a
scientific system of wage payment should supply.

Facing these successful wage systems (outlined merely

in principle here[1]), the manager can make a wise decision only by keeping a tight grip on all the factors involved. His product may be of such a type that the day rate is the only possible method of maintaining quality or satisfying his production conditions. His organization may be of such size or character that the cost of installing and maintaining a differential piece rate, with all the conditions involved, would be prohibitive. Between these extremes there are a score of alternatives. The conditions in different departments of the same business, in fact, often call for different wage systems. In choosing the one or more than one which fit his situation, the executive must keep his principle of balance always in mind. The fresh point of view, too, is of more than usual importance, since the wage systems of most industries are traditional compromises or guesses developed like all other rules of thumb. Its value, indeed, has been generally recognized: witness the recent widespread interest in the Taylor system of shop management and other efficiency methods, and the associated movements in many industries to reduce labor costs and conditions to something like common and reasonable standards. With the overhead charges on factory operations averaging as much as the direct labor costs, the rewards are for the manager who can hasten production and thereby reduce the proportion of rent, light, heat, power, and other fixed charges which each unit of product must bear. There, in countless plants, the zone of profit lies.

But a wage incentive, however alluring, is not enough to get results from factory labor. With the best will in

---

[1] For a fuller discussion, see C. B. Thompson, "Scientific Management," and the works cited in the Bibliography beginning on page 863 of that book.

the world, a workman must have the knowledge and skill his job demands, or his output will suffer in quantity or quality. This knowledge and skill can frequently be hired in the larger markets; with a certain amount of "breaking in," a new workman becomes capable of handling the tasks for which he was employed. Quite as often competent mechanics or machine operators are not to be had; or, if available, they cannot be engaged except at rates higher than conditions in the business will justify. The only alternative, then, is for the manager to train unskilled labor to the level of efficiency required.

Every factory organization confronts this situation at more or less regular intervals. For at least a generation the apprentice system, limited in its application by the rules of the unions and neglected by self-centered employees, has been inadequate to provide the skilled workers our industrial expansion called for. Hundreds of thousands of English and German mechanics, emigrating in answer to the call, helped to supply the lack. The division of labor and the development of automatic machinery of endless variety and countless functions further served the need. But the burden of getting and retaining men was not lifted from the manufacturer. Each machine required an operator; and its output in no small degree was measured by the thoroughness of the training grafted on his natural intelligence and dexterity.

This fact gives the Taylor system and similar efficiency programs their chief significance. Their standardizing of materials, machines, processes, and methods by means of time and motion studies is all preliminary to the final task of teaching each worker how to perform his operation with the least possible outlay of time and energy. They approach each process, each separate motion, indeed, from the engineering viewpoint. Is it necessary? Is it the most effective way of doing the thing? By observation, analysis, and experiment they arrive at a standard method. This method they demonstrate to the worker, helping him to master it. They watch him try it time after time, day after day, if necessary, correcting his mistakes, explaining the how and why of each detail, holding him to the exact technique they have determined as the best. As we have seen, they get the man's coöperation by paying him his full wage while he is under instruction and showing him how he will profit by following the new procedure. The increase in wages, so graduated that the highest premium can be gained only by the fullest coöperation with the management, supplies the incentive to effort. But the fixing of the standards and the training of the workmen are indispensable to the success of the plan.

Under the best systems, indeed, the training of the worker never ends. He is not allowed to earn the maximum bonus one week and slump the next. An instructor-foreman, having a limited group of men in charge, keeps close watch on his output and exerts all his knowledge, tact, and authority to keep it up to standard. As the instructor's own bonus is based on the success of his men in earning theirs, the efficiency level is usually maintained. In addition to the instructor or gang boss, there are other functional foremen, such as speed and repair bosses, inspectors and planning-room men, each of whom contributes his special aid in achieving standard efficiency.

AN APPROACH TO BUSINESS PROBLEMS

One of the indictments brought by sociologists and humanitarians against the modern factory system of production is that the minute subdivision of labor dwarfs the development of the worker and makes him a one-operation specialist rather than an all-round mechanic. At first sight efficiency systems would seem to exaggerate this tendency. On close observation, however, the opposite would seem true. The fresh viewpoint which standardization proposes to the workmen, the mental exertion required to master the technique of the new methods, the processes of analysis and synthesis which take place under his eyes, all open new channels of thought and transform him from a creature of habit to a man awake, with a mind open to new things. If he has average intelligence and ambition, after mastering one process or series of operations he "gets the hang" of the new idea and finds it easy to master a second and a third or any number of operations which shop exigencies may propose.

This should eliminate monotony of occupation and supply something like an equivalent of the training an apprenticeship or a trade school might have given him. From certain factories where the Taylor system has been installed come reports of individual progress of this sort which would indicate the possibility of all-round training for employees without any sacrifice of output while their education was going on. It is said that at the Tabor Manufacturing Company, Philadelphia, two young men who gave promise of executive ability were "passed through" all the departments of the factory in two years, reaching during that period the efficiency standards of every operation in the plant.

This development of capable, "all 'round" men, first

for the performance of single processes and finally for the supervision of groups of workers engaged on a whole cycle of operations, has long been recognized as an important phase of the management's labor problem. The subdivision of labor as carried out in a great many industries has meant that the apprentice or the unskilled man learns only to tend certain special machines which perform a limited range of operations on an unending succession of similar jobs. His work becomes automatic; there is nothing to cultivate skill outside his narrow field, to develop his thinking power, or to help him to see his own detail in its relations to the general production scheme. Take him off his machine or away from his bench and he must start all over again.

Coupling this tendency with a general breakdown of the apprenticeship system, many of the older and larger industrial organizations, like R. Hoe & Company and the General Electric Company, have established apprentice schools in which selected boys are not only taught a trade, in the former sense of the phrase, but are given regular class-room instruction in shop arithmetic, geometry, algebra, drawing, physics, mechanics, strength of materials, and subjects directly related to the technique of the industry or calculated to fit them for understanding all its shop processes. This class work, which occupies usually from three to twelve hours a week, is partly or wholly on the employer's time, and the apprentice is required to give it the same attention and show the same progress in it as in his shop work.

At the General Electric works, the courses are planned to produce expert machinists, pattern makers, iron molders, core makers, and draughtsmen, though a few boys in every class are taught blacksmithing, tin-smithing, and steam fitting. The course lasts four years, during the first three of which the boys are given experience on the various machine tools and are put to work on as many different processes as possible. In the fourth year of service they are rated as competent work-men, so far as quality of work is concerned, though still under direct charge of the superintendent of appren-tices. The draughting apprentices serve their second year in the shops doing the same class of work, under the same direction, as the machinist apprentices. An-alogous courses for "student engineers" are also conducted by this same company with the object of giving graduates of technical schools, when they enter its employ, experience in all its production depart-ments and an intimate grasp of their activities.

Because the cost of equipping and maintaining effec-tive schools for apprentices puts them beyond the reach of the ordinary business, the manufacturers of Fitch-burg, Massachusetts, have adapted to their local needs the "half-time" plan of education conceived by Dean Herman Schneider for the University of Cincinnati's engineering school.

Under the Schneider plan, seventy-five or more in-dustrial plants, construction companies, and transporta-tion lines coöperate with the university in the training of the engineering students. The latter work in pairs, one man attending the university while the other works for wages at one of the coöperating plants. They alter-nate bi-weekly at study and service in their common job and thus get an opportunity to "hitch their theo-retical knowledge to practical things and bring a prac-tical viewpoint to their studies." Incidentally some of

LABOR

them earn enough on the various jobs they have, during
their sequential training through the departments of
the coöperating concern, to keep them in school, and
they all have the valuable experience of turning out
commercial products under actual working conditions.
The manufacturers secure high-grade intelligence practically and theoretically trained at the wages which
they pay any one else for the same class of work; also
they have a chance to pick possible executives, designers, salesmen, and other high grade employees
among the student graduates. At the same time the
university is spared the expense of equipping its lab-
oratories with expensive machinery and of maintaining
a staff of machinists and instructors to direct students'
practice work.

Fitchburg's manufacturers have a similar coöperative arrangement with their city high school. The first
year of the four-year course there is no interchange
between school and shop; but during the last three
years the pairs of pupil-apprentices serve alternate
weeks under teachers and foremen. The school does
not attempt to teach anything about practical shop
work; but concentrates on mathematics, mechanical
drawing, elementary physics, and chemistry, and other
branches which give the pupil a grip on theory and interpret shop practice, broadening his outlook and increasing his capacity. It tries to answer his "why"
questions and leaves the "hows" to the mechanics and
foremen of the different factories.

Some manufacturers have brought trade schools into
their schemes of training labor. Knowing that the
conditions under which factory production goes forward make it difficult for the apprentice or young

helper to get more than a smattering of the underlying trade, not a few pick out at intervals boys of more than average character, force, and intelligence and help them to put themselves through a trade school in order to master their chosen craft. The purpose, of course, is to secure workmen of wider experience, skill, and knowledge than can be developed in their own plants and to train possible executives. There are numerous cases where specialists of various sorts, chemists, factory engineers, and the like have been developed from the ranks by employers observant enough to notice unusual aptitudes in factory workers and keen enough to give these exceptional men the backing necessary to secure them special technical training.

A most important general policy governing the problem of labor has to do with the manager's attitude toward trade unionism. As already suggested, it is in this connection that the personal factor is most difficult to discount. Opposition to organized labor, to collective bargaining, to contracts secured and enforced by implied or expressed threats of strikes may be said to be one of his normal habits of mind. For the organization of his employees on occupational lines is certain to bring about interference with his free hand in running the business. In some businesses, however, compensating factors have arisen from recognition of the unions and a surrender of a portion of the employer's power over shop discipline and conditions. In a notable clothing concern in Chicago, for example, the establishment of machinery for adjusting disputes is said to have brought peace, stability, and production betterments to an industry in which antagonism and unstable conditions have always obtained.

LABOR

From the viewpoint of the manufacturer, it may be worth while to surrender part of his authority and control in order to gain a spirit of contentment and coöperation in the factory.

Frequent "turn-over" of labor is the outward expression of another serious labor problem. Manufacturers in both small town and city experience much difficulty in holding competent operators of certain standard and widely used machines, screw-making machines, milling machines, and so on. These are men above the unskilled in intelligence, though lacking exact knowledge of a trade, and therefore more sensitive to the monotony of repeat operations indefinitely continued. Relief from this monotony is denied usually by factory conditions and the lack of training; it is found by moving on to the next city where there is a steady demand for this kind of labor.

Efforts to hold these "floaters," usually most restless in seasons of maximum production, have taken many forms. Company "thrift clubs" and other plans for encouraging and financing the purchase of homes is one avenue of approach. So-called "welfare work" designed to make the factory more attractive from the standpoint of comfort, convenience, and social and working conditions is another. An eastern manufacturer comes closest, perhaps, to the root of the difficulty by studying methods of restoring variety to the day's work. Instead of putting through work in quantities as large as is commercially possible, he takes the monotony factor into consideration and manufactures in lots small enough to allow frequent shifts to new tasks for his machine operators. This plan, he has found, reacts as well on other production difficulties, lessening to a large extent the proportion of spoiled parts in each factory order.

With many managers, it is a settled policy to try by other means to hold workers who have made their honesty, industry, and good will evident by service. Before a man can be paid off, even when leaving on his own initiative, either the manager or some one in his confidence has a talk with the employee about his motives for leaving. If the reason is a condition which can be corrected, the change is made. If a transfer to another department or another task will remove the employee's dissatisfaction, the change is made whenever possible. In many successful organizations, indeed, discontent on the part of the worker is anticipated and it is made one of the chief duties of the employment official or department to discover the capacities, ambitions, and desires of all workers and to endeavor to place them, as soon as practicable, in the positions which will bring out the fullest measure of their interest and productive powers.

After adjustment of the wage factor — which may or may not include profit-sharing — the placing and training of workers are the two policies most vital in the building up and holding of an efficient factory force. Give a man the work he wants to do; help him to fit himself for its effective performance; pay him fairly for what he does, and the other factors in the equation will almost lose themselves; so strong is the creative, the productive instinct, so real the joy in doing the work that fits.

CHAPTER VII

ORGANIZATION

STARTING with a factory, a working force, and a supply of raw materials, the manager faces a final production problem, that of effectively organizing his operating activities. He has a definite end in view. To the smallest necessary amount of wood, metal, clay, or fiber he wants to add the fewest motions required to turn out a properly balanced unit of product. To do this he must so coördinate and direct the application of these motions that there shall be no duplication or loss, no waste of time or stock or energy. And he must further provide a permanent method of controlling both motions and materials in order that this equilibrium of means and results shall be preserved.

Inefficient management involves either the application of too much power or labor to a given unit of material, or the use of too large or too valuable a quantity of raw stock in the manufacture of a standard unit of product. In flagrant cases it may mean that all the elements which enter directly into manufacture — material, labor, power, machinery, space, light, and so on — are entirely out of proportion to the result which is obtained. Efficient production, on the other hand, is always the consequence of establishing and maintaining a balance of all the elements that count in the making and, to a lesser degree, in the marketing of an article.

The factory head must so organize his plant and processes that he can turn goods out economically. Yet in his attention to cost he must not lose sight of quality, accuracy, durability, beauty, or whatever is the characteristic which measures the service to customers. In the building of machinery, for instance, it may be possible to increase output substantially by permitting small deviations from standards in cutting gears, reaming out bearings, and like finishing processes. But laxness in this respect is almost certain to be followed by the development of lost motion when the machine is operated by the purchaser, and lost motion always means greater consumption of power and a shortened life for the machine itself. This inevitably reacts on sales and sometimes brings disaster, as in the recent experience of a great industrial concern whose chief product was sold on long-time payments.

In an effort to bring output up to a quota based entirely on selling and financial considerations, this factory was enlarged and its working force increased to a point where the old plan of organization was inadequate to insure efficiency. Relaxed or incompetent inspection allowed many faulty parts to be incorporated in machines. Tried out by the purchasers, so many of these were thrown back on the agents' hands that the company's reputation suffered, a financial crisis followed, and complete reorganization was necessary to protect creditors and stockholders. Other factors, besides too rapid expansion of the working force and scamped workmanship, undoubtedly contributed to the failure. The same emphasis on volume led to general overselling by the field force and a breakdown of the plan for financing deferred payments on orders. Both of these weaknesses might have been corrected, however, if the plant had shipped standard and satisfactory machines to all buyers. It was the flood of returns which shook confidence in the company's products, neutralized its selling efforts, and ultimately destroyed its credit. Because its factory organization lost control of production and failed to maintain the right ratio between cost, quality, and service an industry of almost national scope collapsed like a house of cards.

Control of operations, then, is the culminating function of production. The man at the head of a small plant has need only of a personal system or a personal routine, perhaps, which will bring him into contact at frequent intervals with all his workmen and all the jobs they are engaged on. If he has a real knowledge of the technical processes and a certain amount of personality — the typical "one-man" business seems to be built largely on these two elements — he can at the same time control the quality and cost of output, hasten production, and accommodate it to sales or financial exigencies to a degree which few large businesses can hope to equal. But when he finds it necessary to delegate authority because important details have so multiplied that he can no longer handle all of them, a more formal organization becomes essential if his plant is not to lose efficiency. As Alfred Marshall senses it, the crucial point in business expansion arrives when orders must be written instead of being spoken.

To keep control of operations while delegating supervision and authority is the manager's broad problem in organization. Once he has determined the lines on which the latter can be divided and has established his underlying policies in accord with the principle of balance and the principle of interdependence, he can hire or train men to whom he can turn over the direction and the responsibility of all or nearly all his operating activities. Experience indicates that this is naturally the first step taken toward the division of labor in the field of management. This, it has already been shown, is for two reasons: first, because production (while much is still to be done) has so largely been standardized and so many of its processes and reactions reduced to generally accepted and measurable terms; second, because classes of specialists have been developed who are competent to take charge of operations and hold them to any predetermined balance of cost, quality, and service. When the growth of his business or the initial size of his undertaking forces the executive to substitute organization for personal supervision, then it is in the factory that he finds it easiest and most profitable to share his functions and responsibility with subordinates. His problem, therefore, is to discover how best to delegate his authority in order to retain effective control.

When he consults the experience and practice of other manufacturers, he finds in use three distinctive types of shop organization. These differ in the manner of delegating authority and control, in the extent of the responsibility fastened on individual executives and foremen, and most of all in the philosophy of business which informs them. Widest apart are (1) the line type of organization and (2) the functional type. Midway between these and having characteristics in common with both is (3) the line-and-staff. In considering which kind of organization is likely to prove most applicable and most efficient in his own factory, there is hardly need to say that the factors which determine his choice should not be personal in their nature or relations and that the decision should not hinge solely on the manager's experience or familiarity with a particular type of organization or on the usage of the district or the industry in which he is engaged.

In breaking up his problem of organization into its constituent problems and assembling the factors which enter into the solution of each, he will find it necessary to analyze and consider from the viewpoint of his own business the principles and the working of the three types of control just named. In the line organization — the traditional form, and until our own generation the only common type — the authority and responsibility are delegated throughout. The head of each department and sub-department is held responsible for all that happens within his jurisdiction. It follows that his functions are of many kinds and large in number. He must hire his men, place them where their capacities will be most useful, determine what is a fair day's work for each and what payment should be made for it, watch his machines to see that they are in proper condition, plan his work in such a way and keep material so moving in the shop that the men and equipment are always producing. He is expected to be able to show a workman how an operation should be carried out to secure maximum results with the least expenditure of time and energy, and in an emergency to give exact instructions for meeting it.

This list of duties, incomplete as it is, illustrates both the advantages and disadvantages of the line type of organization. It unifies work by concentrating authority and definitely fixes responsibility upon certain individuals. As the shop grows larger, however, the demands made upon the foreman's time, skill, intelligence, and patience increase to a point where it is difficult to satisfy them. He may carry the hardest of his problems up to the superintendent or even to the head of the business, while his responsibility for groups or cycles of operations is frequently divided by putting these in charge of job or section bosses. But the foreman's mental and physical limitations remain; and the efficiency of the individual workman and of the factory as a whole suffers unless the size of the shop or the special character of the operations allows each boss to master the technical details and oversee the performance of all the processes for which he is held responsible.

If an industry is to satisfy these conditions and best lend itself to economical application of line organization, it seems obvious that the processes must be virtually standard and continuous, one operation following another in regular order and all of nearly routine character, while the machinery must be largely automatic. There must be no extraordinary demands upon the intelligence or initiative of the foreman and his duties must include little outside keeping his men at work, preserving discipline, and seeing that materials or parts in process move according to schedule. But in factories where assembling operations form an important part of the production cycle, the line organization offers few advantages. It is in the assembling industries, indeed, that the functional system and the different systems of line-and-staff shop organization chiefly have been developed.

The functional system is simply the application of the principle of the division of labor to shop management, while the line-and-staff may be considered either as a modified form of the functional scheme or as a grafting on the traditional line organization of functional principles. In succeeding chapters we shall see this same tendency toward the division of labor in management revealing itself in the gradual division of the activities of distribution along functional lines, and the unrecorded and almost unnoticed development as such of functional middlemen, like bankers, insurance underwriters, and transportation and express companies. For the moment, however, we are concerned only with factory activities.

The first functional division of production is a separation of planning from performance, with the aim of relieving the foremen of the duty of arranging and routing materials through the shops. A further functional division then takes place within the planning department. In the Taylor system of management, which is a typical functional scheme, the work is divided among an order-of-work clerk, an instruction-card man, a time-and-cost clerk, and a shop disciplinarian. The names of these foremen, for that is their real rank, indicate the duties which each performs. Auxiliary to the planning department are the time-and-motion-study men, upon whose investigations, analyses, and experiments are based the standards which govern all the shop activities, whether these are ordered by the planning room or actually applied under the eye of the foremen in immediate charge of the operations.

The function of the order-of-work clerk is to plan the route which each piece or lot of material shall take through the shop. But his task is not simply to indicate the sequence of the movements. He determines what processes the material shall pass through and in what order, and maps his conclusions on route sheets which illustrate this order graphically and chronologically. With these charts before him, the instruction-card man works out the details of each operation, even to the particular machine and tool to use, the speed to be observed, and the order in which the cuts are to be made. All this from standards already set by preliminary time-and-motion studies and kept at hand for instant reference in the case of new or unfamiliar work.

The instruction cards have two purposes: they are work orders for the proper functional foremen out in the shop, and they also give exact directions for the mechanic to follow in his work. After the latter has finished the job, a return of the time consumed in both labor and machine-hours goes to the time-and-cost clerk, whose function it is to make up the pay roll, including the bonuses earned, and to determine the cost of each separate operation performed on the job. Lastly there is the shop disciplinarian (frequently the head of the planning room as well) to deal with any dispute or insubordination which the other bosses are unable to handle satisfactorily.

In direct contact with the men, the machines, and the work in process are four other functional foremen, the gang boss, the speed boss, the repair boss, and the inspector.

The gang boss is more a teacher than an executive. It is his part to interpret the planning room's instructions on unfamiliar work, to demonstrate if necessary the standard way of carrying on the process as indicated on the instruction card, and to continue this demonstration and supervision until the workman is able to turn out the job in the standard time. Moreover, on familiar or repeat operations in which the workman is likely to lose interest and efficiency, it is the duty of the gang boss to hold him to the efficiency level where he will earn his own bonus, and allow the gang boss to earn the premium gained when his group makes more than a specified minimum of individual bonuses. No need to say that the workman's bonus is an imperative part of the functional system of management; without such an incentive to effort, the efficiency level could not be permanently maintained.

The function of the speed boss is to see that every machine moves at the exact speed called for by the instruction card. This indicated speed is the one which has been shown to be the most effective in the tests and experiments carried on when this particular operation was submitted to time-and-motion studies and thus standardized for all future repetitions. The business of the repair boss, naturally, is to keep all machines, tools, power transmissions, and the like in such perfect order that processes can be performed in the standard times. The inspector, last of the four shop bosses, has jurisdiction over the manner of performing the different operations as well as over the finished results. The idea here is to prevent mistakes rather than to penalize them by rejecting parts or assemblies which fall below specifications.

In some plants, where modified forms of functional management are in use, the work of the speed boss is assumed by the gang boss or instructor. Sometimes, too, the repair boss and inspector have diminished functions and the gang boss is restored to much the same authority as that which he holds under line organization. It is here, indeed, that the line-and-staff system emerges as a virtual compromise between line and functional management. Keeping the line organization to supervise operation, a staff of technical experts is added to analyze every factor and detail in production — materials, machines, methods, routing, arrangement, and the like — to determine standards for each of these and to secure the adoption of these standards by the officers of the regular line organization.

In every sense of the word, these specialists are functional foremen who do not come into direct contact with the working force except when they are making their time-and-motion studies of processes, or demonstrating the standard methods of performing an operation. The greatest advantage of the line-and-staff system, perhaps, is that a beginning can be made in the betterment of shop practice without disturbing the regular factory organization and that the betterments can be carried forward at whatever rate the manager deems advisable. In this it differs from functional management, the advocates of which declare that it must be adopted or rejected as a whole. Both systems are as one in insisting on the bonus method of wage payment, a factor in efficiency which was discussed at some length in the previous chapter.

To the business man approaching the subject of functional management from the outside, the apparent amount of clerical work required, the opportunities offered for mistakes and for the shifting of responsibility, the amount of preparatory work demanded, and the long interval before marked results can be expected should not be absolute deterrents. Functional management, unabridged, may be beyond the present scale or needs of his business as he is conducting it or proposing to start it. But the principle behind both the functional and the line-and-staff systems of management — the finding and using of the "one right way" under present conditions of doing things — cannot be ignored if his business is to meet competition grounded on this fundamental of efficiency.

In this discussion of production little attention has been given to strictly intra-departmental problems. As suggested in earlier chapters, plant and operating activities are relatively well organized, and technically trained factory experts are available to carry the burden of these internal problems. The purpose, indeed, has been less to outline the policies of production and the principles on which they are based than to suggest in a known and standardized field a logical classification of the activities of business and to illustrate how a systematic approach may be applied to the problems disclosed as the classification develops.

PART II

THE PROBLEMS OF DISTRIBUTION

CHAPTER VIII

DEMAND CREATION AND PHYSICAL SUPPLY

WHEN economic life was organized on a basis of barter, both traders inspected and took over the actual goods involved before the transaction was complete. One or the other carried his surplus of food or skins or weapons to the point where the second man had need of it and a store of some desirable thing to exchange for it. Or both transported their merchandise to a recognized market place where the bargain was made and the transfer effected. For a long time, indeed, after the first broad division of labor along functional lines had brought the merchant into existence and the evolution of a medium of exchange or "money economy" had displaced barter, the buyer had personal contact with his purchases at all stages of the transaction and viewed, handled, and tested them before assuming possession.

This was distribution in its simple phase — literally, the application of motion to change the *place* and *ownership* of material which production had already changed in *form*. The two chief functions of marketing, demand creation and physical supply of the merchandise, were all but performed simultaneously. There was no necessity of distinguishing between them or of considering their activities separately, since the sale proper and the delivery of the goods merged into one operation.

Development of the range and means of distribution,

however, has enlarged the original scope of these two functions. Each has given rise to a distinct group of related activities, with corresponding problems for the man who must coördinate and control them. The primitive producer solved all problems when he conveyed his cattle or corn or tanned skins to the market place. For the most part, his goods were common utilities, mere sight of which stirred desire for ownership, even among those already adequately supplied. Under normal conditions, therefore, he was sure of a market at the prevailing market price. If this were unsatisfactory, he could take his merchandise home again and wait for a more favorable occasion.

The problem of distribution to-day is more complex. Broadly speaking, it divides into two sub-problems closely related and interdependent but each having to do with a different set of factors and reactions. The first takes shape in the question: Given a particular article, how can a demand for it be created of sufficient volume to make its production and distribution profitable? The second is: Through what channels can the article itself be conveyed from the factory warehouse, where it is of least value, into the hands of those consumers who will pay the most profitable price for it, though this price may not be the highest at which a more limited volume could be sold?

The activities of demand creation focus on the consumer. Their purpose is to communicate to his mind such ideas about the product as will arouse desire for it and cultivate willingness to pay the price and make the effort required to secure possession of it. This aroused demand would have no commercial or economic value, however, unless provision were made for satisfying it by actual transfer of the goods to the consumer through one or more of the agencies available.

The relations between the activities of demand creation and of physical supply, in fact, illustrate again the persistence of the two principles of interdependence and of balance. Failure to coördinate any one of these activities with its group-fellows and also with those in the other group, or undue emphasis or outlay put upon any one of these activities, is certain to upset the equilibrium of forces which means efficient distribution. Nor must it be forgotten, in organizing these activities and establishing the policies which shall guide them, that both groups present situations which involve the production activities discussed in previous chapters and the activities of administration to be taken up in another section of this book.

In approaching the problems of distribution, greater consideration must be given by the manager to strictly departmental policies than was necessary in dealing with production. In the first place, the standardization of processes and materials, which has been carried to such length in the factory, has hardly touched the major operations of distribution. Relatively little progress has been made, for instance, in observing and compiling the essential facts about demand creation, in classifying them, coördinating them, and establishing their mutual relations; and in tracing and defining the broad tendencies and principles which analysis of a sufficient number of cases would disclose.

It is true that many intensive studies have been made of various functions, processes, and reactions concerned with distribution. But these investigations generally have been made from the viewpoint of a single business or a group of similar businesses. They have concentrated in the main on promising territories and avoided those where the chances were unfavorable. And as a consequence, the results are so subject to qualification that few significant rules capable of general application have been formulated. Promising beginnings have been made — the investigation of retail selling by the Bureau of Business Research at Harvard University, the experiments conducted by the schools of commerce at various universities, the constant gathering, sifting, and organizing of practical methods by business magazines, the trade press and trade associations. By comparison with the work yet to be done, however, they are only beginnings, trial efforts valuable chiefly because they point the way and demonstrate the feasibility of an adequate, organized study, perhaps under the national government's leadership, of all the activities of business.

The present lack of standards is due largely to the difficulty of analyzing a structure so intricate as our system or distribution, complicated further by geographical, seasonal, and other physical conditions, and by the presence of the changing human factor in every individual transaction. Consider, for a moment, how many and various are the elements presented by the United States as a consuming market. Here are about one hundred million people distributed over an area of more than three million square miles. Some are gathered in the large cities, where millions jostle elbows. Some are scattered over great areas with considerable distances between them and their neighbors. Some daily pass hundreds of retail stores; some must ride miles to reach the nearest store. Wide extremes in purchasing power exist. Millions have a purchasing power barely sufficient to obtain for themselves the necessities of life. A few can satisfy the most extravagant whims of the imagination. Between these extremes lie all degrees of purchasing power, the number in each class becoming greater as you descend in the scale of purchasing power.

Their desires are as varied as their purchasing power. Besides the great colonies of immigrant folk in every large city — Poles, Bohemians, Hungarians, Italians, Scandinavians, and Russian Jews, each race with transplanted tastes and standards and a language barrier to make more difficult the approach — the native-born consumers present a complex problem, with environment, education, social customs, individual habits, and all the variations of body and mind tending to make their wants diverse.

In each individual certain conscious needs are constantly gratified by the purchase of goods produced for such gratification. Then there are the conscious needs which go ungratified because of the limitations upon buying power and the necessity of satisfying other needs of greater felt importance. And finally, there are the unrecognized needs which fail of expression because the individual is ignorant of the existence of goods which would gratify them. Twenty years ago, to illustrate, there existed in the farmer, far from a barber shop and clumsy of touch, an unformulated need for a safety razor. To-day a score of manufacturers bring to his attention the existence of such devices and the recognized need finds expression in effective demand.

The existing system of distribution was built up along the line of least resistance, aiming always at the satisfying of known wants. As suggested in a previous chapter, the capacity of the market to absorb goods has generally exceeded the ability of manufacturers to produce them. This at least was true from the introduction of power-driven machinery into English industry until the closing decades of the nineteenth century. Pressure of demand made it unnecessary for the business man to devote his time to searching out unformulated needs. Only in recent years, when the development of production has potentially outstripped the available market and shifted the emphasis to distribution, has the manufacturer-merchant become a pioneer on the frontier of human desires and needs.

To-day the progressive business man makes careful, intensive studies not merely of the consumer's recognized wants but of his tastes, his habits, his tendencies in all the common activities and relations of life. This he does in order to track down unconscious needs, to manufacture goods to satisfy them, to bring these products to the attention of the consumer in the most appealing ways, and finally to complete the cycle by transporting the goods to him in response to an expressed demand. His problem is chiefly one of adjustment. He must bend the materials and forces of nature to the end of human service. And, most difficult task of all, he must shape his making and selling policies alike to satisfy contradictory conditions and methods and to employ without waste the divergent and overlapping agencies through which present-day distribution is carried on.

In marketing identical products and appealing to identical classes of consumers, for instance, no one method of sale is recognized as the right or the most profitable way. Sale by bulk, sale by sample, and sale by description are often carried on for the same commod-

ities, at the same time, by the same organizations. Not
from choice, certainly, nor from lack of thought put
upon the question of simplifying the problem of creating demand and supplying it. But rather because, with
a few exceptions, the gathering of the necessary information, the analyzing of the data secured, and the building
up of a standard method of marketing which would
satisfy all the conditions, is a task beyond the resources
of any but the greatest of our businesses.

Sale by bulk goes back to the first dim beginnings of
trade — the barter of a rude stone ax, perhaps, for an
ill-tanned deerskin beside the tribal campfire. It persists in all the stages of advancement and occasional
retrogression through which commerce and civilization
have come together — when buyers and sellers met
personally at the market places or fairs, when the traveling artisan went to the home of his customer and there
constructed the cart or chair or coat of which the latter
stood in need; when shops were set up in the towns and
the situation was reversed, the customer seeking the
seller. The significant factor in the process was the
same in all cases, however. There was personal contact
and the buyer saw the actual goods which he was asked
to purchase.

Later came sale by sample, where the customer examined and judged, not the actual goods to be received, but a sample which the merchant guaranteed to
be similar in type and equal in quality and in every
other essential respect to the product which he would
deliver. The development of this method of sale was
dependent on progress in several apparently unrelated
directions. New manufacturing methods made possible a standardization of product as the market widened.

AN APPROACH TO BUSINESS PROBLEMS

It was possible to produce substantially identical articles in large quantities. Grades and standards thus could be established. At the same time there came into being the higher code of commercial ethics necessary to the extension of sale by sample. For the purchaser must have confidence not only in the ability of the producer to furnish goods identical with the sample, but also in his intention to do so.

In sale by description, the purchaser does not see even a sample of the goods. Instead, ideas about the goods are communicated to him by the distributor through the use of salesmen (his own or those of middlemen), advertising, catalogues, booklets, or letters. Spoken, written, or printed symbols take the place of the sight of the goods themselves or a sample of them. The use of the term "symbols" rather than "words" is necessitated by the fact that photographs and drawings to-day are important factors in sale by description. For a picture of the commodity is frequently able to convey to a prospective purchaser a more vivid impression of the product than could pages of verbal description. In the case of complicated machinery, indeed, the blueprint, with exact dimensions set down and the exact relations between parts made plain, is used to supplement and make clearer the conception which the engineer purchaser acquires by examination of the machine itself.

Sale by description demands a still higher plane of business conduct than is required for sale by sample as well as a higher level of general intelligence. The purchaser must have enough of understanding and imagination to grasp ideas conveyed either through spoken, written, or printed symbols and to visualize the article described and its projected effect on his own business or pleasure. In the backward community, where education is at a low level, sale in bulk and sale by sample must continue as the chief method of distribution. In a sense, therefore, sale by description, whatever its beginnings, is in its modern application a by-product of the public school and of the printing press.

At this stage of progress in selling methods, too, the distinction between the demand-creating and the demand-supplying functions of the distributor becomes obvious. Barter is largely the matching of wits and commodities by the two participants; demand creation and actual supply are merged in the minds of both. But in sale by sample and sale by description the line of division is clear. The functions are differentiated and can readily be distinguished.

The ideas to be conveyed to the prospective purchaser in sale by description are such as will awaken an effective desire for the product thus exploited. The arousing of desire is the essential element in selling, though the distributor has the further task of providing machinery for the meeting of the resultant demand. He must make his goods physically available to the buyer. In sale by bulk, this activity merges with selling, since the goods are physically present when the sale is made. In sale by sample and sale by description, the physical distribution of the goods is a problem distinct from the creation of demand, though it is one which must be considered at every step in any solution arrived at.

All three methods of sale, however, are in use in modern trading. The consumer still purchases a large part of the commodities he uses under conditions which make them sales in bulk. He views and inspects the goods in a retail store before he buys them, though thousands of farmers and small-town folk depend for their supplies on mail-order concerns, which sell by description. The middleman, buying in larger quantities, generally purchases from samples, often manufactured singly or in small lots long before the season of sale to consumers begins. This is the rule also with products classed as specialties — vacuum cleaners, cash registers, coffee percolators, and a thousand other products which need a demonstration to clinch the prospective's desire to possess them for the sake of utility value. To be sure, this difficulty has been solved in part by the extension of the approval system. But sale by description becomes each year of increasing importance in every phase of distribution. Even where the purchaser examines a sample or the merchandise itself before the sale is concluded, the earlier steps in the creation of interest and desire probably have been by means of description.

In marketing motor cars, for instance, sale by sample is the method most generally used. Demonstration cars are shown at the agencies and at the annual automobile shows held throughout the country — modern equivalents in a single line of the medieval fairs — and orders are taken for future deliveries. Early in each successive season orders are frequently booked, however, before the new model has been completed, the customer buying on the designer's specifications for both chassis and body, backed up of course by the manufacturer's reputation for turning out efficient and beautiful machines. This is nothing more or less than sale by description, since extensive magazine and newspaper advertising campaigns (sale by description, again) contribute not a little to the prestige of the leading cars and unquestionably stir the desire to possess a motor, which is the genesis of every purchase made. Finally, when the driving season is under way and the agency is stocked up with machines manufactured and delivered during the winter and early spring, hundreds of buyers give their orders after examining the cars and participating in a road test of the identical cars which are to be delivered to them. It may fairly be said, therefore, that the automobile industry, barely twenty years old as yet, uses all the methods of sale which have been developed through many centuries in the marketing of staples.

This evolution in the mechanics of distribution is graphically shown in Chart I (page 165). Though the diagram summarizes the changes which have taken place in marketing methods, it does not tell the whole story. The forces behind the advances made are not to be overlooked. The higher standard of business ethics — what Veblen has called "mitigations of the maxim, *Caveat emptor*"[1] — has meant a growth in public confidence. The factory system and machine processes have made possible a high degree of standardization, distinct differentiation of quality, and a volume of production which has lowered factory costs and thus brought innumerable articles within reach of wider circles of consumers.

Most important, perhaps, have been the improvements in the means of communication. The development of the steamship, the railroad, the telegraph, the telephone, and the post office have opened virtually an unlimited market to the individual business man.

[1] Thorstein Veblen, "The Theory of Business Enterprise."

And this has meant further division of labor in marketing and further differentiation of functions. In fact, specialized institutions have grown up, concerned with finance, transportation, insurance, and other sales functions originally assumed by the merchant producer himself, but now surrendered to groups of what may be termed functional middlemen.

Broadly, then, the problem of distribution is to bring about an effective adjustment between demand creation and economical supply, to arouse the desired maximum of demand at a minimum of expense, and to supply without leakage the largest possible percentage of this demand. The second phase of the problem involves the elements of time, convenience, and service. If the demand which has been aroused among consumers is to be fully utilized, it must be possible for them to obtain the goods promptly and without undue effort at the moment when the demand shows itself. In many cases certain collateral services must be provided, such as instruction in their use, subsequent repairs, and the like. If the consumer's interest and desire to try a certain food product have been stimulated through an advertising campaign, but the product itself is not to be had at a convenient grocery store when the buying impulse is at its strongest, the resulting leakage of demand, if it is at all general, is bound to defeat the manufacturer's purpose.

Not a few costly failures in distribution campaigns have been due to such a lack of coördination between demand creation and physical supply, to the producer's neglect either to provide stocks of his commodity at points easy of access to the consumer or to enlist to the same end the interest and the coöperation of the middlemen who are the usual sources of supply. Instead of being a subsequent problem, this question of supply must be met and answered before the work of demand creation begins; otherwise the leakage may endanger the result. Middlemen do not cover all fields efficiently. The branch house or store is an expensive undertaking. An exclusive sales force means a constant outlay. Mail orders and direct shipments are effective only in distributing certain kinds of merchandise and in reaching certain sections and classes of consumers.

The supply plan adopted may use only one of these agencies; it may employ all. In any case, it must correspond with and serve the districts, the social strata, or the special classes of consumers at which the selling appeals are directed. It follows, as a corollary, that the demand-creation campaign must likewise be shaped to fit the available facilities of demand supply — another outcropping of the principles of interdependence and of balance. Otherwise there is waste through over-stimulation of demand where no adequate or economical means have been provided to satisfy it, and this means a proportionate increase in the burden of distribution expense.

The consumer pays, of course. Yet it is neither sound business nor ethical business that the price of any commodity or service should be loaded with the cost of duplicate or unnecessary functions or of any other preventable leakage or waste. Stripped down to essentials, a business succeeds only as it serves. Unless it adds to the sum of human happiness or comfort or progress something which no other activity or agent can supply so cheaply or so well, its end is forecast; a more efficient competitor is building to take its place.

AN APPROACH TO BUSINESS PROBLEMS

On the other hand, each access of value, each price reduction made feasible by the elimination of lost motions, widens the market of the article, brings it another degree nearer the status of a necessity for daily use or consumption by the multitude. Forty years ago — to take one instance in a thousand offering — a woven wire mattress ranked as a luxury, costing fifteen dollars at wholesale, ten days' pay for the man who constructed it. Now a better mattress, machine made, is sold to dealers for eighty-five cents and no day laborer can find a cheaper substitute. Similar achievements in organization, in invention, in ceaseless pruning of expense and adaptation of materials, have driven soaps, collars, cottons, kerosenes, books, furniture, and an endless list of other things down from the plane of semi-luxuries to facilitate and enrich our daily life.

SECTION I

DEMAND CREATION

CHAPTER IX

LOCATION, CONSTRUCTION, AND EQUIPMENT OF THE PLANT

ALL the activities of distribution, we have seen, have to do with the two functions of demand creation and physical supply. If we apply to each group the same systematic approach used in our analysis of production, an interesting parallel is developed. In both groups, we find, there are plant and operating policies to be determined. Further, the plant policies are governed, as in production, by the factors involved in location, construction, and equipment; while the operating policies are shaped by considerations bearing on materials, agencies (grouped labor), and organization. This is true broadly of both demand creation and physical supply. The parallel may not extend to all the factors involved in either case. Our knowledge of distribution does not carry far enough to say definitely what are all the factors. But at least the analysis will be sufficiently complete to give direction to this discussion.

The problem of demand creation may be stated simply: How shall we transmit to the possible consumer such ideas about the goods we have to sell as will arouse a maximum demand for them at a minimum expense, present and future sales both being considered?

Starting with the plant activities, as in our analysis of production, we find that we have to deal with the location, construction, and equipment of the "plant" for demand creation — in other words, the quarters for the sales department and such other departments as contribute directly or indirectly to the work of demand creation. Like all other general business problems, that of location proves to be a complex of several sub-problems. At least four simple solutions are found to be common practice: the sales plant may be at the factory, at the largest neighboring city, at the largest trade market, at the chief city of the country. Still another recognized plan combines a central sales plant at one of these locations, with auxiliary district or branch organizations, each of which concentrates on the peculiar distribution problems of its own territory. Quite as successful campaigns have been conducted from one location as from another; offhand choice of any one of them, therefore, without study of the comparative advantages offered by the others, would be shortsighted and possibly ineffectual. For there are definite factors governing the placing of the sales departments which should be recognized and weighed by the management before a decision is made.

To reduce the problem to concrete form, let us consider the location of the selling plant of a company making furniture in a small town in southern Michigan. Taking the first step in our systematic approach and eliminating, or at least recognizing, the personal equation, it is obvious that the placing of the sales department should be influenced principally by the marketing needs of the business.

Personal conveniences should not dictate its location at the factory; nor should prejudices or prepossessions be allowed to weight the decision. The ambition of the owner's wife or family to exchange life in a country town for the greater social opportunities of New York or Chicago should count for no more in fixing the location at either point than should personal associations or the traditions of the trade tip the scale in favor of Grand Rapids. True, man does not live by business alone, and personal considerations frequently supply valid reasons for preferring one location to another. Even here, however, the manager who recognizes the personal element, when it enters into his handling of a question, is in a fair way to eliminate it or take precautions to compensate its effects. If he yields to interests entirely foreign to his business, at least he can measure the cost of his yielding in definite terms.

Breaking up his problem into its constituent problems — the second step in the approach — he discovers that in the placing of his sales "plant" he must consider not only its relation to the activities of demand creation, but also to the physical supplying of the consuming market and to the activities of production and administration. There are innumerable sub-problems arising out of the interplay of these various activities and the necessity of establishing policies for their coördination and direction.

Consider, in the first place, the influence of demand upon the product, an influence which is felt by all specialties and by not a few established staples. Styles are an essential factor in the furniture business; the sales department which keeps in constant touch with middlemen and consumers can sense the changing tendencies of demand and transmit this information to the production department. Under normal conditions, the more frequent and intimate this contact, the smaller will be the chance of mistaking the current drift and of manufacturing a stock which does not coincide with the public's desire for chairs and tables and dressers in one or another "period" style. From this viewpoint, a selling plant at Chicago will have advantages over one in New York; while location at Grand Rapids will further lessen the danger of launching models in which retailers will put none of the faith that is expressed in orders and which housewives, therefore, will encounter only in post-season clearance sales. For Grand Rapids is the seat of the seasonal furniture expositions which virtually establish the styles for the general trade. Would it not be possible, then, to place the permanent selling plant at the factory and display samples and keep representatives at Grand Rapids during the semi-annual exposition periods in January and July, when nearly all the initial buying by the trade is done? Few dealers come to market at other times, except to conduct hotel men or other large private buyers who have special contracts to place. If a manufacturer's line and prices are likely to appeal to such contract buyers it might be profitable to keep a permanent display room at Grand Rapids.

From the viewpoint of administration, which must also be considered, if the balance of cost, quality, and service is to be maintained, the location should be tested on the basis of expense and of effect on organization. A location at the plant would probably mean less outlay than one at Grand Rapids, Chicago, or New York; it is the part of the manager to determine whether the saving more than compensates for the possible selling advantages sacrificed.

Or considering the problem of organization, would it be more effective to have the salesmen focus at the factory, at the principal market, or at one of the two chief cities? If the selling force were handled by districts or if the sales department were at Grand Rapids, Chicago, or New York, could not semi-annual conventions be held at the factory to familiarize the salesmen with all the new numbers in the line, changes in style, materials, construction and finish, and similar new selling arguments, thus also at the same time giving the designers and foremen at the factory the benefit of the salesmen's knowledge of what dealers and ultimate users seem to favor or dislike? Information of this sort can be gathered in other and more stable lines through salesmen's daily reports and inspection trips by the salesmanager or by special investigators. Many successful manufacturers of specialties, like adding machines, cash registers, and typewriters, supplement all their other means of gathering information with factory conventions of the sales force at which certain sessions are devoted entirely to discussion of existing weaknesses and possible betterments in the machines and of the future service needs of users.

The effect of location on the sales department and its allied departments cannot safely be ignored. The practical business man frequently must adapt his policies and methods to the temperaments and personal needs of his valuable men. With the factory near Grand Rapids, the center of the furniture district, men work and live in a furniture environment. Furniture is the absorbing interest, not merely of one community but of several; competition is intense, and the result is a stimulation of ideas and a constant interplay of opinion which is clearly lacking in great general markets like Chicago and New York. Such an atmosphere naturally makes for enthusiasm and efficiency; the personnel of the sales office feels it all the time; the members of the field force feel it at each visit.

On the other hand, Chicago and New York are important centers of the trade. The competitive element is not lacking. The standards set by the exclusive shops and great retail stores which buy abroad as well as at home are high. Advertising, perhaps, is on a plane of greater efficiency. The interchange of information and the discussion of sales problems in association circles is more free and the experience of one line is more accessible for adaptation by another. The cities, too, are magnets for men of initiative and capacity; able salesmen, or the raw materials of salesmen, are more easily secured. Here, however, the angle of expense must not be overlooked; higher salaries must be paid as a rule to men whose homes are in the city.

A further factor to be considered is the effect of the manufacturing organization's opinion and moral support on the temper and effort of both sales department and selling force. With the sales plant at the factory to maintain this contact without break, to represent the field men there and in turn to interpret the production departments to the salesmen, it is less difficult to cultivate a company spirit and solidarity which will react on every man employed and bring about an unusual degree of coöperation and mutual interest. With certain of the larger industrial organizations, this contact has become an important factor in both sales and production. More than one agent has been carried across the last barrier separating him from an order of consequence by the knowledge that the factory flag will be raised in his honor and that a thousand company workmen will comment appreciatively on his exploit.

Workmen, too, feel the thrill of accomplishment when new production records for the day or week or month are celebrated in a special letter to the field force. Recently, for instance, the executive officers and selling plant of a big specialty house were moved from a mid-western town to New York to accommodate the personal desire of the president, who insisted on keeping in close touch with all sales activities. A significant falling off in orders, an increase in points of friction between the making and sales departments, and an obvious slump in the organization spirit during the ensuing year convinced him that he had made a mistake in policy; and the general offices and selling plant were hurried back to their old quarters across the court from the assembling departments.

Another vital sub-problem in location harks back to the relations between the sales and production departments. If the selling policies are fixed at a distance from the factory, there is the increased possibility of tangential development on the part of both, which we saw as a danger in earlier chapters. Separated, there is a strong chance that the two forces will drift apart. The factory is likely to plan a product which will occasion the least trouble or expense in process. Production considerations may govern, such as the length and width of lumber in stock or offered by supply houses, the gauge or quality of steel which is easiest or cheapest to buy, the finish most readily applied, and so on, without particular regard for demand as expressed by the sales department.

The factory's emphasis is nearly always on cost; the sales department is concerned with service and the impression, first and last, which the product makes on the customer. The requirements of the market, as registered by the sales department (within the limits set by the principle of balance, of course) should be satisfied by the factory. Otherwise the burden on the selling force is too heavy and the cost of closing orders likely to be out of all proportion. On the other hand, the sales department must not misrepresent the product; it must sell what the factory is able to deliver.

With the sales plant at the works, this danger of tangential development is minimized; only blind obstinacy could prevent the sales and production managers from getting together and reconciling any differences. Where the factory is near the principal market, the situation is still more advantageous, since the plant for demand creation can at the same time keep its contact with the trade and with production. Where the factory must of necessity be located at a considerable distance from the market, as are the cotton mills of the South, for instance, the coördinating function of the general manager is called into play to compensate for the obvious difficulty in maintaining contact. As a matter of fact, the character of cotton cloth produced in the South simplifies the question of demand creation. Moreover, proximity to raw materials, and equable climate, and in some cases lower wages, when translated into smaller manufacturing costs, give a price margin which equalizes the marketing disadvantages.

Other constituent problems enter into this general problem of where to place the plant for demand creation: the sales prestige of a big city location, its superior facilities for the preparation of advertising both general and direct, its transportation advantages, and the like. There are also local sub-problems which must be settled: whether or not it is better, for example, to maintain the sales department in the high-rent central district, on a fashionable avenue, or on the Millinery or Motor or Machinery "Row" where your trade naturally congregates; whether the saving in rent due to the separation of your production and demand creation plants will cancel the loss in efficiency and mutual inspiration; whether ease of access for the customer is an essential in sales departments (as in the case of millinery houses, which seem to consider a central location absolutely necessary), and so on through a series of detail problems which will vary with the nature of the business and with the physical factors of distance, transportation, and quarters available.

It is interesting to note contradictory tendencies in different businesses.[1] There is, for instance, the typical concentration of manufacturers of women's garments on Fifth Avenue, New York, with the obvious end of capitalizing the selling prestige such a location gives. But, contrariwise, a great mail-order merchandise house removed the sales department, general offices, and stock rooms (the latter used to impress visitors and forming, therefore, part of the plant for demand creation) from a "show" building in the heart of a western city to a dingy neighborhood much less accessible to the out-of-town customers whose visits were desired. Here administrative considerations commanded the change. The company's building was being outgrown, trucking costs were high, a prompt service of shipments was difficult to maintain, and the fixed investment, as measured by the constantly increasing market value of the ground

---

[1] See the discussion in F. W. Taussig, "Principles of Economics," Vol. II, pages 78–80.

and building, was out of balance with the business done. New warehouses, with direct railroad connections, were indispensable; the entire establishment, therefore, was transferred to the river front, where rail and water transportation met, and the sales value of the central location was sacrificed to the more vital considerations of cost and service. Analysis of these sub-problems is necessary, of course, in the placing of an actual selling plant. The purpose of this chapter, however, is merely to illustrate how a systematic approach can be applied to a business problem rather than to pursue a typical case through all its phases and conceivable variations.

Completing this analysis (in an actual case), the next process is to assemble all the relevant factors, listing them if their number or complex character renders them difficult to keep track of and giving each its approximate value in a scale of comparison. Many of these were touched upon in the discussion of factory location in the previous section, since the interdependence of the activities of production and distribution is so close as to make it almost impossible and, in fact, inadvisable to fix a guiding policy in either field without first weighing its probable effects in the other.

There follows, then, the final step, the adoption of a fresh point of view. That the majority of furniture sales departments are at the factory, for instance, is not conclusive evidence that this is the best policy. It may be due to a tradition which has persisted without adequate reason. A man with sufficient courage and initiative to challenge the tradition and marshal the factors for and against such a location may find that this trade usage perpetuates the best balance between cost and efficiency in the creation of demand; or under certain circumstances and in certain lines he may discover that the advantage lies with separation.

If it were the purpose of this book to indicate general policies, broadly applicable, I might be tempted to write that the weight of opinion and experience favors the location of the selling plant at the factory. For specialties, at least, this would seem true, since a specialty is the result of closer adaptation of a product to the needs or the unformulated desires of the consumer, and the more constant and intimate the relations between the department which arouses or interprets the market's demands and that which manufactures the commodities to satisfy them, the more complete should be the coordination of their efforts and the more successful the final outcome.

Compared with the problem of the location of the plant for demand creation, the problem of construction, the housing of the plant, is much less complex, though still made up of several constituent problems. When it comes to expressing his business in terms of architecture, the feeling of the average successful man is all for achieving as much of dignity, beauty, and originality as utility and his financial resources will permit. So strong is this feeling that it amounts to a personal bias which frequently has handicapped the growth of the business by diverting money needed for more essential uses and given rise as often to the cynical prediction that the builder was erecting a monument for his undertaking. Approaching the question, then, the prudent manager will recognize this very human tendency and will try to eliminate the personal factor, or at least to bring it into balance with factors more vital to the main purpose, which is the erection of the most effective building for housing the plant for demand creation.

Analyzing his main problem, the manager finds himself, as in his approach to the construction of his factory, confronted first with the necessity of determining the size, type, character of construction, and cost of the building to be erected. These general considerations are for his decision; the technical building problems he must necessarily leave to an architect or engineer. If the selling plant is to be located at the works, in style and materials the building will match, or at least harmonize with the general group. It may even occupy part of one of the factory buildings, finished and fitted up in a manner commensurate with the impression it is desired to make on customers and prospective customers visiting the works.

Broadly speaking, all these matters of size, type, character, and cost are governed by considerations similar to those outlined in the study of factory construction; just as the important administrative problem involved, the financing of the selling plant, is also parallel. In the construction of the factory, the accommodation of the equipment was the first purpose, and efficiency of operation the main end. In the housing of the plant for demand creation, the same guiding motives appear. The factor of advertising value, however, takes on much greater importance.

The manager, in shaping his construction policies, must consider the effect on customers, especially if his industry happens to be in a line like furniture, silverware, or motor cars, and customer visits to the factory are encouraged. Even where advertising or the work of traveling salesmen is the chief factor in demand creation, the prestige obtained from imposing or unusual buildings is often important. Indeed, entire groups of buildings occupied by houses like Butler Brothers; Sears, Roebuck and Company, the Strathmore Paper Company, the National Cash Register Company, and the leading automobile manufacturers are brought into the scheme of demand creation and are exploited in direct and general advertising to emphasize the importance and the volume of business transacted and to enhance the reputation of the product or the merchandise distributed.

In assembling and striking a balance among all the factors that enter into the solution of these sub-problems, an unbiased and individual point of view makes for safety. What other men or other industries have done is not always a safe guide. It may be necessary to break absolutely new ground to arrive at the most effective solution. Undue weight given to traditional standards or trade usages is likely to prove as unfortunate at this stage as would failure to recognize and make allowances for the personal factor in the beginning.

Sometimes, indeed, the history of a single organization supplies examples of absolutely opposed policies. Fifteen years ago a large industrial concern provided quarters for its sales department at the factory by rearranging and refinishing one of its earlier mill-construction buildings, choosing to add a new steel-and-brick unit for manufacturing purposes rather than build a special demand-creation plant. For ten years the revamped structure served every purpose, including that of impressing thousands of prospective customers who visited the works and tens of thousands who viewed the factory group in advertisements. Then came the idea of completing the factory group and providing a sort of monumental entrance to the works by erecting a new home for the administrative and sales departments at another point. What was virtually a high-grade metropolitan office building was conceived and executed on a scale so lavish as to provide space for generous expansion for many years.

Officials of the company insist that the new structure has been a wise investment, from the standpoint of publicity as well as organization efficiency and inspiration. This is probably true. It is entirely possible to reconcile the earlier policy of investing the company's resources in factory buildings with the later policy of lavish outlay on an office structure. The decisive factor in both cases may have been administrative, the necessity of utilizing the first appropriation where it would reduce manufacturing costs, and the subsequent growth of a surplus which could be devoted to a selling plant. As the advertising of this concern identifies the whole factor with its sales and promotion activities, such a building would adequately express the strength and dignity of the business. It is obvious, however, that the business man seeking facts on which to base his own construction policies must exercise care and judgment in his choice of examples to follow.

Equipment is the third main problem in this managerial sequence for supplying the concrete needs of the plan for demand creation. What the manager must aim at is to furnish the sales and allied departments with tools of a quality and effectiveness proportionate to the results sought. His own experience with this or that kind of lighting or ventilation, with this or that system of filing or follow-up, with this make of typewriter or that model of desk, may be of great value in determining his equipment standards. But personal preferences alone should not inform his choice. Quality and quantity of output are the two chief problems into which the main question resolves itself. The parallel with the results of our analysis of factory equipment is very close. Even competent men are powerless to hold output to a given standard unless their tools are of corresponding capacities. It is the manager's task not merely to put aside groundless prepossessions and prejudices, but to analyze and master the elements of each sub-problem. Knowing these, he can assemble all the factors bearing on the main issue and match and reconcile them without regard for any solution which has ever been offered before.

This fresh viewpoint, indeed, is vital in considering equipment for the reason that in this activity of business the principle of balance is rarely observed. Too often the governing factor is cost rather than quality or service. The average manager entertains no doubt of the value of factory units whose production he can measure in terms of lowered costs. He approves the requisition even when it involves the exchange or scrapping of costly machines. In buying equipment for demand creation, however, he is frequently ultraconservative.

Salesmen for office appliances say that while the purchase of plant equipment is left more or less to subordinate executives, the buying of office equipment is usually under the direct control of the management. The reason for such inconsistent policies is not hard to find. An expenditure for machinery devoted to demand creation is looked upon as "unproductive." The possibility of saving time and money or of increasing output as a means of increasing sales is not realized in its true proportion. The only way to correct this shortsightedness is to put the fresh point of view into play. The manager must coördinate his problem of finance with that of equipping for effective demand creation.

So much for what may be called the plant policies of demand creation. Lengthy as this chapter has become, the principal factors have been no more than indicated. The method of analysis worked out in our earlier approach to the plant policies of production has been applied to one set of distribution problems — in this instance concrete problems which allowed of a relatively simple procedure. But in the following chapters we shall consider the more intricate operating policies of demand creation. Here again the method of approach and analysis worked out in the consideration of production activities will be applied to the policies governing materials, agencies, and organization, the operating problems of demand creation.

CHAPTER X

MATERIALS

WHEN a factory starts to turn out goods, its static, preparatory phase ceases and its dynamic stage begins. Up to that moment the management has been preoccupied with policies bearing on the plant itself, where to place it, how and of what to build it, how to equip it, though all these policies are shaped and colored by the requirements of the operating activities which are to follow. Once the plant policies are expressed in brick and mortar and machinery, their broad outlines for the time at least remain fixed. The guiding policies of operation, on the other hand, are subject to constant change to accommodate varying influences affecting materials, labor, and in lesser degree organization.

In the activities of demand creation a close parallel to these production conditions exists. We have seen that the same method of approach, the same scheme of analysis can be applied to both; that the same language can be carried over from one field to the other. In each, plant policies have to do with location, construction, and equipment, and operating policies with materials, agencies for applying motion to materials, and organization. In both, plant policies practically crystallize after they are established; while operating activities present fresh problems for the manager every day. In demand creation, these claims on his attention are mul-

131

tiplied and the difficulty of analysis and decision intensified because of the general lack of standards and because the factors engaged are largely abstract quantities not easily measurable, unstable human relations, or the unexplored complexities of market psychology.

The materials of demand creation are ideas which, when put into circulation by certain available agencies, will cause consumers to want the goods. Like finished products piled up in a factory warehouse, these ideas are of no value until they are transferred to prospective buyers. This, indeed, is the whole process of demand creation — the transmission of ideas about a commodity through the various agencies of distribution, middlemen, salesmen, and general and direct advertising.

Any one or all of these agencies may be used. Problems of organization are involved, therefore, including analysis of the market, determination of price policies, the most effective combination of agencies, and coördination of the effort and money expended through each. In the interests of simplicity, however, ideas about the goods will be regarded, for the time being, simply as materials for possible and not necessarily for specific and actual use. For the same reason, in the chapters immediately following, the agencies of demand creation will be viewed merely as agencies, leaving the problems of organization and coördination, of establishing the right relations between the agencies and materials employed, for later discussion.

To consider ideas about the goods as the materials of demand creation is, I think, a new conception. If it holds in practical business, it should simplify all the processes of our analysis, since ideas about the goods are the selling points from which salesmen, middlemen, and advertising men develop arguments and demonstrations to arouse in the consumer's mind interest in a product and a desire to possess and enjoy it.

Despite the fact that demand creation is largely a problem in applied psychology, the analogy between factory materials and selling points is close. Ideas about the goods can be handled as definite, almost tangible things. The results they produce can be measured with a fair degree of accuracy, particularly in advertising, where the personal influence of the salesman does not enter to confuse the issue. This means that the effectiveness of each idea can be tested, that different arrangements of the same ideas can be compared and measured by the results attained, and that the relative efficiency of the agencies employed for their transmission can be accurately determined.

The parallel may be continued still further; the written or printed symbols which represent a given idea or series of ideas can be classified, indexed, and filed as readily and as definitely as the different materials used in manufacturing are classified, inventoried, and put away in bins until they are needed.

Here enters the value and significance of the concept that ideas about the goods may be treated as the materials of demand creation. Considered as materials, they can be subjected to an analysis similar to that which was applied to the problem of materials in production. There we found that the governing factors had to do with the kind, the quality, the sources, and the control of materials, with their handling and utilization in the factory, and finally with the determination of laboratory standards to guide the activities involved and to insure economy and efficiency. Utilizing the same approach, the manager finds that his problem of demand creation is simplified, that it becomes to a great degree one of definite measurement rather than of opinion and personal judgment.

Considered in this way, the problem, so far as it is concerned with the materials themselves rather than with the means of transmitting them, breaks up, as in production, into two groups of sub-problems having to do (1) with the kind, quality, sources, control, and utilization of the ideas in the sales department (including their development, accumulation, arrangement, and handling) and (2) with the adoption and development of laboratory standards in the treatment of these ideas. This last is by no means the least important step. It will be seen that something analogous to the laboratory methods of analysis, employed to determine what are the most effective and economical factory materials, may be applied with corresponding advantage to the less obvious field of market distribution.

First, then, is there a choice as to the kind of materials to be employed in demand creation, the kind of ideas? Clearly, yes. The selling points of soap and sewing machines, of rolled oats and window shades, are certainly not interchangeable. Besides its general class character, each product has special qualities or utilities which should form the basis of the appeal to the consumer and, through the hope of quick and profitable sales, to the middleman as well.

It is quite as incumbent on the manager to discover what are these special qualities or utilities as it was to canvass the possible sources of factory materials and determine whether wood or clay or alloy steel should enter into the composition of the product. But not so easy. In choosing his manufacturing materials, he would have the advice and experience of his factory superintendent, perhaps of an industrial engineer or chemist as well, to supplement his own inquiries and conclusions. In many lines where the raw materials of manufacture will be the finished products of more basic industries, he can command the counsel of experts employed by these sources to analyze his needs and facilitate their supply. Above all, he has the recorded knowledge and practice of his own and allied trades in the solving of like problems and in the handling and processing of the same or similar raw stock.

It is here, indeed, that the manager sees his two problems as to material diverging most emphatically. His sales and advertising managers will give him help comparable to that of his superintendent and factory specialists; his advertising agency and the service bureaus of various mediums of publicity will supply further counsel. But in determining and measuring the value of his materials of demand creation, neither he nor his aids can find the experience of other manufacturers recorded and available in anything like the same degree as in production. Standards are so few that they may almost be regarded as non-existent.

Yet the kind and the quality of the materials used in demand creation are matters of utmost importance. Salesmen frequently have it forced upon them that some casual argument, some apparently minor selling point, seems to engage the attention of prospects much more readily than do those on which he and the sales department behind him have placed their reliance. In other words, their conception of the consumer's wants and the motives likely to lead him to purchase does not coincide with the facts. Somewhere the analysis has gone astray, and the most available materials for demand creation have not been appraised at their true value or assigned to their rightful tasks.

It is clear, therefore, that a test of quality is needed. But is such a test practicable in dealing with quantities so abstract and so variable as human motives and mental reactions? My own experience and knowledge of what other business men have accomplished convince me that it is practicable. The best ideas are those which arouse the maximum of demand at a given expense or a required demand at a minimum of outlay, all things considered. Definite methods can be applied to the measurement of the response made by prospective purchasers to any particular selling point or combination of selling points, especially when the vehicle of communication is direct advertising and the conditions under which the tests are made can be regulated or their influence on the result can be traced.

At this point the considerations having to do with quality merge with those governing the establishment of standards in materials. The latter is the decisive problem, indeed, in the manager's quest of the most effective selling points. The standards thus developed not only are criterions by which to guide judgments, but represent actual, proved materials for demand creation — individual or associated ideas about the goods, the reactions of which have been tested and demonstrated, ideas which can be used over and over again in diverse ways by the different agencies employed.

Before approaching this problem of standards, the gathering, control, and utilization of the materials of demand creation should be attended to. First of all, sources of ideas about the goods and some dependable method of bringing them together must be developed. Reports from salesmen, letters from customers, the results of prize contests, transcripts of sales convention speeches and demonstrations, and direct, intensive analysis of the product by the sales and advertising departments are the commonest sources of materials. It is feasible, indeed, to work out as definite a routine for assembling and classifying selling points and making them accessible for use as the routine which the purchasing agent employs in keeping his factory supplied with the steel or lumber or lubricating oil which it consumes.

The parallel with production continues in the utilization of ideas. When a manufacturer determines that one particular material is the best the market affords for his product (cost, quality, and service to the consumer all considered) he adopts this as his standard and keeps on using it just as long as results are satisfactory and a better material is not discovered. Yet a striking cause of waste in advertising and selling lies in the fact that many distributors are using demand-creation materials of secondary value because they conceive that the appeal of their primary ideas has worn out.

They cast about, therefore, for new ideas about their goods, forgetting that consumers buy again and again to satisfy the same basic needs, and that long after you are tired of your reiterated selling points, the majority of the public is probably still unacquainted with them. Nearly all the great and successful modern campaigns have exploited persistently the dominant ideas about their products. Just as the hundreds of novels published each year have the common theme of love but achieve interest and distinction by reason of new settings, new situations, and new characters, so the most effective advertisement or selling talk is that which is based on the primary appeal of the goods to the consumer, no matter how often that appeal has been used before. So long as Ivory soap floats and is $99\frac{44}{100}$ per cent pure, these qualities will count most heavily in keeping up its volume of sales.

When analysis of your product has uncovered all the elements of service, advantage, or pleasure which it holds for the consumer, there is relatively little profit in having these selling points in stock unless each is used in the right place, at the right time, and in the right way to produce maximum demand with the least possible expense and waste. This achievement frequently involves the planning of a series of intensive campaigns, each designed not only to employ effectively some one of the agencies of demand creation, but also to make the most of the available ideas about the goods. To stimulate curiosity and make the first sale of a five-cent cigar or a ten-cent cereal is obviously an easier undertaking than to perform the same function for a high-priced motor boat or player piano. Belief in the worth of such a product, even a strong desire for that product, is not enough to make a man purchase it.

The average consumer will risk at any time a small amount to try a new substitute for a personal or household necessity he is buying regularly. The lure of novelty or a single outstanding selling point may suffice to fix his attention and complete the sale. When he faces a considerable outlay for some article lacking vital appeal, however, or when to buy it means the expenditure of money he had no intention of spending and feels no necessity of spending, it may require a protracted campaign through magazine and newspaper advertisements, through letters, catalogues, house organs, and salesman's calls to educate him to the point of purchasing. Manufacturers of cash registers, adding machines, typewriters, and other business utilities sometimes pursue a "live" but unresponsive prospect for several years before the order is finally booked.

It follows that in any extended campaign of demand creation the directing minds will have many alternatives in selecting, combining, and arranging the selling points suitable for use by each agency and in fixing the order in which the various combinations shall be brought to bear upon the prospect. Judgment and experience will go a long way in guiding these decisions, in marking the superfluous idea whose elimination will strengthen the advertisement or sales talk, and in providing a logical program for the presentation of the various arguments by the coördinate agencies. Yet a high degree of efficiency in utilization will not be attained unless the methods as well as the materials of demand creation (here the finished letter, advertisement, or sales talk) are tested and reduced to standards — a not impossible enterprise, as we shall see a few pages further on.

Making the materials of demand creation available for use may be considered a process of utilization and control closely akin to the handling and storing of materials in the factory. The ideas, reduced to written or printed symbols, must be classified and kept ready for easy reference. In many cases the memory of the salesman or advertising manager serves both as inventory and storage place; in others, scrap books or filing devices of various sorts preserve the materials and make them accessible when needed. The most advanced sales organizations maintain filing and index systems which group similar ideas about the goods in the order of their pulling power and provide means of automatically bringing these to notice at intervals.

One sales manager of my acquaintance files every scrap of information bearing on the functions and known uses of his machines according to subject, supplements this material with such clippings from magazines, newspapers, and letters as contain suggestions or idea-germs, and keeps a master index to all under the glass top of his desk. To this store of ideas he adds from his correspondence, his reading, his contact with men inside and outside the organization; and he is able to bring the whole to bear when planning an elaborate campaign or dictating a single sales letter. A signally successful industrial concern improves on this practice by displaying all its live sales material on multi-leaved fixtures which permit the bringing together of all the associated ideas, thus making the members of each group visible at the same time and facilitating choice of the best for the current purpose. Further, this company has gathered into an indexed pocket volume several hundred selling points for its various products, the most effective answers to prospects' objections, and the approved methods of demonstrating its machines. This is used for the refreshment of the memories of seasoned salesmen as well as for the information of new recruits.

In both these instances the attitude toward the materials of demand creation is practically the same as that of the average factory organization toward its raw and partly processed stock. The guiding purposes are virtually identical: to insure an adequate supply of materials, to classify these according to their character, properties, and uses, and to keep them instantly accessible through an inventory or master-index.

Quantity is a further factor in utilization. In manufacturing the chief element in determining quantity is the cost of the materials consumed. The solution is not reached until each unit of product contains the minimum amount of raw stock consistent with the kind of product desired. In demand creation, on the contrary, quantity is a question of economizing the prospective buyer's time and attention. Too many selling points will tire him. Too few will certainly fail to persuade him that he must purchase or else sacrifice a possible advantage.

Every executive has had contact with the salesman who "talks himself out of an order" as well as with the young or mediocre man who does not know how to present a convincing case for his merchandise. Both are recognized types in business; both are victims of defective analysis. In the first case, the process stops with the gathering of a stock of ideas about the goods and fails to discover the proper proportion in utilizing them. In the second, there is probably no conscious analysis either of the prospect's needs or of the qualities in the merchandise which might engage his attention.

Analogous types of advertising are also common. There is the letter, magazine page, or booklet which crowds so many arguments upon the potential buyer that he is repelled by the mass or is fatigued after he begins to read; and at the other extreme is the advertisement which puts forward so few or such general ideas about the goods that no positive impression is made upon the prospect's mind. In a word, the problem of quantity is largely one of elimination and selection. The necessity of establishing the right balance between the materials used and the result desired is no less imperative than in manufacturing operations.

This brings us to the final problem confronting the business man in his consideration of the materials of demand creation, that of establishing standards comparable with the laboratory standards so common in the industries. The possibility of formulating such standards may be challenged by the average producer, no matter how carefully he has standardized his factory materials. For here as elsewhere in the field of distribution too many business men are guided by rule of thumb. They guess at the most effective sales ideas which analysis of their product discloses, guess at the most forceful forms of expressing these, and guess at the most efficient agencies and mediums for transmitting them to prospective purchasers. They spend hundreds of thousands of dollars on selling campaigns based on a series of approximations or opinions arrived at in this hit-or-miss fashion.

This means an enormous waste of money, effort, and product, due simply to the general lack of standardization. Nor is waste from this cause confined to the materials of demand creation. It is characteristic of our distributive organization as a whole. In the aggregate, it constitutes an overwhelming case for a thorough and systematic study by government and coöperating private agencies of all the activities of market distribution.

The abler business man, to be sure, makes an effort to determine those properties of his goods which should attract the attention of the possible buyer and awaken the desire for possession which is the root of market demand. He discovers by a general inquiry, if not by intensive study, the points of superior quality, utility, or service inherent in his products as distinguished from competing goods. He turns for guidance as to the form in which these ideas are to be conveyed to his own experience, to the principles of English style, and to the practice so far as he can ascertain it of other men who are marketing commodities appealing to the same classes of prospects, under conditions similar to his own.

From the observations of successful sales and advertising managers, psychologists, and students of business he gathers the fundamental rule that the mental energy of the prospective buyer must be conserved by cutting down to a minimum the labor attendant on the assimilation of new ideas and concepts. He learns to avoid abstract statements and vague general claims. He seeks short, familiar words which will convey in homely phrase the exact meaning he wishes to transmit. He employs apt illustrations and figurative statements whenever they will help the prospect to visualize the product and its effect on the comfort, the pleasure, the health, or the safety of himself or those he holds dear. And he uses the imperative mood judiciously when the reaction desired is at length suggested.

These are only a few of the many precepts put forward tentatively or more decisively by the psychologist and by the specialist in sales. Their weakness lies in their *a priori* basis. What the business man requires is a practical test for certain ideas about his goods under conditions approximating those of the physical or chemical laboratory. He wants a workable method of trying out selling points alone and in combination, in diverse forms, and with varying degrees of emphasis, before staking thousands of dollars on the effect they will produce in an actual sales campaign.

In making these tests, the manufacturer can borrow the methods by which statisticians in many fields of social and business endeavor arrive at their results. These latter are familiar with what are termed mass phenomena and put their dependence in the law of averages. They know that they can approximate the average height of a country's population, for example, by measuring a few thousands of representative folk drawn from the larger body. If the smaller group is really typical of the mass, the statistician knows that its average height will coincide roughly with the average height of the total population.

The business man can apply this method to tests of his demand-creation materials. In direct advertising, the mailing of sales letters, circulars, catalogues, samples, and the like to prospective buyers, orders for the goods are proof of an awakened demand which is capable of direct statistical measurement. Each piece of advertising posted is a stimulus; the number of responses per thousand of communications can be determined as exactly as though the operations were conducted in a physical or psychological laboratory. It is a simple matter of so framing and keying the advertisement that every response can be identified and only those due to it shall be counted.

It is possible also to isolate a group from the general mass (just as the sociologist isolates a group for study of its stature) to test the average reaction induced by any unit or series of advertisements, thus forecasting the results that will be attained when the campaign is extended to the mass. If the test is unsatisfactory, it demonstrates either that the selling points put forward lack persuasive or convincing power, or that the form in which they are cast is defective. A third alternative hinges on the chance that the group of individuals selected for the test is not representative of the mass. The trial list, however, can be revised again and again until it is truly typical, until the average of responses per thousand of letters or catalogues mailed does not vary greatly between test and full campaign.

Once the business man secures a representative test list or series of lists, he can try out at relatively small expense all his materials of demand creation and determine which selling points and what forms of each are most effective in stimulating the market for his products. This method of "sampling" has been successfully employed so often that its value and accuracy are beyond question.

Take the case of a producer of a food specialty planning a campaign to reach, not the consumers, but the grocers of the country. The whole body of dealers in this line falls little short of a quarter of a million. After working out a series of selling points expressed in such forms as he thinks likely to be effective, let the manufacturer test this material by mailing it to say one thousand grocers. The group selected must be large enough to give typical results and it must be so selected as to be of the same general character as the whole body of grocers.

Assuming these conditions, the number of orders or inquiries received from the thousand grocers can be tabulated, and the probable response per thousand can be estimated when the same ideas in the same form are conveyed to the two hundred and fifty thousand. This can be followed or paralleled by another direct mailing, to another test list similarly constituted, of an alternate campaign built on different selling arguments or on the same arguments differently expressed. Half a dozen test campaigns, indeed, might be profitably conducted at the same time. The greater the number of tests (always assuming that the trial lists are representative and of about the same character) the more certainly the results will define the weightiest selling points and the happiest ways of conveying them to the prospect.

Intensive study of the reactions produced by individual units in each test may even result in a composite final campaign which will far exceed the returns from the best of the trial campaigns. It is thus possible to determine what ideas about the goods and what arrangement and phrasing of those ideas are most effective in arousing demand — in other words, to select your materials of demand creation with little more dependence on guesswork than obtains in the choice of raw materials in a standardized factory.

That such tests are practical is indicated by the typical records presented in the table on the opposite page. Here are shown the results of several "try-outs" and complete mailings of various letters and circulars making the same specific offer of certain commodities. The tests and mailings covered five well-defined functional groups of business men and two additional groups of members of large local merchants' associations. In all but two instances, B[1] and D, it will be noted, the results of the tests and full mailings were practically parallel. In one of these, B[1], mailed to master printers in June,

1915, the orders fell far short of what the test forecast; yet the same letter and inclosure mailed to credit men in May, 1915 (B²), brought orders corresponding very

TESTS AND MAILINGS TO RATED BUSINESS MEN
MINIMUM STANDARD, 16 ORDERS PER 1,000
Test lists, each 500 names

Note: In the column headed "Material Mailed," it will be seen that the same letters stand for identical material, the exponent numbers designating the different mailings. The unit of sale was $5.00.

MA-TERIAL MAILED	CLASSES ADDRESSED	TESTS			MAILINGS		
		DATE	ORDERS RE-CEIVED	ORDERS PER 1000	NUMBER MAILED	ORDERS RE-CEIVED	ORDERS PER 1000
A¹	Printers	4/19/15	9	18	5,368	117	21.8
A²	Credit Men	9/14/14	13	26			
A³	" "	10/19/14	13	26	16,376	342	20.9
A⁴	Advertisers	10/22/14	9	18	13,890	295	21.2
A⁵	Architects	4/29/15	7	14	1,478	21	14.3
A⁶	Association No. 1	4/29/15	16	32	2,770	75	27.1
A⁷	Association No. 2		Not	Tested	2,972	100	33.9
B¹	Printers	6/1/15	14	28	5,296	93	16.2
B²	Credit Men	4/15/15	9	18	15,412	271	17.6
B³	Advertisers		Not	Tested	13,848	197	14.3
B⁴	Manufacturers	6/1/15	7	14	8,492	148	17.3
C	Credit Men	8/20/14	2	8			
D	" "	9/14/14	15	30	16,439	348	21.1
E¹	" "	1/25/15	4	8			
E²	Advertisers	1/25/15	4	8			
F¹	Credit Men	3/25/15	6	12			
F²	Advertisers	3/25/15	2	4			
G¹	Credit Men	7/22/15	4	8			
G²	Advertisers	9/20/15	7	14			

closely with the results of the test mailing and also with the final results of B¹. Mailed also to a selected list of manufacturers in June (B⁴), the materials again brought the standard result. In this last case the test fell under the minimum, but because of the uniform performance of B^1 and B^2, a chance was taken and the letter sent out. In B^3, mailed the same day to advertisers, without a special list test, the returns fell under the minimum standard allowed.

Study of this and hundreds of similar tests would seem to indicate that lists classified along functional lines require individual tests even for materials generally effective. In A^5, for instance, the test result of fourteen orders per thousand was disregarded because the list was small and the letter and circular used had been uniformly successful on several other lists. Yet here the final result was almost identical with that of the trial and netted only fifty-seven per cent of the average from other lists.

As final evidence of the value of classifying lists according to functions or dominant interests, observe that A^6 and A^7, the same material sent to the members of two large associations of business men, after a single test, brought very satisfactory results from both lists. Another important fact to note is that when the minimum standard of orders is as low as sixteen and the test group numbers only five hundred, there is danger that the average will be disturbed where one individual influences the giving of several orders. The larger the trial group and the more clearly classified the various lists used, the more exact an index will the test give on the results from the complete mailing. Experience with the varying factors involved teaches one to sense the abnormal, whether in composition of mailing list or ratio of responses.

This method of studying ideas and forms of expression in direct advertising would be important even

148

though its use did not extend to other agencies, since it permits the business man to guide an extensive advertising campaign by means of an investigation relatively inexpensive. But the importance of the laboratory method does not end with direct advertising. The root idea is the same whatever the agency for selling employed. Selling is accomplished by communicating ideas about the goods through middlemen, salesmen, general advertising, or direct advertising. The ideas remain virtually the same in all instances. The business man, therefore, can determine in his direct selling laboratory what ideas and what combinations of ideas constitute the most effective selling material. He can then carry over the results obtained to his selling by other agencies.

To illustrate: An extensive promotion campaign is under consideration. The producer contemplates spending thousands of dollars upon advertising in certain periodicals. What can the "distribution laboratory" do to determine the ideas to be conveyed and the forms of expression to be used to create the desired demand? The circulation of a single periodical used may run into the hundreds of thousands or even into the millions. It is the part of prudence, therefore, to test the response that will result from the communication to this enormous body of subscribers of ideas about his goods. Accordingly he works out the most effective selling points, the most effective arrangement, the most effective form of expression through direct trial mailings. He can even test the final "copy" itself, just as it will appear in the periodical, by mailing it direct to relatively small groups and noting the reaction which it produces.

Moreover, he can determine in this way the response from differing economic strata. Ideas adapted to build up a demand for a commodity on one economic or social plane may fail utterly with another. The value of a "try-out" for each lies in the fact that most periodicals circulate within well-defined economic and social limits. The ideas and forms of expression which created a demand in direct advertising addressed to these strata is likely to have a similar effect when used in periodicals circulating among the same classes.

The application of laboratory tests to the selling arguments used by salesmen is equally practicable. One need only appreciate the fundamental identity of the selling function, whatever the agency employed, to realize that the results obtained in experiments in direct advertising can be carried over into distribution by salesmen. The whole structure of the selling talk can be built up on the ideas, the order of arrangement, and the forms of expression demonstrated as most efficient in creating demand through the medium of direct advertising.

Many progressive organizations, indeed, insist on all salesmen mastering a standard approach and selling talk which marshals certain basic arguments in a settled order and phrases them in a definite way. This is impressed upon the new salesman as more likely to secure the order than would any argument he could frame impromptu. It serves chiefly as a foundation for the argument he makes to possible buyers. The assumption of the laboratory point of view by salesmen, the conscious testing of ideas and methods and the recording of results, may in turn strengthen the entire sales organization.

The general principles upon which the testing or sampling of ideas depends apply also when the possibilities of the whole market are studied by the intensive cultivation of one section. It is only necessary that social and economic conditions be broadly identical. Other things being equal, the result of a test in Kansas should hold true for the states immediately north and south, though it would not apply to Georgia or Alabama. On this basis a localized selling campaign, narrow in extent, will give relatively exact data from which the possibilities of a general campaign of like character may be forecast.

Again, the laboratory method here suggested lends itself to a determination of just what elements of quality and service in a given product are deemed most essential by the consumer. The effectiveness of the ideas conveyed in building up a demand reflects the intensity of human wants as to the elements of quality and service described. The producer can sound the consumer and can adapt his product to the latter's expressed demand. In other words, the entire selling campaign can be planned and directed by guarded tests comparable to the laboratory investigations of the scientist.

It may be possible in time greatly to extend and simplify this analysis of materials. As yet the professional psychologist has addressed himself to few of the problems which engage the attention of business men. The conclusions arrived at, too, are rarely of much practical value, chiefly because the psychologist, in framing his tests or phrasing his questions, is not always cognizant of the thing the business man wants to know. In some of these experiments a series of advertisements has been submitted to a group of thirty, forty or fifty students, themselves, perhaps, far removed in character, tastes, and purchasing power from the average consumer, and they have been asked to indicate which is the most attractive or effective of the lot.

The question should have been more specific: "Which advertisement would get your attention first? Which one, if any, would hold your interest? Which one, if any, would stir curiosity or make you want the product enough to ask for it, by letter or at the nearest store?" And so on, breaking the one question up into perhaps a dozen specific inquiries which would give definite information as to the size, the shape, the quantity and character of ideas, the kind of illustration, and the style of argument which would secure and hold the reader's attention and induce the desired action, whether this be the filling out of a coupon or the inclosure of a signed order and check.

Some encouraging attempts have been made to eliminate from such laboratory experiments the factors which reduce the value of the results and to check up these results by repeating the experiment under actual business conditions. One of the most interesting of these studies, conducted at the University of Michigan in 1913, minimized the chances of error by submitting the questions to five hundred and sixty persons, fifty of whom were outside business men. The questions, too, dealt with specific things, like the attention value of various sizes of copy, from full pages to quarter pages, and the efficiency of the coupon in securing answers. The man who conducted the experiments was himself a successful advertiser and the copy which he submitted to his subjects was tried out a little later in an advertising medium of known pulling power.[1]

It is significant that the results of both tests cor-

[1] See W. A. Shryer, "Analytical Advertising."

MATERIALS

responded closely. The large number of subjects in the test undoubtedly reduced the percentage of error. Divided into groups of about twenty-five persons, it was found that the opinions of a few of these groups varied widely from the average, thus indicating the danger of depending for a decisive test on a single small body of subjects. At the same time, further illustration was given the principle that specific problems in demand creation can be solved by laboratory tests conducted under carefully guarded conditions on a sufficient number of representative subjects.

CHAPTER XI

AGENCIES OF DEMAND CREATION — THE MIDDLEMAN

DEMAND creation is a problem in the transmission of ideas. Here is a business man seeking a market for his product. It may be a standard article somewhat improved, but at the usual price. It may be the usual grade at a lower price, or a frankly cheaper substitute depending on a marked price reduction for its appeal. Or he may offer a specialized commodity invented or adapted to satisfy a specific want not yet fully realized by the consumer. The seller, as a rule, believes that in one or more of the three essentials — quality, price, or service — the product offers advantages over any other article of its kind. Else he would not undertake the endless labor of stimulating demand for an inferior commodity. It may sometimes happen that an article not otherwise superior reflects only the prestige or charm of the seller, or more energetic selling power overcomes the attraction of greater intrinsic merit in competing merchandise. But even here faith in the goods is generally recognized as indispensable. "First sell yourself" is an axiom in the practice of salesmanship.

Now "selling one's self" is the rule-of-thumb equivalent for the series of activities described in the last chapter — the gathering, classifying, testing, and standardizing of the materials of demand creation. With these proved ideas about the goods in hand, the mana-

154

ger's task is to transmit them effectively to the minds of possible consumers. When he thus leads consumers to adopt his viewpoint as to the utility and desirability of his wares, he induces them to become purchasers. For this work of transmission, he finds that three important agencies have been developed, the middleman, the exclusive sales force, and direct and general advertising.

His problem is to determine which one of the three will best perform the function of demand creation without undue interference with other necessary activities of production and distribution. He may discover that two or more can be combined advantageously, or that different agencies will be most effective in different sections of his selling field. Following the analogy already indicated, they may be considered as corresponding to the labor factors in production. To these ideas or selling points, also, motion must be applied through human effort in order to perfect and transmit them to the minds of prospective users and thereby create desire for the goods.

In any extended study of the agencies of demand creation it becomes evident that the sales record of a single industry frequently includes all the significant functions and operations which have marked the development of distribution since exchange of commodities began. The surplus product of a country blacksmith shop in the early fifties — to quote a classic illustration in American business — consisted of several farm wagons which the neighborhood had not been able or willing to absorb. A local demand for a number of such vehicles had been created with little effort. A simple demonstration which convinced the prospective buyer that wheels, axles, and other members were of sound timber equal to the rough usage before them, was usually sufficient to complete the transaction, since the product satisfied a known and imperative want of the customer. When all the farmers in the district who needed and could afford new wagons had been supplied, however, the makers faced the alternative of finding a market further afield or of suspending manufacturing operations and reverting to the odd jobs with which the average forge of the time occupied itself.

Had they been ordinary blacksmiths, they would have taken the easier way, or probably would have failed to realize that they had any choice in the matter. But they possessed initiative, intelligence, and that pride in their product which has been, I believe, an important motive in the expansion of American business. One of the brothers, therefore, hitched a team to a string of the surplus wagons and drove forth in quest of buyers. He found them on this and on subsequent excursions within the county and without, in villages and towns, on farms along the way, at crossroads stores, and even at smithies whose owners had not the craft or capacity to build wagons in numbers to supply the local demand.

Wherever conditions seemed to warrant and a competent man could be interested, a representative was appointed, at first to take orders on commission for the wagons which the brothers learned to trade-mark and guarantee, but later as a wholesale or retail dealer who bought his stock and assumed all the functions and risks of demand creation and supply in his territory. From such homely beginnings the Studebaker business has grown to international proportions, manufacturing a long line of horse-drawn and motor vehicles and distributing them to every civilized corner of the earth. In developing this world market, virtually all the agencies of demand creation have been employed: middlemen of various sorts, wholesalers, retail dealers, and exclusive agents; a direct sales force, including not only salesmen, but branch houses, district sales organizations, and even retail branches in the larger cities, as well as direct and general advertising of every kind and class.

Whether the ideas about the goods are communicated through spoken or written symbols, by middlemen, salesmen, or advertising, the ultimate purpose is the same. For the time being, however, we shall consider only those problems which arise when the middleman is used as the agency of demand creation. It cannot be overlooked of course that this is by no means the only function which he has exercised in the past and continues in many cases still to exercise.

The present tendency of many producers to go around the middlemen and eliminate him entirely or as fast as possible from their schemes of distribution cannot rightly be understood without review of what these historical functions are. Nor can the current conditions which enter as factors in the problems of demand creation be explained without analysis of these functions and their influence on the producer's relations with the middleman. These functions may be listed as follows:

1. Sharing the risk.
2. Transporting the goods.
3. Financing the operations.
4. Selling or demand creation.
5. Assembling, assorting, and reshipping the goods.

Each of these functions was at first divided among a series of middlemen, the selling agent, the wholesaler, and the retailer each assuming his part in turn. Each middleman took the risk that the goods might lose value or go stale on his hands, just as he bore the hazard of destruction, damage, or theft of the goods while he held title. Each took the chance of credit losses. Each paid a proportion of the transportation charges from the producer's stock room to the consumer's hands. Each had a part in financing the entire operation. Each assumed a share of the work of selling, of creating for the goods he had purchased a demand in an outer circle of middlemen or the final circle of consumers. And each performed part of the task of assembling, assorting, and reshipping the goods to make them physically available for consumption.

In many instances the middleman exercises these same five groups of functions to-day. If he overestimates the probable demand for an article or line, he pays the penalty for his bad judgment when he clears his stock at the end of the season. If he encounters a season of depression with heavy stocks, the loss is his so long as he remains solvent. And unless he transfers his liability by paying an insurance premium, he assumes the risk of loss or damage in his warehouse or while the goods are in transit. Frequently he delivers the merchandise to his customers by team or motor truck, especially if he is a wholesaler supplying a large city and suburban trade, or a retailer in a city where consumers are accustomed to such service. All along the line, the middleman (except when he makes a virtue of demanding cash payments by offering reduced prices) lends his credit to his customers and thus finances the selling operation.

His business is primarily to sell, but at times his manner of performing this function presents one of the producer's gravest problems in distribution policy. The attitude of many middlemen toward a new product or a new line seems to be one of indifference or even latent hostility, unless it offers for some standard commodity a substitute which can be handled more easily or at a greater profit. Middlemen of this type virtually say to the manufacturer: "Create a demand for your goods and I will handle them. I am here to give my customers what they ask for, not to make a market for something they know nothing about."

There is no denying that they have sound and practical reasons for this attitude. Hardly a day passes that the wholesale merchant is not importuned to buy and push some new branded product which can hardly be distinguished from one or perhaps a dozen like it which he already has in stock. If he yields, it means that he puts an additional load, however small, on his financing, on his stock-keeping, on his selling, and indeed on every department of his business. One item, of course, would not be much of a burden; but multiply that item by five hundred or a thousand in a year (the latter is not an impossible estimate in many lines) and the risk of loss and spoilage becomes so great as to justify a defensive policy. The same problem on a lesser scale confronts the retailer. No wonder, therefore, that middlemen of all classes look with disfavor on a new substitute for established brands unless they can see in it an extra profit or a ready market.

Because they exercise the final functions of assembling and forwarding merchandise stocks, assorted according to their customer's needs or expressed desires, the influence of middlemen on the choice of commodities is very great. Their negative attitude toward demand creation in many lines, coupled with this power of influencing purchasers, has already affected the relations between manufacturer and middleman and will undoubtedly work further and radical changes in our system of distribution.

In certain lines the middleman frequently takes on the constructive function of financing the producer directly and indirectly. Many of the cotton mills of the South were built with capital furnished by northern selling agents and their associates. Often, too, the wholesaler indorses the commercial paper of the manufacturer and thus indirectly finances production. In the textile industry of New England, such "two-name" paper is quite common, and it is frequently met with in other trades where the design and manufacture of the goods and their movement to the ultimate consumer occupy a considerable cycle of time. Certain it is that in all cases the middleman materially shortens the period of investment on the part of the producer and enables him to make more rapid turn-overs.

At a relatively early date in modern distribution began the taking over entire of certain single functions, which each middleman had been performing in part. The most notable functional middlemen to emerge thus far are the insurance companies, the direct transportation companies, and the commercial banks. The insurance company in a real sense performs a middleman's function when it assumes the hazard of damage or loss by fire, by flood, by theft, by wreck, by non-delivery on time, and by all the other mishaps to which goods are exposed on their journey from factory to consumer. Further, the insurance company is ready to assume practically the entire element of risk, to guarantee credits, to warrant the honesty of salesmen, agents, delivery men, and other employees, to assume the liability for injury to persons or property incident to operation, even to reimburse a commercial institution like a department store or specialty shop for failure to earn profits because of weather unfavorable to seasonal trade.

In much the same manner the great transportation companies, railroads, ocean steamship lines, express companies, and more recently the domestic and international parcel posts, undertake and perform an important office originally shared with the producer by successive fractional middlemen.

In financing the operations of distribution, too, the bank has gone a long way toward relieving the middleman of his burden. By making advances on merchandise stocks, on open accounts, and on commercial paper, it has absorbed much of the function of finance in distribution. There are exceptions, as noted above in the textile and other long-cycle industries, but in the main the bank, with associated agencies like commercial-paper brokers, has been long recognized as an indispensable functional middleman in the marketing process. The establishment of the federal reserve bank system, with its power to rediscount acceptable "two-name" paper and bills of exchange, has led to further extension of banking activities in this field. The application of the corporate form to industrial organization has also contributed to the producer's financial power by making it possible for him to secure adequate working capital without sharing or surrendering control of operations at any point.

Development of these functional middlemen has relieved the wholesaler and retailer of certain onerous activities; in theory, at least, he is left free to concentrate on his remaining functions of demand creation and physical supply of the merchandise which his customers require. In a measure his field of demand creation has been encroached upon, either as a consequence of his indifference to particular commodities based on wide possible choice among rival products or because of the manufacturer's compelling interest in maximum sales. Beyond question, producer advertising can be regarded as a general or direct appeal, according to its character, which tends to supplant the dealer's efforts in the stimulating of a consumer market.

The advertising medium or agency is in this sense as truly a functional middleman as either the insurance company, the railroad, or the bank. But it is more recent in origin and more undeveloped in operation. Advertising has as yet few dependable standards to direct the use, for instance, of coincident newspaper, magazine, letter and circular campaigns — especially when they are conducted in coöperation with middlemen.

This inability to coördinate activities which can only partly be controlled (though the entire expense must be charged up against the product as delivered to the consumer) and thus reduce duplication of effort, counts heavily against the efficiency of advertising. Coupled with the indifferent attitude of the middleman, it may account for what seems to many keen students an apparent tendency to eliminate the middleman in demand creation. It is one phase, perhaps, of a general movement looking to the integration of industries, to the control and coördination of all the activities involved in production and distribution, from the supply of raw materials for the factory to the laying down of the merchandise at the consumer's receiving platform or the back door of his residence.

This, indeed, is the producer's vital problem: Shall I sell direct or through the trade? And if my goods move to the consumer through the recognized channels, shall I depend on the successive middlemen to do all or any part of the work of demand creation? Or can I take on the entire burden of advertising and selling without prohibitive increase of expense and leave to the wholesaler and retailer only the function of physical supply, of stocking my products and handing them out to the customer when they are called for?

Modern practice embraces the entire range of possible procedure, from absolute dependence on the middleman for demand creation through every degree of coöperation in selling to complete assumption by the manufacturer of the task of developing and holding a market for his goods. A great number of branded and nationally advertised food products illustrate this last stage; trade-marked and advertised lines of clothing, tools, household appliances, and the like occupy the intermediate positions marked by coöperative selling; while thousands of commodities prepared by concerns which limit their activities to production alone represent the first extreme of marketing dependence.

Price and conditions of supply being equal, the middleman will naturally prefer to handle those products which require the minimum of effort to move along to the next circle in distribution, which necessitate the exercise only of those functions of assembling, assorting, and reshipping which fall under physical supply. And here lies the crux of the producer's problem. The system of discounts to dealers which has been more or less traditional assumes that the middleman performs his share of all the functions of distribution. The middleman may readily consent to delegate all the work of demand creation to the producer, but in doing so he only reluctantly surrenders any considerable part of his customary recompense.

On certain branded and widely advertised products, the dealer perforce accepts a reduced unit profit, partly because this is compensated by the large number of unit sales and partly because the consumer allows him no choice. When a customer asks for Ivory soap or Holeproof hosiery, Kellogg's corn flakes or Uneeda biscuits, the retailer must either supply the requested product, sell a substitute against a definite prejudice, or risk the customer's departure and a black mark against his store. The wise dealer stocks the popular brands, therefore, even though the profit per sale is less than for a non-advertised substitute. The difference is his contribution to the manufacturer's campaign of demand creation, though he does not always recognize it as such.

The wholesaler in his turn feels the pressure of the consumer's demand when the retailer orders; he also makes contribution to the demand-creation fund of the producer. In the case of established, advertised brands, middlemen as a rule accept the situation; to new trademarked products they are generally less hospitable. With both, many of them put all their emphasis on the promotion of competing articles which they themselves control or which carry a higher margin of profit. Consumers can often be influenced to buy these.

That the wholesaler and retailer should expect payment for a function which they have wholly or partially

THE MIDDLEMAN

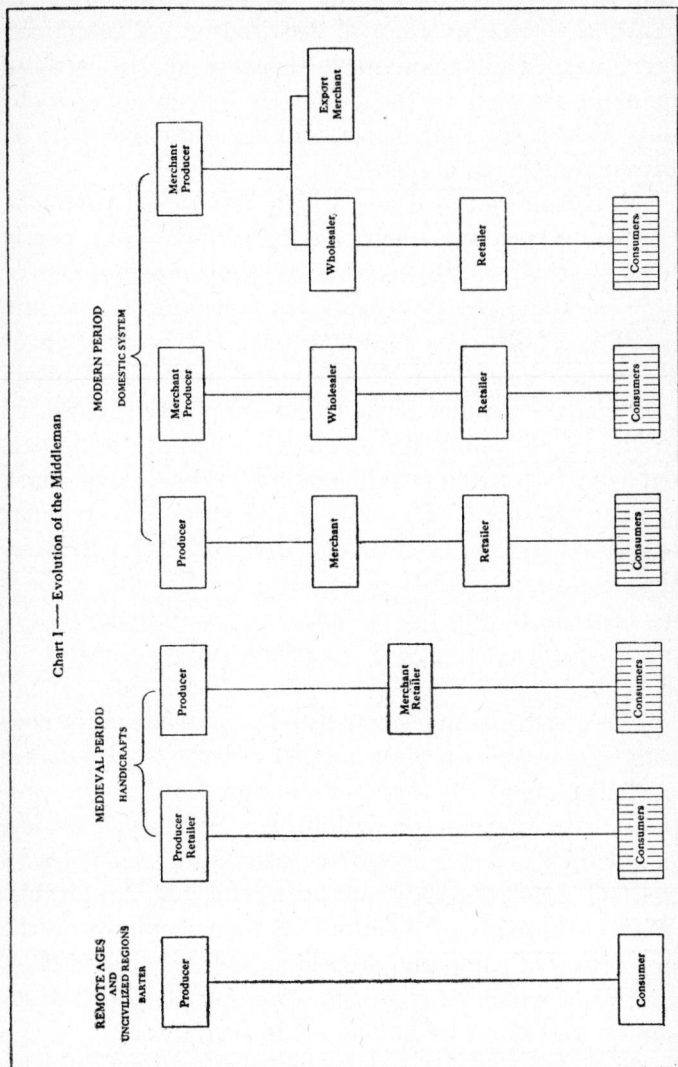

Chart 1 — Evolution of the Middleman

ceased to perform is explicable on the ground of tradition. The middleman has had a long-established though shifting position in the development of organized distribution. It is true that the history of his functions has not been adequately studied and that only tentative outlines of his evolution can be drawn. Pending the fuller study which the subject should receive, even a cursory and incomplete sketch may assist in giving the manager a sense of direction.

The middleman, as we know him, is a product of a complex industrial organization. Chart I attempts to give in graphical form a rough notion of his evolution from the remote time when producer dealt directly with consumer to the rise of the factory system in England and the development late in the eighteenth century and early in the nineteenth of what may be called the orthodox type of distribution. Under the primitive rule of barter, the producer became a trader only at intervals when he had accumulated a surplus of skins or cattle or hunting gear and conceived these as of less value than something a neighbor possessed. We find him as a craftsman, traveling from house to house to make up the consumer's own raw material into shoes or harness or clothing, or attaching himself to the household of some nobleman. Then as the crafts became specialized and settled occupations and the town appeared, the craftsman producer took on the functions of retailer, making to order or on occasion selling directly from stock.

As the market widened and the merchant appeared as an organizer of trade, the producer concerned himself solely with making things, in many cases becoming practically an employee of the merchant who provided

THE MIDDLEMAN

the stock and capital, took all the risks entailed, and sold the finished goods in his own shop and at neighboring town markets. Steadily this system of trading widened until there was a metropolitan market for goods of certain recognized types and qualities. While on one side the merchant became more definitely a wholesaler, disposing of the goods he took from the producer to distant retail merchants, who in turn distributed them to the consumers, on the other side the merchant-producer gradually strengthened his financial position and grew in importance. Assuming all the risks of production, he distributed his product through various wholesalers who sold in turn to retailers, the latter supplying the consumers. As a world market appeared, the producer disposed of a part of his product to the exporting and importing houses which carried domestic goods beyond the seas and brought back foreign luxuries and necessities for home consumption.[1]

[1] In Defoe's "Tour of Great Britain," written about 1725 (Volume II, Letter II), also quoted in C. J. Bullock's "Selected Readings in Economics," beginning on page 325 we get vivid and entertaining glimpses of the activities of both merchant wholesalers and retailers full two generations before the industrial revolution gave its tremendous impetus to English trade. In one chapter he reports the departure of a merchant's representative for a trip through the provinces, which might outlast a year, in such state and splendor as no modern salesman could hope to emulate. In another passage he describes the manner of retail and wholesale trade at the great Sturbridge fair, one of the typical markets of the time, with the same feeling for detail which makes "Robinson Crusoe" seem a transcript from the experience of a shipwrecked sailor. Here is his picture of the retail section:
"It is impossible to describe all the Parts and Circumstances of this Fair exactly; the Shops are placed in Rows like streets, whereof one is called Cheapside; and here, as in several other Streets, were all Sorts of Traders, who sell by retail, Brasiers, Turners, Milaners, Haberdashers, Hatters, Mercers, Drapers, Pewterers, Chinawarehouses, and, in a word, all Trades that can be found in London. I might proceed to speak of several other Sorts of English Manufactures, which are brought hither to be sold; as all Sorts of wrought Iron, and Brass Ware from Birmingham, edged Tools, Knives, etc. from Sheffield; glass wares, and Stockens, from Nottingham

167

AN APPROACH TO BUSINESS PROBLEMS

After the advent of the factory system, producers tended to lose their character as merchants and to devote themselves wholly to the management of their works and the invention and betterment of methods and machines. The chief reason for this, as we saw in an earlier chapter, was that the market constantly outran production. The problem was not so much to create a demand as to manufacture goods to supply it. The pressure was all to increase the rate of output. With the division of labor and the growing intricacy of operations, manufacturers found it both necessary and profitable to concentrate their attention on production.

To relieve them of the alien task of merchandising, the selling agent appeared as a new link in the chain of distribution. He undertook to dispose of the total product of the factory to wholesale merchants. These in turn supplied retailers, and the retailers the consuming public. So long as the demand exceeded output, this arrangement satisfied all hands; but as mill capacity outgrew the market, the producer discovered him-

and Leicester; and unaccountable Quantities of other things of similar Value every Morning."

His account of the wholesale market has added interest because it sets forth as an established trading process what must have been sale by sample, if, indeed, it was not that most modern of merchandising expedients, sale by description. And this was a century before the widespread use of power machinery in the industries made uniformity of product easy of attainment.

"Besides," Defoe writes, "the prodigious Trade carried on here by Wholesalesmen from London, and all Parts of England, who transact their business wholly in their Pocket-books; and, meeting their Chapman from all parts, make up their accounts, receive Money chiefly in Bills, and take orders. These, they say, exceed by far the Sales of Goods actually brought to the Fair, and delivered in Kind; it being frequent for the London Wholesalemen to carry back orders from their Dealers, for 10,000 Pounds-worth of Goods a Man, who deal in heavy Goods, as Wholesale Grocers, Salters, Brasiers, Iron merchants, Wine-merchants, and the like; but does not exclude the dealers in Woolen manufactures, who generally manage their Business in this Manner."

self at a serious disadvantage. The outlet for his goods was controlled by middlemen; but while he had been designing machinery, reducing costs, perfecting quality, the middleman had intrenched himself with the trade as the source of its supplies. The manufacturer, isolated from the consumer and with fixed charges which compelled him to operate continuously or lose money, found the intervening middleman exerting pressure to force him to accept a narrow margin, even at times to operate without any profit at all.

The middleman, too, was the creator and definer of demand. Any attempt of the manufacturer to differentiate his product and thus lift it out of the ruck of staples was subject to the approval of the middleman, who might veto it because it introduced an untried element into his selling plan. To escape this limitation, the stronger producers in many lines have assumed the neglected function of demand creation and have sought ways of going round the selling agent, the wholesaler, and even the retailer in order to establish a closer contact with consumers of their goods.

The development of this tendency to reduce the number of factors intervening between the consumer and the sources of the goods he needs is one of the distinguishing characteristics of modern business. Producers assert that the movement has been an effort not so much to get rid of the middleman as to eliminate payment for functions which the middleman no longer performs. The question narrows down, they declare, to this: Shall there be double pay for a single performance of the function of demand creation? Since the product pays the charges, it is vital for them to discover a more economical way of creating and supplying

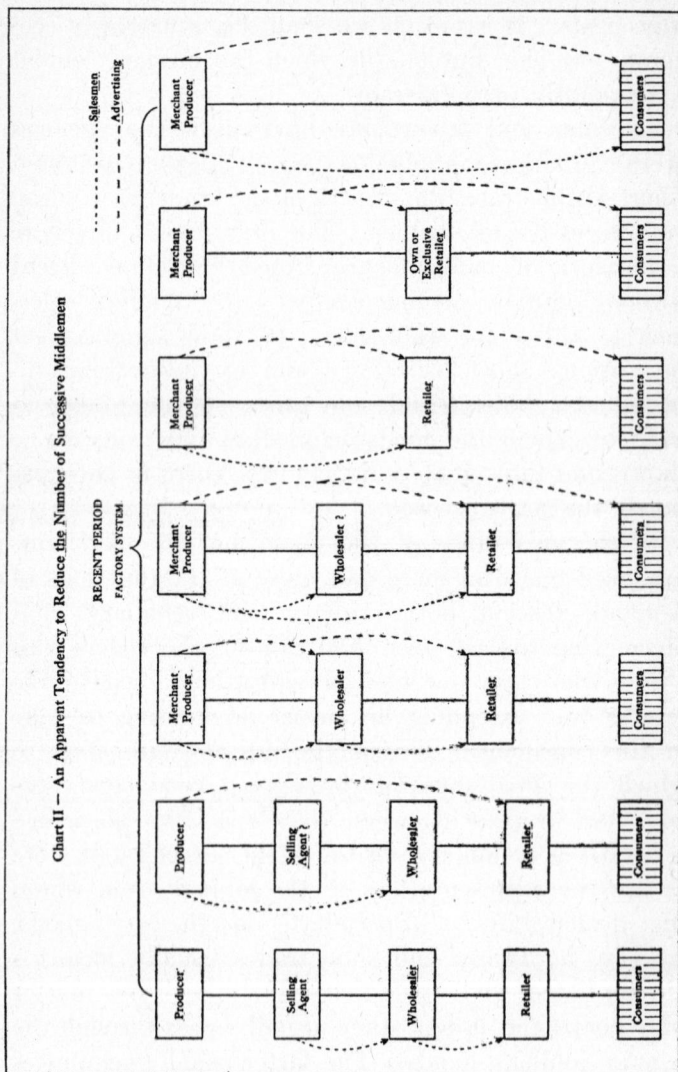

Chart II – An Apparent Tendency to Reduce the Number of Successive Middlemen

demand than through the orthodox channels, if such a way exists. It is not, as we shall see, a narrowly economic problem, but one in which the human element is frequently preponderant.

Salesmen and advertising have been the agencies of the producer's gradual approach to the consumer. Chart II illustrates the growth of the tendency to drop out successive middlemen. The first step is to secure a measure of independence from the selling agent without actually parting company, by sending salesmen to call upon wholesalers, to show samples, get suggestions and book orders, and by advertising directed at retailers (and sometimes at the jobber as well) to exploit the goods before they are ready to be shown and thus create a demand for them in anticipation of the market season.

In the next stage of the evolution the merchant-producer takes on more and more of the functions of demand creation, both primary and secondary, supplementing the salesmen who call on wholesalers with others who carry the work of education down to the retailer and extending his dealer advertising to take in the consumer. This is the intermediate stage to which the great mass of progressive producers have advanced at present, when the "specialty salesman" is almost as common a visitor in the larger retail store as are the representatives of the jobbers from whom the dealer buys. "Specialty" in the dry goods, grocery, hardware, and shoe trades usually means a differentiated and trade-marked staple. No matter who books the orders, they usually pass through the regular jobber's hands. The latter usually acquiesces in this plan because it relieves his road men of the burden of selling and gives them more time to push other lines without sacrificing profit.

Often this results in another step in the evolution of the merchant-producer. Having direct and satisfactory connections with the retailer, the producer decides to eliminate the wholesaler and save a discount, especially if his product has no great weight or bulk and reorders can be forwarded quickly by express or parcel post. He keeps in touch with his dealers through salesmen and advertising, using the latter and frequently the former to stimulate and renew the consumer's appreciation of his goods. If he has a widely advertised and very desirable line, he can even demand a contract with a sales quota guaranteeing a certain volume of orders, and can secure the adoption of those methods of display, promotion, and selling which experience has proved best for his products.

From this vantage ground the manufacturer can make one further advance, to complete independence of middlemen and absolute control of his trade. He can establish his own retail stores — witness the success of certain notable shoe and tobacco "chains." With a smaller outlay of capital he can make exclusive contracts with going concerns, as in the drug trade, which insure his goods against competition in that store through a profit-sharing clause. Again, he can take the mail-order route, using general and direct advertising to reach consumers and create his demand, and railroads, express companies, and the parcel post to deliver his merchandise. If he be a manufacturer of another class of "specialties," such as machinery or labor-saving devices for the office, factory, store, farm, or household, which require a high order of intelligence and skill to sell them to selected prospects, he will find it economical to employ both salesmen and advertising in his work of demand creation.

This tendency to decrease the number of distinct ownerships through which goods pass on the way to the consumer will probably show further development in the future unless new factors appear. The attempts of wholesalers and retailers to check the growth of direct selling or semi-direct selling through the mail-order houses, while in many cases raising the efficiency of the middlemen themselves, have not seriously inconvenienced the rival agencies. Concerted action to force the producer to dispose of his output through regular trade channels has taken at times the form of a virtual boycott. But even if this were of itself the most effective method, the attitude of the federal and state governments would probably discourage it.

Much more significant is the movement among jobbers to establish their own house brands, thus reviving the conditions which obtained in production and distribution before the manufacturer sought emancipation from the middleman. Neither this nor the remarkable growth of the chain store nor the growth of the coöperative trading associations should be left out of the manager's calculations. Buying associations have been organized by the "regular" retailers of many cities and districts to meet the new condition. How nearly each of these systems will balance the others and what effect antagonistic factors will have on the final adjustment of distribution are still matters of speculation.

For the individual manufacturer, however, they have a practical aspect. In many localities the chain store and the retail buying association present immediate problems. Is it sound policy, for instance, to ignore the tremendous distributive power of the "chains" in a city like Philadelphia, St. Louis, or New York because of the prejudice the regular trade holds against them? The sales manager of one of the large cereal companies not long since declared that the profits which his company sacrificed by refusing to sell to chain stores in Philadelphia alone amounted to tens of thousands of dollars yearly. He put his problem and the problem of every manufacturer whose product by its nature must be handled through middlemen into a single query to the trade.

"Will you," he asked in substance, "coöperate with us and push our breakfast foods a little harder to make up for a loss which is due to our policy of protecting your interests in this respect? Or shall we throw down the bars to chain stores and take all the orders which rightly come to us?" It happens that this cereal company has been most scrupulous in avoiding sales policies which were not frank and fair to middlemen. This extraordinary appeal of the sales manager, therefore, would seem to indicate that in the orthodox machinery of distribution there is sometimes serious leakage of good will and the spirit of coöperation.

This orthodox system is organized on a basis of hastened profit. In normal seasons the selling agent, in touch with the market and its current wants or fancies, takes over the producer's output at a price which allows him to dispose of it to wholesalers at a substantial advance, yet still leaves the jobber a satisfactory margin when the goods are moved along to the retailer. Again, the dealer's inducement to purchase is not primarily the quality or service the merchandise offers, but the opportunity to resell to the consumer at a profit.

Not until the storekeeper displays the commodity before the customer or considers what shall be the appeal of an advertisement does the stress fall on style, utility, durability, or service as a buying argument. In brief, the demand-creating ideas about the goods vary at different stages in the process of distribution, by reason of the different viewpoints of those who buy for resale and those who buy for use or consumption. Price and salability are the essential factors to the middleman; with the consumer, quality and service must balance cost, or dissatisfaction ensues.

Analysis, not indictment, of current practice in the distribution of unbranded commodities is the purpose of these paragraphs. I do not mean to convey the impression that wholesalers and retailers generally consult no other standards than price and salability when they lay in their stocks. Within certain limits price is here also a question of comparative values; and the merchant who does not employ some measure of value in his buying will soon have the mistake called to his attention by the complaints of his customers or their neglect of his offerings. He may capitalize for one or two seasons an earned reputation for fair prices and foist on his trade goods of inferior quality; or if he be a retailer with a store in a large city, he may continue this policy indefinitely because he has a mass of fresh prospects to draw upon. As a matter of fact, the most successful wholesale houses and retail stores in the country are those which apply rigid tests for quality and service to the commodities they purchase, both for their own protection and for the benefit of their customers.

Before buying goods not trade-marked they go so far as to inspect minutely the factories where they are made, the raw materials, the processes. They count the number of threads to the square inch in textiles, the number of knots in carpets. They use chemical tests to determine the proportion of cotton in mixed silk and woolen goods. They expose colored fabrics to the action of sun, wind, and weather to determine the permanency of the dye and their wearing qualities. They sample canned goods and packaged foods of all kinds to make sure of their character and freshness. They even employ production engineers to analyze the items in their principal lines and estimate the factory cost of each as checks on the prices quoted by the manufacturers.

Because of training and superior intelligence, too, their buyers usually are keener judges of value than the factory inspectors who spend their lives passing on the same kinds of goods; and this knowledge and judgment is exercised every time a new sample comes under their eye or a new consignment is received in the stock rooms. The big department stores recognize three grades of quality in their major lines, a best, a medium, and a low-priced line, but no effort is spared to make each grade represent the utmost of value which can be bought within its price range. The average wholesaler or retailer is content to supply full lines in two price ranges, grading upward or downward from the medium according to the character of his trade. The measure of value in many instances is based on personal judgment, experience, and rule-of-thumb, but it is applied with painstaking care.

Thus equipped, the large retailer, knowing that his customers look to him to make good any defective merchandise, even when it carries the maker's name, frequently takes the final step of assuming all responsibility and finds an anonymous manufacturer to turn out his clothing, hardware, toilet articles, silverware, shoes, or what not, according to specifications and at a lower price usually than that which the trade-marked product commands.

Summed up, this struggle for integration — the integration of industry on the one hand, and opposing it the integration of trade — hinges on the division of profit. The manufacturer is sometimes forced, as he views it, to take over the function of demand creation because he sees the work neglected or ineffectively performed. Naturally he is averse to paying the middleman for something the latter no longer is required to do for his product, though he recognizes that jobbers and dealers are effective instruments of physical supply and is quite willing to pay them for the performance of this function. On the other hand, so long as they continue to be paid for creating a demand for his product he naturally desires to see them actually and adequately doing so.

CHAPTER XII

AGENCIES OF DEMAND CREATION — DIRECT SALESMEN

WHEN a manufacturer considers the problem of building permanent demand for his product, he looks first to those elements of quality and service which will render his goods more desirable to the consumer and more likely to be bought repeatedly as the latter reënters the market. Without neglecting the factors which appeal to the middleman, since the latter must be reckoned with in innumerable lines as the established agency of physical supply, he adds as much of style, finish, or special utility as his cost and production conditions will permit and takes steps to insure that his entire output shall conform to this standard.

If he trade-marks the resulting product and its superiority to competing commodities is evident, he can count on a certain proportion of repeat orders. Consumers who have bought it will recall its excellence and will try to secure it when they have need of such goods again. The middleman also can be trusted to make an effort to stock it in order to satisfy the consumer's desire to buy.

He finds, however, that at first the chances of his specialized product suffer in about the same degree as its adaptation to the specific needs of the final user (often latent or unrecognized needs) differentiates it from the bulk of similar products. A soap for washing woolens without shrinking them is likely to prove more difficult to market through the regular channels, for instance, than would a laundry bar of the conventional size, shape, and color. First, because its specific claims are likely to inhibit its purchase and use for any but this particular purpose. And second, because the "how" and "why" of its non-shrinking properties, to be effective in the creation of demand, must be conveyed accurately and vividly to the minds of prospective users.

Orders from wholesalers and retailers, therefore, will not entirely bridge the gap that separates the article and the consumer. They and their salesman, as a rule, do not have sufficient time either to master its essential selling points or adequately to present them to their customers. The qualities which appeal actively to middlemen, who buy for resale, are often quite distinct from those which attract the consumer, who is directly interested in value and service as well as appearance and price. The ideas that the retailer must communicate to the consumer, therefore, in order to create in him a desire for the product are not necessarily the ideas with which the wholesaler interested the retailer. Not until the latter addresses himself to the consumer is emphasis laid exclusively upon the special features which the manufacturer is counting upon to make the final sale.

This does not mean that wholesalers or retailers are indifferent to conspicuous quality in a product when it does not bear an established trade-mark or a quality price ticket. Quite the contrary. Such "good buys" strengthen any merchandise line or department stock and add luster to house and personal reputations. Frequently, too, they provide opportunities for better-than-regular mark-ups and corresponding immediate profits.

But the great hindrance to maximum sales for a specialty through orthodox channels is that it is difficult by this system to secure the individual handling at every stage of demand creation which a differentiated product requires. The jobber's salesman has hundreds of items to display to each dealer in the course of a few hours. The retail clerk's value is usually measured by his sales totals and his skill in serving a maximum number of customers in a limited time. The transmission to the consumer, therefore, of the ideas necessary to sell any given specialty call for the intelligence, efficiency, and good will of at least four persons, the jobber and his salesman, the retailer and his clerk. If any one of the four is careless or indifferent or incompetent, the chain of transmission snaps and the product is left to make a dumb appeal to the consideration of the consumer.

For an increasing variety of non-staple articles, then, the special salesman is recognized as an essential agent in demand creation. If the product is simply a bettered staple, retaining its familiar characteristics and depending on refinement of design or finish to recommend it, no particular urging is necessary to stimulate the middleman's interest and secure his order. But any advance in price or decrease in quantity operates against this easy acceptance, even when its specialization gives the product an added utility.

Where the character, quality, or use of the article is not evident but requires demonstration or the development of ideas unfamiliar to the trade and the consumer, the work of transmitting its selling points to the final user through two or more middlemen becomes difficult and uncertain. And finally, the minimum of sales effort is all that can be expected from the middleman, when a trade-marked product is in direct competition with his "house brands" or with accustomed articles which with a larger percentage of profit satisfy his customers.

The producer's problem, therefore, is to determine whether a direct sales force is necessary to create maximum demand for his goods with a minimum outlay of money and effort. Enough has been said to indicate the sub-problems which he must address and the factors to be considered in their solution. Too much stress cannot be laid on the importance of a fresh point of view. The great initiatives in distribution during the last thirty years have all been breaks with merchandising traditions. The Butler system of wholesaling by catalogue, for instance, was a new departure. So also was the Larkin method of selling soap and similar household and personal requisites through consumers' clubs. Another notable case was the long-range retailing of staples and specialties by mail-order houses. These revolutions in marketing custom have substituted advertising for personal solicitation of orders, the written for the spoken word; yet at the same time the exclusive salesman has become a most important agency of demand creation not only for invented specialties but also for innumerable lines developed from the staples which were formerly distributed entirely through middlemen.

Whether advertising and the producer's sales force have usurped the middleman's function of demand creation or were evolved to perform a neglected task is of no immediate moment. All three agencies exist and are likely to continue active as long as individualism holds its place in business. This chapter is concerned primarily with the direct salesman and with the problems which his employment in demand creation set up for the management. His relations with the other agen-

cies or activities of distribution, production, and administration, because of their number and complexity,
can only be touched upon here. The broader question
of when and how the different agencies of demand creation can be used independently or in combination must
be reserved for discussion later.

Nowhere do the policies of production and distribution
seem to approach so closely as when the common human
agent in operation is considered. In an earlier chapter
dealing with the policies of production we saw that the
manager's labor problems have to do with four chief
contacts with his men: (1) hiring, (2) training, (3) paying, and (4) directing. The common purpose guiding
him in all these functions is to secure for each dollar expended the largest regular day-by-day return in productive effort. But the workman is interested mainly
in the amount of money in his pay envelope; the success
of the manager, therefore, is measured by his skill in
utilizing this dominant motive to further his own purpose. His method of fixing and paying wages may add
to their pocket value by making clear the definite relation between the sum paid and the amount and quality
of the effort received. Pride, ambition, loyalty may be
awakened; latent capacities may be developed. But
the range of motives to which the employer of factory
labor can appeal remains narrow; the wage system is
the pivot on which most of these must be swung.

The employer of salesmen has a larger margin of
psychological values (if the phrase is permissible) with
which to work. As a group or class, efficient salesmen
have marked characteristics. The well-worn proverb, "A
salesman is born, not made," had as its kernel of truth
the fact that conspicuous success in selling, before

analysis was applied to salesmanship and training courses were developed, was usually attendant on certain personal or temperamental qualities.

The typical salesman was ambitious, intuitive, quick-witted, capable of enthusiasms, and sympathetic, or at least was able to see his product or service from the other fellow's viewpoint and in terms of the latter's needs. He was willing to take a chance, not only on the closing of an immediate or future order, but also on the possibilities of a new connection for himself. His function was to sell, to persuade prospects to buy his merchandise in maximum quantities; and frequently the lack of balance which comes of over-emphasis on one function led him to oversell his customers.

Now all these qualities, tempered by experience and training and by a saner conception of customer service, survive in the salesman of to-day. Twenty years ago they were the natural qualities which marked a man as a potential salesman until some discerning employer supplied him with a sample case, a price list, and a set of mileage books. To-day they have been cultivated as part of their selling equipment by thousands of men and developed in other thousands by astute employers. Whether native or acquired, they may almost be considered stock characteristics on which managers can build plans to secure sustained and maximum efforts from their field forces.

Not that the economic motive can be overlooked in dealing with salesmen, any more than in handling factory workers or customers. But the economic element is nearly always relatively constant; everyone must pay the market rate of wages and be satisfied with the approximate market price of his commodity. The efficient business man, then, is likely to give his attention to getting extra production or extra sales volume by appealing to motives outside and beyond the money involved.

It is a commonplace of management, indeed, that added pay alone, unless it be a considerable addition to the market rate, will not secure this desired extra effort continuously. Mechanics and "handy men" will work at top speed over long periods in plants like the Ford motor works, not merely because the pay is good, but largely because their jobs are coveted by so many other men outside the organization. This outside pressure reminds them constantly that their pay and condition are exceptional and that exceptional service is demanded of them. But only in extraordinary situations can the average man be prevailed upon for higher day wages or a better salary to put forth all the productive energy he possesses. To tap his reserves, something more than a money reward is required.

This is especially true of men who sell goods. The typical salesman is keen about money. He insists on receiving as much from his present employment as he can command elsewhere. It is a point of pride with him that he is paid as much or more than the average man in his line and grade. He is more interested as a rule in his gross income than in the net, a fact that must be weighed in deciding his method of payment. If he receives a salary of $5,000 a year and an allowance of $2,000 for expenses, he is likely to consider himself underpaid as compared with a friend who gets $7,000 a year salary but pays his own expenses. Straight commission or a lump sum for salary and expenses, therefore, is likely to prove the more effective method of compensation, not only because the results bulk larger in the salesman's eyes, but also because it supplies a curb on his class extravagance, his liking for the best hotels, the fastest trains, taxicabs, parlor cars, and the like.

But a fancy salary will not always obtain a salesman's best efforts unless the connection between these efforts and the consequent reward is visualized for him. That is one reason why the high-grade specialty man nearly always works on commission. The plan suits his temperament. He is willing to take the risks involved in return for the opportunity of independent action. And the experience of manufacturers would seem to show that no other method of payment gives such dependable results and allows such varied appeals to the motives which stimulate sustained effort.

The plan, it is true, has its drawbacks. Salesmen working on commission are more difficult to control, are inclined to resent interference with their personal programs of work and play. Their time, they consider, is their own. If they "let down" in their pursuit of orders, they know they pay for the lapse in lessened income. That the house also loses in volume of sales is an incidental thing. So vital is this matter of control that many concerns prefer to pay salaries, depending on regular advances backed up by daily reports and other checks to insure a fair level of industry and initiative. Bonus systems similar in principle to the Taylor method of paying factory workers have also been developed for the encouragement of salaried salesmen. Whatever his method of payment, however, no manager can afford to neglect the psychological appeals open to him for the incitement of his men.

Ambition is primary among the motives which can

be enlisted. The salesman on commission, with a guaranteed territory, is virtually in business for himself. Of every order closed he knows he will retain a fixed percentage for himself. The wise manager makes the most of this fact in urging him to continued activity after he has reached the monthly or seasonal volume which as a rule he sets for himself. It is those plus orders, of course, that make the difference between ordinary profits and extra dividends. And it is usually the salesman's tendency to self-indulgence or some similar mental handicap which stands between the management and this "velvet."

Salesmen, as a rule, have individual conceptions of the amount of money they should earn monthly or yearly or during a trade season. One is a $2,500 man. Another puts himself in the $5,000 class. A third fixes his earning power at $10,000. And when they have reached the self-appointed mark or its monthly fraction, the tendency to self-indulgence is ordinarily so strong that they slacken their efforts, begin to go to ball games, quit their territories on Friday nights, and neglect out-of-the-way or doubtful prospects.

These slumps in activity ordinarily come at the end of the month or near the close of the selling period, when the desired goal is within easy reach. But many salesmen of the lower grade unconsciously adopt daily schedules that include a certain amount of loafing because they have learned that so many hours of "hustling" will in the average give them the $25 or $30 or $40 a week which they decide on as their standard of compensation, or, if they are on salary, the volume of orders which will satisfy their employers.

This indeed is the chief problem the manager of sales-

men faces — how to keep each salesman in his territory
and at work after he has secured the volume of orders
which he has set for himself.

A manufacturer of my acquaintance has tried again
and again to get added endeavor by added payment.
Individuals have here and there responded, but as a
group the effort failed. Originally he paid straight
commissions. Reducing these commissions in certain
fertile territories, he found that his salesmen continued
to make about the same income as before. Apparently
their margin of leisure was large enough to allow considerable increase in activity without making undue
demands on their time and energy.

But high levels in sales are not reached and maintained by cutting commissions, any more than maximum production is attained in the long run by lowering
the factory piece rates. So the manufacturer went at
the thing from the other angle. To hold his men and
get the best they had he would enable them to make
more money. So he increased commissions; but the
increase did not bring the results he expected. Instead,
the number and volume of orders went down — an
outcome that is difficult to understand or account for
unless you consider how strongly the inclination to
self-indulgence operates when the accustomed standard
of life has been attained.

Nor was this experience out of the common; it can
be matched by almost any business which pays its
salesmen on a percentage basis. For years the "inside" slogan of the organization which probably has
developed more high-grade salesmen than any other
company in America has been: "Time not spent in the
presence of prospective purchasers is time lost." And

AN APPROACH TO BUSINESS PROBLEMS

I once heard a great sales manager, now many times a millionaire, put all the emphasis of an important sales convention address on this same point.

"When I was an agent myself," he said, "I started each month with the thought that I was in debt until I had earned commissions enough to meet my office, home, and traveling expenses. I couldn't rest until I was even with the board. Sometimes it took me ten working days, sometimes three weeks or more to get square. But when I did get square, I simply could not quit because I realized that I was just beginning to work for myself. In every dollar I made beyond that point one hundred cents belonged to me. And what a fool I would have been to waste one hour loafing or amusing myself, when I had slaved the best part of the month to pay for this opportunity to work for myself!"

That in substance was the message of a $50,000 sales manager to two hundred agents, no one of whom could retain his territory and earn less than five or six thousand dollars a year. I quote it simply to show that salesmen of all grades have "the defects of their qualities" and that the unending problem in managing them is to find and utilize the motives which will stimulate them to do their best. There is even the danger, as suggested above, that their compensation can be made so liberal that it will defeat its purpose.

Personal pride and social emulation are motives generally appealed to in this vitalizing of sales effort. By substituting for the individual salesman's conception of what his territory should produce a sales quota proportionate to its population or the number of live prospects it contains, a sound basis is established for comparing the personal records of all members of the field force.

Then by means of prize contests open to all on these equalized terms, the instinct of competition and the desire of leadership are aroused in the interest of individual efficiency. The prize itself is the least of the incentives. In many cases it is no more than the printing of the winners' portraits and the announcement of their records in the house organ or in a circular letter. Even when it takes the form of money or some article of personal equipment, its chief value is as a symbol of the distinction attained.

The sales contest is a thing so familiar that no analysis of its technique or effects is needed here. The most successful competitions have been those in which the struggle was visualized as a game or sport, like a hundred-mile motor race, a baseball or football game, a flying machine race, or any other form of contest that the season or the current news suggests as certain to enlist the interest of the field force.

Frequently this individual competition is varied by appeals to organization spirit. District is marshaled against district, city territories against country territories, the East against the West, and so on. In one concern, at least, the rivalry has been carried across international boundary lines. Before the present European conflict began the big biennial competition was a three-months' "war" between the American and the foreign sales forces. Even here individual achievement was the burden of the "news from the front"; the skill and courage of this or that agent or salesman in landing large orders was acclaimed.

Coincident with these monthly and quarterly team contests an individual competition was carried on against a special yearly quota averaging forty per cent above the regular quota. This contest was primarily against a monthly "bogy" of one hundred points; as soon as a man secures twelve of these, or orders totaling twelve hundred points, he takes his place among the stars of the "Hundred Point Club." The instinct of personal emulation was further enlisted by awarding the presidency and the lesser offices in the club to the first winners of the coveted title of "Hundred Pointer." The material "Hundred Point" prize was a trip, free of all expense, to the annual sales convention at the factory.

The average manager has to determine whether conditions in his organization make it sound policy to carry on such sales contests. It has been argued that salesmen soon tire of them and refuse to respond to them. As a matter of fact, they have been conducted month after month and year after year by certain sales organizations; success seems to depend on the character of the contest and the vitality and tact of the management rather than on novelty to the sales force. It must be remembered, however, that not a few houses of high standing object to the principle of pitting employees against one another; while others find it difficult to standardize conditions so that fair quotas can be established.

In fixing quotas it must be borne in mind that some salesmen are more militant than others, and that while you are directing them in groups you must also take their individual characteristics into consideration. The quota which will stir the fighting qualities of one man to supreme effort will merely discourage another; and the figure which will be quite easy to secure in March or October may be entirely beyond reach in July or January. The most effective quota, therefore, is likely

190

to be a compromise, a little higher than the average for normal months, with a margin of increase in "rush" periods and particularly favorable seasons.

Whether it should be a standard based on population, or the number of rated prospects, or a more flexible quantity based perhaps on past performances of each salesman, would depend on the number of men involved, their relations with the house, and the advantages of individual arrangements and individual treatment. Of the wisdom of a carefully adjusted quota there can hardly be a question, no matter what method of payment is in use. For one thing, it supplies a standard of industry and ability for each salesman, it fixes a definite volume of sales for his territory instead of depending on his hazy personal notion of what he ought to earn. And again, it gives a more accurate statistical basis for the fixing of salaries and commissions and for the comparison of individual records.

Mention has been made of a bonus system of payment for salesmen adapted from the Taylor and Gantt systems described in Chapter VI of this book. These have taken varying forms, from the primitive salary-and-commission method to more scientific plans. The fundamental principle in all is recognition of the excess profit in sales made over and above the ordinary volume of the industry. On his quota of this ordinary volume the salesman receives the usual commission or salary; on all sales above this quota he is paid at a much higher rate.

Certain companies have gone further, working out for their salesmen a close parallel of the Taylor differential piece rate, with marked increases in commissions as the bonus standard is reached and passed and corresponding lowering of the rate when the salesman falls short. Here daily quotas and bonuses keep the advantages of application constantly before the individual. But such an intensive use of the motives of utility and money gain is practicable only in lines where the salesman has a number of regular customers or definite prospects to see every day and where the demand for the product is continuing and susceptible of increase.

Fearing over-emphasis upon these group methods of control, payment, and stimulation, there is another school of management which puts its faith in individual analysis of the salesman's character and abilities first, followed by individual training and placing in the territory to which each man seems best adapted, and individual managing when the latter has taken hold. Broadly speaking, this is the method of the successful old-school manager, who frequently is an uncommon judge of men and has sufficient force and personality to command the loyalty and enthusiasm of his subordinates.

In such cases, however, the securing and holding of salesmen is largely a process of "trial by error"; if the man fails to "make good," he is dropped and another candidate takes his place. In a small organization, this is a practicable method, particularly when the direction of sales is in the hands of the man who built the business. In a large sales force, it might easily lead to disorganization, loss of sales, heavy expense, and sacrifice of prestige and good will, unless it were backed up by an efficient system for taking care of records and all the routine activities of selling. Supplemented in this fashion, individual hiring, training, and managing of salesmen, without attempting any group incentive, is a practical ideal which has been realized with rather large forces by sales directors who concentrate on this one function and leave routine to assistants. In such an organization records and results are considered only as they demonstrate individual selling efficiency.

Whether he shall stress group or individual management of his salesmen, therefore, is a question which each executive must settle for himself. He will first eliminate the personal equation so far as is possible, then he will break the main problem up into its constituent problems, analyzing these and assembling the factors which influence them, and he will adopt a point of view independent of tradition, trade customs, and even personal experience. The decisive factor may be the character of the salesmen available or actually at work, the trade requirements which must be satisfied in marketing his product, the quality, price, simplicity, or complexity of that product, or any one of a score of conditions or combinations of conditions which it is imperative to consider.

Whatever his choice, he will face certain stock problems which every sales manager faces. These problems arise from the ambition of salesmen to make records, from their readiness in particular cases to rely on their own judgment rather than to observe the house policy, from the lack of balance which often goes with the valuable quality of enthusiasm, from the tendency to oversell or unconsciously misrepresent the product to customers, from the narrow view of sales possibilities which holds to accustomed paths in the search for prospects, from the itch for change which makes the investment value of a new salesman an uncertain quantity, from the lack of self-discipline which crops out in careless expense accounts and in the slighting of tasks which have no immediate influence on sales or compensation.

It is problems like these that put a premium on training courses and carefully organized systems of supervision, which leave nothing to the salesman's initiative except the actual face-to-face dealing with customers. So much has been written about the schooling of salesmen, and the methods employed are so familiar, that they are referred to here only to emphasize the need of making this training as comprehensive as it can be and of continuing it as long as the salesman represents the company.

To acquaint him with all your ideas about your goods is naturally the first purpose, since it is his function to transmit these ideas to consumers or to the middlemen who will aid in distributing your product. This might be a mere memory exercise for him, and for you the gathering and compiling of a manual of selling points. Only this is not enough. To reduce a mass of information to an orderly store of living knowledge, each idea instantly accessible when occasion arises for its use, requires on your part careful analysis and logical arrangement of the material, and intelligent study and practice on his.

Goods can be sold and are sold by the million dollars' worth without either. It is merely a question of your taking the pains to analyze your product and to prepare beforehand an approach and a series of selling points which are convincing, or else allowing your salesman to make the same analysis in the presence of a dozen or a hundred or perhaps a thousand prospects before he learns all the possible contacts and reactions and is able to perfect his exposition. If you leave it to his initiative, he may be years discovering and putting to use the selling points which a month or two of schooling at the factory or in selected training ground would have given him. And every business man who has bought merchandise or equipment for any length of time has met salesman after salesman whose goods had to sell themselves in spite of an awkward approach and blundering demonstration.

I am not advocating the crude, ready-made canvass and selling talk which is as ineffective as it is common. But experience both as seller and buyer and some acquaintance with the best current sales practice have persuaded me that every step in the selling process can be standardized, from analysis of the product and its market to the closing argument which clinches the order.

All that was said in a previous chapter about the development of laboratory standards as applied to the materials of demand creation holds true for face-to-face selling as well as for advertising. Not only can the most effective arguments be determined, but also the most effective order in which they can be brought to bear upon the prospective customer. There may be forty cogent reasons, for example, why the detail sales strip in a cash register is a record of value to various merchants, yet only four of these may be of direct interest to a certain storekeeper. The salesman's task is to discern the special conditions which govern in the case and to put forward the selected arguments of greatest weight.

It is obvious that a standard selling talk could not be framed to fit equally well all the store situations and personal idiosyncrasies which an equipment salesman will encounter. But if he has a logical method of approaching his prospect and uncovering the latter's business needs and mental attitude, if he can draw from a store of tested selling points the illustrations and arguments which fit the case most exactly, and if he knows the proper sequence in which these should be introduced to bring his prospect to the point of buying, his chances of landing the order are decidedly and measurably increased.

Between such a skilled approach and demonstration, with its definite plan and its wide latitude in the use of selling points, and the parrot-like recital of standard sales talk there is all the difference in the world. Part of this difference lies in the faulty analysis and scanty materials on which the latter is built; a large part, however, lies in the difference in the training given the salesmen — a careful and persistent instruction, with the development of mental poise and initiative on the one hand and the hasty cramming of a sales formula on the other.

Not every business needs or is able to develop training courses for salesmen like those which the large specialty companies maintain. Products may be so simple or the items in the line manufactured so few that an elaborate analysis would cost more than it would make. Customers and prospects may be confined to a single trade and be so nearly of the same type that a salesman of moderate resource can deal with them satisfactorily. As the product becomes complex or the line longer or an expanding market takes in prospects engaged in many different kinds of business, the value of analysis, classification, and organization of your materials of demand creation increases rapidly and the necessity of a definite method of instruction grows.

Even where a formal school for salesmen is out of the question, other means are successfully employed for their training. The commonest and the most effective in small organizations is personal attention on the part of the sales manager, both in the "breaking in" of new salesmen and in the aid and supervision given to seasoned members of the force. The house organ and the sales convention are also widely used. The former ranges from a weekly or monthly mimeographed record of individual sales, with a "ginger talk" and new selling points added, to admirably edited and printed weekly or monthly magazines, full of new facts about the products, personal mention of salesmen and their achievements, and inspirational messages and editorials. When contests of the spectacular sort are on, the house organ frequently becomes a daily paper, with every appeal to the social emulation, ambition, and sportsmanship of the individual salesman intensified.

Every possible change, too, is rung on the sales convention. There may be daily and weekly meetings of city salesmen, monthly gatherings of district forces, annual visits to the factory for three days or a week of instruction, with interchange of ideas, good fellowship, and judicious cultivation of organization spirit and personal enthusiasm.

To do more than indicate the broad problems and policies involved in the hiring, training, and management of salesmen would be impossible in a single chapter. If I have seemed to slight the problems of hiring, it is because there is less of agreement among business men and psychologists as to many of the specific qual-

197

ities which make a salesman and as to the tests which reveal these qualities than in almost any other department of business.

Certain qualities which are recognized as fundamental have been suggested earlier in this chapter. But even here dependable scientific tests to determine whether or not a salesman possesses them have not been developed. Promising experiments and investigations are under way by the psychological departments of several universities in coöperation with industrial concerns. The results thus far are meager, however, and the average business man in hiring a new salesman must still depend on the old process of a personal "sizing up," checked up by the record of past performances and references as to the subtler qualities of character which limit or enlarge the salesman's usefulness in demand creation.

No methods of hiring, training, paying, and directing, however, can result in satisfactory relations with salesmen unless backed by a certain human friendliness and understanding. If this quality is present, the salesman inevitably senses it; nor can any amount of simulation long conceal its absence. Analyzed, it may be found largely a keen perception of the salesman's pleasure in effective functioning, and of the house's interest in supplying him the most favorable conditions. But it must include a generous measure of simple good will. Without this, true loyalty and coöperation are not to be expected.

CHAPTER XIII

AGENCIES OF DEMAND CREATION — ADVERTISING

ADVERTISING is the communication of ideas about the goods to possible purchasers by means of written or printed symbols. As in the transmission of like ideas through middlemen and through direct salesmen, its purpose is to create a demand for a product or to divert a demand already existing. It has been developed not solely to take the place of the middleman or salesman in demand creation but as a means of doing quickly, cheaply, and effectively much of the work these other agencies have done in the past and much which neither could profitably undertake at present.

Like them, it has its limitations and its spheres of special utility where it satisfies all selling requirements. Apart from these specific fields — mail-order selling, for example — the manager's problem is to determine what part of his work of demand creation can be done more cheaply or more efficiently by advertising than by his sales force and what kind or class of advertising is best adapted to perform each of these tasks. There is the further problem of coördinating the different elements in his selling plan, in order to eliminate the duplication of effort which pyramids distribution costs to-day. But that is matter for a succeeding chapter on organization.

Two broad classifications of advertising are recognized — general and direct. The first aims to find new prospects, either addressing the broader public through magazines, newspapers, painted or electric signs, posters or street-car cards, or appealing to a special social stratum or a professional or business group through the class periodical or trade journal.

The second seeks to turn known prospects into purchasers and to cultivate good will and stimulate increased buying among regular and occasional customers. Various mediums are used, either independently or in combination — personal letters, booklets, circulars, and mailing cards, house organs, catalogs, premiums, and novelties. Direct advertising is intensive advertising in that it is aimed at individuals selected from the mass, whose needs, tastes, and inclination to buy have been fairly well established and each of whom has a local habitation and a place on the mailing list.

For all practical purposes, both direct and general advertising can be treated as one phase of sale by description. All advertising, indeed, is a logical outgrowth of sale by description. So long as prevailing commercial ethics made sale in bulk the only practical method of distribution, the middleman was indispensable. As business morals bettered and manufacturing methods improved so that standardization of products was possible, sale by sample appeared. The producer found that he could send his own salesman to the prospective purchaser instead of depending solely upon the selling efforts of a middleman to obtain an outlet.

When sale by description appeared, with a still higher code of conduct and a higher level of general intelligence, a third selling agency took form in advertising. Its development as an important tool of business falls well within the last fifty years, with its significance greatly increased toward the end of the period. In advertising, as in selling through salesmen, it is the communication of ideas about the goods to the prospective purchaser that creates demand. When the purchaser insisted on seeing and testing the actual goods before purchasing, sale by advertising was impracticable. This remained true, on the whole, even after sale by sample became common.

Increasing general intelligence, however, has made it possible to picture and describe merchandise so clearly that the prospective purchaser is able to buy what he wants and to know what he will receive without having a sample for examination. Confidence, of course, is the fundamental thing in such buying. For purely selfish reasons, therefore, to say nothing of the current code of business ethics, the merchant can usually be depended upon to supply the goods described. Under these circumstances, advertising becomes in many businesses the most economical agency of demand creation. Even where the actual sale is made by a salesman from a sample, advertising is used beforehand as an agency to stimulate the desire which the salesman by his selling talk and demonstration turns into expressed demand. Sale on approval makes it possible also to create effective demand through advertising even when the prospect insists on seeing the goods before concluding his purchase.

It follows that advertising may be employed either as a substitute for middlemen and salesmen or as an auxiliary force to aid them in their exercise of the selling function. It tends to displace these other agencies, in whole or in part, whenever it is a less expensive or more direct means of communicating ideas to the consumer. It cannot be dismissed as mere "puffing," because its substantial usefulness in our present scheme of distribution has been demonstrated.

That there are wastes and abuses in its employment may be frankly admitted. It is a new economic force, as yet only partly understood, which has brought change and readjustment in all our machinery of distribution and is itself undergoing constant modification and adjustment. It has been used extravagantly in not a few instances to exploit commodities having a wide margin of profit. In others it has been expected to prove a panacea for weaknesses in departments remotely related to selling. And in a great many cases the failure of individual campaigns has been charged up against advertising as a marketing force when the blame was due to ignorance or neglect of some important factor or element on the part of the advertiser.

Against some advertising campaigns the indictment has been brought that they were simply "weapons of destructive competition," [1] serving no useful purpose. Professor Taussig, observing that "mere effrontery in puffing your wares is an important factor in modern trade," offers this illustration of such action:

"Among articles equally good, that which is systematically paraded is likely to be most readily sold. People are led to buy Smith's wares rather than Jones's. One might suppose that if Smith's wares were equally good, and were sold at a lower price (made possible by eliminating the advertising expense) he would hold his own in spite of Jones's preposterous puffing. But, in fact, Jones's wares are preferred; some vague impression of superiority is produced by the incessant boasting.

[1] F. W. Taussig, "Principles of Economics," Vol. II, p. 428.

Plentiful cash is the *sine qua non* of an effective advertising campaign."

But from the standpoint of the business man, Jones's advertising, if it be typical of most campaigns, does not accomplish its full and proper work if it simply diverts demand which would otherwise go to Smith's product or be divided with the latter. If the advertising has convincing selling quality, it will, with the great majority of products, create demand which did not exist before and will thus widen the market for all makes of the article it describes. Numerous instances could be quoted in support of this statement, covering a wide range of human wants and appetites, from breakfast foods to farming implements.

I feel sure, too, that something more than "a vague impression of superiority" is produced by any advertising campaign worthy of the name. With many low-priced articles, frequently bought and quickly consumed, repeated statement of their merits may be enough to influence the first and succeeding purchases. In any case involving greater expenditure, however, the impression built up by the advertising would have to be positive and convincing to overcome the prospects' natural inertia and disinclination to change his buying habits. With utility values equal, too, there is the question of psychic value. Because advertising has given Jones's product a vogue, there is to the purchaser a distinct element of satisfaction in the certainty that it will be recognized as a standard product needing no apology or explanation.)

From the viewpoint of economy alone advertising has made possible the marketing of thousands of commodities on a national scale, with the consequent savings that always come from large-scale production and distribution efficiently carried out and that are certain to be reflected in the long run in lower prices to the consumer. It has set new and higher standards of quality, utility, and value, not only in the things advertised, but in nearly everything that the ordinary man or woman uses or consumes in everyday life. By the same process it has constantly brought these new facilities and comforts to the attention of those who needed them. And it has accomplished all this by the diversion of a far smaller sum of human energy than any other known method of demand creation would have required—granting that any other method would have been able at all to perform the same service.

It is an accepted truth among advertisers that the creation of permanent demand for any commodity or specialty is impossible, no matter how great the expenditure, unless it is at least equal in value to any competing product. This value may be partly psychic, in the sense that better design or higher finish or an attractive or dirt-proof package is the basis of the special appeal to the consumer. But there must also be solid value to satisfy the consumer's need, or the campaign exploiting it is bound ultimately to fail.

The marvelous expansion of the clothing industry in the United States suggests how advertising reacts on the product and effects standardization and increase in values as well as reduction in marketing expense. To begin with, we have the testimony of the largest makers and distributors of trade-marked clothing, who spend in some cases upwards of half a million dollars a year on publicity, that their selling cost per suit is less now than before they began advertising. Because they are able to manufacture and market suits by the hundred thousand, they have been able not only to reduce their advertising outlay per unit sale, but also to effect remarkable economies in buying, manufacturing, selling, and the handling of reserve stocks.

Differentiation and the development of selling points are fundamentals of successful advertising and hence influence the character of the product sold. If the first analysis of the product does not bring out a convincing array of selling points, the pressure on designers and production men to supply them becomes imperative. Merely general claims may at times close orders when backed up by the salesman's skilled presentation and his personality. But cold type and pictures demand the presentation of specific advantages to the buyer. They may take the shape of reduced factory costs, reflected in lower prices, of added utility, beauty, convenience, or durability, of more careful handling, packing, and delivery, of more intelligent adaptation to the individual consumer's needs or increased service. Whatever the line of betterment pursued, almost invariably the consumer profits. Instead of creating a "vague impression of superiority," any successful advertising campaign must be based on the creation of substantial and demonstrable points of superiority to differentiate the advertised product from the mass of competing articles.

Granting that these added selling features are sometimes of little actual and permanent value, there is no question in my mind that the influence of advertising, particularly in recent years, has been increasingly on the side of betterment and heightened utility in the products advertised. Anyone whose memory is long enough to recall the ready-made medium and high-grade clothing of twenty years ago and compare its style, fit, comfort, fabrics, and prices with the same elements in the clothing retailed to-day has a good measure of the social service which advertising has contributed in this and many other fields.

Consumers and middlemen have been educated to discrimination in their buying; non-advertising manufacturers have had their attention concentrated on the qualities advertised and on the internal conditions in their own businesses which might be standing between themselves and like advantages. Certainly the quality of non-advertised lines, sold under the dealer's label, has been greatly affected by the general advertising of the great houses and by the demand of consumers for style, fit, and materials of a grade appropriate to the prices asked.

The remarkable development of the American motor car is another case in print. Without advertising to call the attention of prospective buyers to the improvements and new features of their cars, thus stimulating demand for the new models and creating desire for possession in non-owners, current standards in design, construction, and price would not have been reached for many years to come. European experience demonstrates this and European prices prove again that advertising, the key to sale volume, instead of increasing the cost to the consumer, almost always reduces the prices and increases the quality or utility of the article exploited. Without exception, it reacts on manufacture, since the pressure is to produce an article which can be more effectively advertised, whether it be quality or price that is the chosen appeal to the consumer.

ADVERTISING

When waste does occur in advertising, it may generally be attributed to one of five things: positive lack in the product of those elements of quality or service which appeal to the consuming public's need or desire; ignorance of the true function of advertising as an agent of demand creation for the particular product in hand; blundering application of recognized principles; failure to develop laboratory standards for the testing of selling materials and mediums; or neglect to utilize and keep in operating balance the other essential agencies of distribution.

It need hardly be said that if the goods advertised are not adapted to satisfy a real want, the advertising cannot produce results; attempting to sell a thing for which no one has actual or potential use is wasted effort. Even with a desirable product, the medium used for the transmission of ideas about it may not be the one reaching an economic or social group in which are many individuals having a latent need for the commodity.

The most serious cause of inefficiency usually lies in the fact that the ideas about the goods or the form in which they are communicated are not adapted to secure the reaction desired. Enough has been said, however, about methods of measuring the value of advertising to indicate the policies whose observance will correct either of these conditions. The final important cause of waste in advertising, neglect to provide for adequate physical distribution and thus realize maximum results from aroused demand, will be discussed in another place. Here, as in all the other activities of distribution, the manager must preserve a balance between the time, area, and volume factors both in advertising and physical distribution, or the leakage of demand will destroy all the gain which should come from the most effective campaign.

I believe that the social disadvantages attributed to advertising do not in the main exist, but that considered as one agency of selling and utilized in its proper place, advertising is a modern social force of high value. To the producer the advantages possessed by advertising over other agencies in demand creation fall under three heads.

I. Efficiency. In advertising there is virtually no limit to the number of prospective buyers who can be addressed simultaneously either through one medium or through many. Intensive cultivation of one or more selected districts is equally practicable. In both cases quick action makes immediate results possible, whether the object is sales volume or the defining of the market in its broad lines. By choosing the right mediums and adapting the appeal to the class addressed, every promising social and economic level can be explored and those who will buy your product for consumption or resale can be discovered.

Besides this selective method of appealing to classes and individuals, a balanced campaign has cumulative force, influencing the public mind as well as individuals. The psychological effect of getting everybody talking about the goods is too well known to require elaboration. Another important by-product of advertising is the stimulus exerted on those to whom it is not directly addressed. The surest road to the interest of the middleman, for instance, is a convincing campaign aimed at prospective consumers.

Where the ideas about the goods are difficult to communicate because they are new and different, or where for any other reason "the trade" cannot be depended upon for their transmission, advertising offers the only available means of rapid and accurate transmission. A further special utility is the stabilizing of the market for a product by inducing the ultimate user to insist on having it and thus limiting the dealer's power to supply a substitute.

II. Economy. For the same outlay advertising will establish a contact with twenty or a hundred prospective purchasers where a salesman or a middleman can call on only one. Granting that the latter contact is usually more likely to show immediate results, it remains true that except where the total of possible purchasers is small or where they are concentrated in a small area the work of finding them and acquainting them with the product can be done much more cheaply by advertising.

In preparing the ground for the salesman's call, in giving variety and interest to the follow-up which continues the education of the consumer, and in supplementing the salesman's efforts in an intensive campaign, advertising has developed an exclusive sphere of action by securing results at minimum cost. In the mail-order field, of course, advertising has demonstrated its ability to market the most diversified lines both economically and efficiently.

III. Controls. The materials of demand creation can be presented in the exact order and in the particular form which tests have proved to be the most effective. The producer's ideas about his goods thus become fixed quantities for the consumer and the middleman. There is no chance of a salesman's failing to transmit them fully and convincingly, no danger of his misrepresenting the product and the policies behind it, or of substituting for sound and honest salesmanship the specious pull of personality, with its bad after effects. Advertising writes a sales platform for the house to which not only the selling force but also the production and service departments must conform.

This permanence of the written or printed word and symbol gives the reader confidence in the claims put forward for the goods, particularly when the medium of transmission is one to which he looks for necessary or valued information. All his training, from schooldays on, has accustomed him to receive important ideas through the eye. The impression made by advertising, therefore, is clearer and more lasting; any complex statement, put in written or printed form, is more easily analyzed and understood. Psychologists are agreed on this point; and salesmen by the thousand apply the principle every day when they use the advertising issued by their concerns to concentrate the attention of customers on some vital point or to reinforce word-of-mouth statements about their products and policies.

The character of the demand created is an important factor in determining advertising policy. This may be either one of three general kinds: (1) expressed demand, (2) unexpressed conscious demand, and (3) subconscious demand.

To illustrate the distinction between them, suppose that a specialized product distributed through retailers is advertised in one or several periodicals of large circulation. In response to this publicity, 30,000 persons go to convenient stores and ask for it, 60,000 make a mental note of its name and qualities and decide to buy it when next they need such an article, and 100,000 get a favorable impression which makes them receptive to further exciting forces, like recognition of the product in a store, plus a clerk's effort to sell it. Here the 30,000 who want to buy the article represent the expressed demand, the 60,000 the unexpressed conscious demand, and the 100,000 the subconscious demand.

This, of course, is the simplest statement of a situation that grows more involved the deeper you penetrate into mail-order selling and other forms of direct marketing. In the case of high-priced office or factory equipment, which ordinarily requires demonstration by the maker's salesman, the briefest request for further information or a salesman's visit would be taken as expressed demand, though the actual sale might be months or years away.

Speaking broadly, however, expressed demand stands for immediate sales and unexpressed conscious demand for future sales if no unfavorable motive intervenes, while subconscious demand means that the field has been fertilized but that additional selling impulses are needed to produce orders. It is quite true that unexpressed conscious demand and subconscious demand are hard to measure or appraise. Yet both must be taken into account in determining the advertising policies of a business. To ignore either or to neglect the available means of turning them into positive demand might spell the difference between success and failure. Here again the principles of balance, of interdependence, and of cumulative differentials come in to govern the emphasis laid on each element of the campaign. Intelligent testing of these elements in preliminary trials will supply a basis for coördination and will furnish standards for anticipating the values of the three kinds of demand created, in terms of actual and potential sales.

Breaking his advertising problem up into its constituent problems, the manager finds that the first of these has to do with the materials of demand creation. Does the product belong to a class that can be effectively advertised? Can it be sufficiently differentiated from others of like use to give it an individuality or a special utility which will commend it to the prospective consumer and induce him to buy it either direct or at his usual source of supply? Is the margin of profit great enough to justify the outlay necessary for promotion? Would increased volume allow such reduction in unit factory and distributing costs as to make up the difference per sale? Are potential consumers or possible new uses numerous enough to render this increase in volume probable?

Here enter the basic elements of price and utility. Take up any problem in any phase of demand creation, indeed, and you will find that it cannot be solved satisfactorily until all the other factors in distribution have been given their rightful weight and value in the general scheme. For instance, a mistaken price policy, if persisted in, may neutralize the effect of a brilliant advertising and selling campaign. A balance between price and utility must be established in fact and in the minds of possible consumers. And utility may be taken to include both practical and æsthetic returns to the buyer, the degree of adaptation in the product to his needs and tastes, its quality, durability, perfection of design and finish, and the service which is the sum of these constituents. Where the middleman takes part in its distribution, its sales utility is also closely related to price.

More of this, however, in a later chapter on price policies.

Such are some of the questions which should be settled affirmatively before an advertising campaign is undertaken, though the necessary adjustments often are made unconsciously. Analysis and accommodation of factors, too, must be carried much further. There is the character of the demand to be created, for example. Is the product one for which only a temporary market can be made, like the fads in women's dress accessories which dominate but rarely outlive the season? Or has it solid, enduring qualities which insure permanent demand and repeat orders at intervals?

In the first case the margin of profit must be greater and the appeal of the advertising more urgent. Since immediate sales are the only sales possible, the effort must be to close the maximum number before the demand fades or competitors enter to dispute the market. In the second instance, all the profit from the first sale may be absorbed by the cost of making the connection, because the initial purchase is depended upon to influence future purchasers and the object is continuous profits over a long period.

The remarkably low price put on some office and store appliances is a development of the latter policy. The machine itself is sold at cost or less than the actual delivered cost, the maker reaping his profits from the subsequent trade in supplies. Manufacturers of food and toilet specialties frequently go much further to introduce a new product. A full-sized unit is either given away or sold at a special price, though the retailer is paid his full profit on every unit distributed. Such apparently extravagant practices are justified when the margin of profit is great and repeat orders can be looked to for long-time returns.

The novelty or familiarity of the product to the prospective buyer raises another problem in advertising. If it be a better or cheaper substitute for something he is already using, the task is relatively simple. The points of superiority must be demonstrated in a convincing way and their effect on the user made plain, the stress on the arguments increasing as the difference in price ranges up from zero. Recent campaigns to exploit men's trade-marked underwear illustrate this.

When a lower price is the basis of the appeal, it must be shown that the essential utility of the article has not been sacrificed. Apart from the design and finish of the cabinet and other parts, the fifteen-dollar talking machine is practically the same, to any but the cultivated ear, as that which retails for twice or thrice as much. But the customer remains skeptical until he has been convinced by advertising, perhaps with the aid of a demonstration for which the advertising has caused him to ask.

The current tendency in marketing goods through advertising is to emphasize not price, but the differentiation from staple types and the closer adaptation to the user's needs. It is only in certain progressively competitive fields, where a national market and a tremendous number of possible buyers hold out opportunities of economy through large-scale operations, that price reduction is made one of the important talking points. The exploiting of safety razors, vacuum cleaners, and dollar watches is an example of this policy. The motor car supplies another striking instance. But here at least the effectiveness of the advertising is increased by the

combination of the two basic appeals already touched
on — extraordinary improvements in the safety, economy, comfort, convenience, beauty, and reliability of
the cars themselves (in a word, their utility) and equally
remarkable reductions in selling prices. And to these
factors should be added the fundamental conscious
need and subconscious demand for the transportation
efficiency offered, both constantly stimulated by a flood
of advertising competitive in purpose but actually
coöperative in its heightening of the prospect's desire
to possess an automobile.

Except for bettered staples, however, few specialized
products encounter a developed need and a waiting
market. The history of modern business is a record of
imagination and intelligence applied to the searching
out of valid but unrecognized needs and the invention
of new foods or furniture, apparel or machines, to satisfy them. The constructive specialty manufacturer is
a pioneer always a day's march ahead of the general
public and usually under the necessity of educating the
public to perceive a particular need it has lying latent
and to apply his product to that need.

For many years this education was carried on through
salesmen. Within the last two decades, however, advertising has been developed into a more effective agency
for the transmission of ideas about the goods both to
consumers and to the intervening middlemen. Some
may prefer to date this development from the second
half of the seventeenth century, when manufacturers
and retail shopkeepers solicited custom through ele-
gant printed dodgers and the weekly newspaper offered
a medium for exploiting books, patent medicines, and
merchandise of various sorts; not a few might insist that

intelligent use of advertising is a thing of very recent years. Whichever opinion the reader holds, there is no ignoring the contrast between the long process of introducing the pioneer models of typewriters, adding machines, and other modern tools of business through salesmen and the rapid expansion of these industries in recent years when advertising has been developed to the point where it can take over its proper share of the work of demand creation.

What constitutes that share in the case of his own product is one of the manager's primary problems. He has certain ideas about his product, which must be communicated to consumers or potential consumers in order to stimulate buying. If he has a going business with an established scheme of distribution, his effort will be to discover where and how he can increase the efficiency of his selling efforts through advertising or where and how he can substitute advertising of one kind or another for a more costly form of demand creation currently employed.

Fundamentally he has the same need for a general knowledge of the advertising machinery and mediums at his disposal as the man just launching a new trading venture. Otherwise his choice and use of mediums are likely to be biased by prejudice or insufficient information. Such a survey, except in outline, is beyond the purpose of this volume, which attempts to deal with the problems of business from the owner's or manager's viewpoint and assumes that he has the aid of department executives in guiding the activities of his business. In this case, a competent advertising manager or an outside service agency would supply in a qualified measure the sort of counsel which a superintendent or works engineer would bring to the settlement of a question of factory construction or equipment.

The distinction between general and direct advertising, as we have already seen, rests on the scope of the appeal made. General advertising is addressed to the public at large or to a considerable section of it. Direct advertising is aimed at a specific individual or a group of individuals who have been sifted out of the mass by one process or another and classified as prospective buyers. It may be said to occupy halfway ground between the impersonal appeal of general publicity and the individual contact of the salesman.

It is in manner of approach rather than purpose or function that general and direct advertising diverge. A perfectly balanced campaign might include the use of every class of general and direct mediums, with a distinct function allotted to each class and a different appeal framed for each medium. And another equally intelligent campaign might concentrate on the use of a single class of either direct or general mediums. Between these two extremes, any one of a great number of combinations of mediums and appeals might be the one to prove the most effective.

The practical plan, indeed, depends on so many factors that only a few can be suggested here. The character and price of the product, for example: is it a necessity, a utility, or a relative luxury? An article of business, personal, or household use or one of pleasure? A thing of daily consumption or of long service? Is its price large or small as compared with the "consumer's surplus?" Can its purchase and use be extended by judicious reduction of its cost and quality? Is it trademarked or otherwise differentiated so that the demand created for it cannot be diverted to similar competing products? And so on through a long list of things to be considered, including the possibility of doing all the work of demand creation through advertising or the necessity of employing middlemen, the agency adopted for physical supply, the existence of mediums reaching the classes who are prospective purchasers, the degree of intelligence and the reading and buying habits of these prospects.

No small amount of the waste in money and effort which has attended advertising in the past was due to the failure of managers to analyze the problem, to break it up into its constituent problems, to list the factors of importance in solving each of these constituent problems, to put aside personal preferences or prejudices in valuing these factors, to refuse to accept precedents as rules, to insist on laboratory standards in both materials and mediums, and to realize that advertising is a distinct and separate activity needing a fresh viewpoint and a new angle of approach to be grasped and effectively performed.

CHAPTER XIV

ORGANIZATION OF DEMAND CREATION
ANALYSIS OF THE MARKET

WHEN the manager of a business has assembled his materials of demand creation and has considered the agencies at his disposal for conveying them to possible consumers, he faces the further task of putting the work of idea-transmission on a sound and efficient basis. Breaking his problem up into its constituent problems, he finds these are three in number: first, to discover how many persons want his goods or can be induced to buy and use them, who these persons are, where they are located, and how often they are likely to come into the market; second, to learn how much these prospective consumers are willing to pay for the goods; and third, to determine what agency or group of agencies will be the most effective in creating an adequate demand.

His problem, in a word, is one of organization; his three sub-problems are analysis of the market, determination of price, and combination and coördination of the agencies to be employed in stimulating demand in the chosen market at the predetermined price. No one of the three problems takes particular precedence over the others, for like all the factors and activities of business, they are interdependent. The extent of the market is determined largely by the price, and the price cannot be fixed without considering its effect on the broadening or limiting of demand. Again the size and character of the market and the price of the commodity (here also the margin available for distribution expense and profit) will go a long way toward deciding what agencies can be used for demand creation; the agencies chosen will likewise have an important bearing on both price and the width of the market.

Nor are these policies strictly departmental in their scope or application. They must conform to the general policies of the management; they cannot be formulated without considering, not alone their effect on one another, but also their influence on all the other activities of the business, on production, distribution, and administration. The principle of balance must be adhered to, the organization of the activities of demand creation must be governed by the same ratio of cost, quality, and service which is observed in production and administration, as well as in that other function of distribution still to be discussed, physical supply.

The market for a commodity is made up of the two classes of customers and prospects, the latter comprising all those who have an unexpressed conscious desire or subconscious need for the goods in question. Demand creation must have for its objective either the development of unrecognized wants or new uses for the product in the minds of customers already on the books or the discovery and transformation of prospects into new buyers. These prospects may be in territory already covered by the selling plan or in territories further afield. They may be buying substitutes or competing goods, or they may not be buying anything resembling the product because an unconscious need or subconscious desire has never been developed into positive demand.

ANALYSIS OF THE MARKET

In the first approach to the problem, individuals do not count except as representatives of the groups to which they belong. It is with the group and its reaction to his product that the manager must deal, since his initial concern is to estimate possible sales volume, the number of product units for which he can reasonably expect to find buyers when his machinery of demand creation has gathered headway.

This first survey is vital. It must uncover a sufficient number of prospective purchasers in the chosen field to insure a fixed minimum of sales; otherwise the business remains merely a project or settles down for "a long pull" while demand grows up to it. The domestic market for aëroplanes early in 1914, for instance, was so restricted and there was such competition for the attention of the few rich sportsmen who were possible buyers, that a new aëroplane business would have been a doubtful undertaking. Since the outbreak of the European war, however, the military demand has brought about such improvement in design and production methods and the safety of flying has been so thoroughly demonstrated that much larger American sales of machines for sport, military, and business purposes may be anticipated when the war is over. This may be the more confidently expected since increased factory facilities, reduced production costs, and the necessity of keeping enlarged establishments busy are sure to be reflected in lower prices — another evidence that the principle of interdependence never ceases to apply in all the activities of business.

In analyzing his market, the business man faces an indefinite body of possible purchasers, widely distributed geographically and exhibiting various extremes of purchasing power, intelligence, and conscious and unrecognized needs. The effective demand of the individual depends not alone on his ability to pay for the product offered, but also upon his wants and tastes as cultivated or repressed by his character, education, habits, occupation, and economic, religious, and social environments. The market, therefore, splits up into economic and social strata as well as into geographic divisions.

Turning first to the territorial distribution of the consuming public, he finds any number of factors influencing the probable demand for his goods. If his product be designed for a special and limited use, like an improved breaking plow or cream separator, his market is narrowed immediately by the exclusion of the millions who live in cities and in industrial districts. Though even here it will be well for him to consider the thousands of business men and investors who own farms and are interested in the latest labor-saving devices for farm work. Means exist for estimating pretty closely the extent of this marginal market and the mediums of demand creation for reaching it.

But town and country are only the first broad geographic divisions of the market. Continuing with agricultural implements, for the sake of simplicity, the New England farmer as a prospect for improved machinery is in a different class from the man in the "corn belt" of Illinois or Iowa, just as the southern planter has very little in common with the dairyman of Ohio or Wisconsin. It follows that the farmers of the United States cannot be successfully approached as a single group, but must be classified as a number of sectional groups, the members of each group having a general likeness in their responsiveness to new ideas, in resources, and in standards of working and living, but breaking up into many sub-groups according to their dominant crop or occupational interests.

All, it is true, have similar fundamental needs for wagons, harness, plows, axes, pumps, and so on. Once away from these necessities, however, great diversity is encountered in felt needs and the mental attitude toward unfamiliar things. Even in buying pumps, where the New England hill farmer would be content with a low-priced wooden or iron pump, the Indiana man would be likely to demand a better grade and then hitch a windmill to it, while the Illinois or Iowa stock raiser would add a gasoline engine to insure him a dependable water supply at all times.

Climate and soil conditions are responsible for further sub-groupings, while the racial origins of the people and the school conditions are further factors in limiting the demands of local sub-groups. The surface character of the land under cultivation and the size of farms must also be considered in determining the market for the larger tools of agriculture like oil tractors, self-binders, gang plows, and motor trucks.

Equally important in such an analysis is a realization of what may be termed the market contour; the market is never a level plain. It is composed of differing economic and social strata, though the distinction between the various levels is not always apparent at first glance. Noting the average size of farms and the land values in the prosperous sections of the middle west, for example, the manufacturer of a moderate-priced heating system for country houses might conclude that here were many prospects for the thing he had to sell. By carrying his analysis a little further, however, easily accessible statistics would show him that a large proportion of the better farms are in the hands of tenants, who might be persuaded to put their surpluses into motor cars or talking machines, but hardly into permanent heating systems. The non-resident owners, of course, would be less apt to make an investment seemingly so unproductive.

Even in the case of farm necessities, like plows or harvesters, tenant farming would be an important factor in the analysis, since many tenants are obliged to operate on credit, and the credit terms usual in the territory might make too severe a drain on the producer's financial resources. At the least, they would influence prices and would present on the whole a more serious problem than the credit situation in a more recently settled district where customers, though lacking ready money, have the landowner's advantage in making loans.

This element of market contour takes on increasing significance when the product is designed to appeal to the general public, without regard for geographic or occupational lines. The distributor of a three-dollar trademarked hat for men must obviously direct his appeal to different economic and social strata, must consider different buying motives, and must adopt different selling policies, as compared with the distributors of two or five-dollar hats. He has this advantage over the latter, that his prospects include dwellers in every village of the country large enough to boast a general store and that a city like New York or Chicago offers him twenty or perhaps fifty neighborhood centers of distribution as against two or three open to the five-dollar hat. But he must keep in mind the fact that he will encounter forceful competition from established hats of the same or lower prices and that absolutely local conditions will frequently determine the volume of his local sales.

Statistics of the population will afford him only initial help, therefore, in arriving at the possible demand for his products in any given district or community. He will have to investigate a number of average neighborhoods and communities, the retailers supplying them, the competing goods bought by them, and the methods used in exploiting those goods. Half a dozen surveys of typical outlying centers of trade would give a fair average of conditions, perhaps, for the whole of Chicago. The fact that New York has been the scene of a greater number of like investigations and "try-out" campaigns would have to be taken into consideration in deciding whether the results of such a "sampling" there would be less dependable. Worcester, Massachusetts, or Dayton, Ohio, should supply data on which to base an estimate of what industrial communities, east and west, would offer in the way of sales.

And so, up and down the population scale, typical cities could be tested at moderate expense to determine how other towns of their size and class would receive a new trade-marked hat and what selling efforts must be put forth to secure the attention of dealers and ultimate users. I need hardly add that an analysis of the market on a national scale would be useless expenditure except for a business contemplating national distribution, or that an analysis of the national market for a general utility must recognize certain broad divisions of the country with distinctive trade and social usages certain to affect demand as well as the processes of demand creation. For the average smaller business the only safe and economical way would be to confine the analysis to its strategic territory and concentrate selling effort on this region, expanding as the manufacturing and sales organization proved themselves capable of taking on more work.

With a product appealing to only a single element of the population, the analysis becomes more complex and the geographical and economic factors are more difficult to align. Take the case of a publisher who is mapping out a selling campaign for a Catholic magazine or encyclopedia. It is essential that he take into account not only the geographic distribution of the Catholic population in the United States, the regions where it is relatively dense, and the regions where it constitutes only a small part in the population, but also the constitution of that population through the economic strata.

A method of distribution successful in New Orleans, where the denser Catholic population includes those of all degrees of purchasing power, might well fail if applied in Maine, where the Catholic population is relatively sparse and is composed largely of French-Canadian mill hands. The irregularity of distribution of the Catholic population, however, would be compensated by the definite information available about its location and its average buying power, the latter influenced in no small degree by its sympathy and responsiveness to church appeals.

Density of population is an element which rarely can be neglected, either in deciding whether a profitable market exists for the goods or in determining how a possible market can be developed and supplied. It is here that analysis of the market, price policies, and com-

bination of demand-creation agencies are most closely
interwoven. Where population is dense the means
of creating demand multiply. Intensive cultivation
by direct salesmen, for instance, becomes possible.
Where people are widely scattered, prospects may be
so few that no practicable market exists unless a combination of agencies can be worked out which will overcome the handicaps of distance, or unless a price can be
secured which will take care of the extra selling cost.

If the manager "lumps" his costs of demand creation
through salesmen or any group of agencies which he
may be using and strikes a balance for the whole market, he may be "playing safe" and insuring himself a
profit. But it is certain that if he ignores or fails to
detect the fact that the salesman is an unprofitable agent
in one or several sparsely settled territories, he is making a double sacrifice of profit — that which he must
subtract from his net returns in densely populated districts to make up these individual deficits and that
which he probably would earn in the unprofitable territories if through analysis and tests he were to discover
the right agency or combination of agencies to cope with
local conditions. Again, if the manager bases his estimate of the average cost of selling for the whole market
on his experience in a few densely populated or easily
accessible territories, he may easily go wrong. Such
a test cannot fairly represent the possibilities of the
larger and differently constituted general field.

The typical business man seldom appreciates the importance of market contours in their relation to the
distribution of his product. His method is the familiar
"trial by error." He sends his salesmen or his direct
advertising to dealer-prospects or consumer-prospects

until he gets a positive or a decidedly negative result. With a large margin of profit, this method, though costly, frequently proves effective for a time. But for the product in a competitive field, analysis of the market is indispensable.

The motives to which a product appeals may differ widely in the various social strata of the market. The materials of demand creation, the ideas about the product which will arouse a desire for its possession in one level or section of a city's population, are not always effective when used to reach another section.

Low price and wearing qualities rather than fineness of finish or exclusiveness of design will appeal to consumers having small incomes, and thus naturally to the retailers who serve them. These arguments would not have the same force on consumers in the higher economic levels, to whom quality of materials and finish and beauty or convenience in design would probably be of prime importance. Many articles of daily use, it may be added, achieve the marketing ideal of general appeal to all classes, either because their enduring quality or essential utility overshadows the price objection or because sentiment or social emulation becomes a factor in the purchase. The presence in our cities and industrial towns of large populations of foreign birth, with traditions, tastes, buying habits, and standards of value all their own, and with varying degrees of intelligence and acquaintance with the English language, further complicates this matter of market location and puts a premium on painstaking analysis.

Innumerable businesses recognize the existence of market contours by putting out their products in two or more grades, retaining as much of the essential utility or style as is compatible with the reductions in price which will bring the various grades within reach of prospects on various economic planes. This is accepted practice among manufacturers of clothing for both men and women, watches, talking machines, cameras, hand tools, and a long list of other products having general appeal.

It is likewise a basic policy in the more advanced retail stores. Some of these not only maintain basement departments frankly offering medium and low-priced substitutes for the more substantial or costly lines displayed on the main selling floors, but also break up their important departments, such as women's clothing, shoes, millinery, and furniture, into sections divided on lines of price and thus advertised. The woman who is able to pay only eighteen dollars for a suit is recognized as a class quite as well worth catering to, because of the number of individuals involved and therefore the sales volume and rate of turn-over that are possible, as the women whose standards of dress make thirty-five, fifty, or one hundred dollars the minimum outlay.

Nor is it forgotten that despite the emphasis put on price, the real standard is one of values and that buyers will cross their customary lines, paying more than usual or making extra purchases when the inducement is sufficient. Accordingly, great technical skill and financial resources are often brought to bear on these basement stores and department sections in providing maximum values within fixed price ranges. They are comparatively recent innovations in retailing, traceable, I think, to the realization by store managers that the local market is made up of several economic levels, and that the problem of sales volume and stability is one of general and particular appeals to all these classes.

There are stores, of course, which concentrate on one or two of the classes at the top of the scale just as there are manufacturers of exclusive pianos and motor cars, jewelry and silverware, who ignore all but the few who can put quality and individuality of product above price. In fact, the specialty shop and the producer of exclusive merchandise, both of them outgrowths of more intensive analysis of the market, have so multiplied in recent years that they have kept pace with what might be called the democratization for profit of the large retail store.

One instance will illustrate the transformation which an intelligent market analysis can effect in an established business. Taking over the conduct of an important St. Louis store, a few years ago, a new manager was amazed at a forty per cent slump in sales during the summer vacation. Railroad statistics indicated that about 55,000 persons went away for a fortnight or longer during July and August. That the absence of seven per cent of the population for a part of the time should cause a forty per cent reduction in sales suggested to the manager that the merchandising plan of the store was badly out of balance.

Checking July deliveries on a route map of the city visualized this lack of balance. Sixty per cent of the deliveries had been made on seven routes in the better residence districts. On five of the seven the July deliveries numbered only half those made in June; on two others the decrease was much smaller. On four other routes which covered two thirds of the total area of the city, the falling off was negligible; but on the basis of the number of parcels handled, these four districts accounted for only thirty-two per cent of the July business.

The outstanding fact from this analysis was that the store was neglecting the great market stratum made up of wage earners and thrifty salaried folk, who did not take long vacations but did buy dependable medium-priced merchandise all the year round. The remedy was obvious; it was to stock the lines and grades that would appeal to these neglected prospects and to let them know about the goods by means of an intensive campaign of direct and general advertising. The problem as to what kinds and classes of merchandise should be stocked was a further serious exercise in market analysis. The correctness of the first broad analysis was proved by steadily mounting store sales and by a vacation business the following year that wiped out the former deficits.

For a new product in an occupied field, analysis of the market involves much more than the classification of economic strata in your selling field, the testing of their reactions to your materials of demand creation, and a survey of the available agencies of demand creation with their relation to your production and sales plan. The following list of factors is suggested by Mac Martin as an essential preliminary to a study of national distribution.

(a) The present annual consumption of similar products or of those for which your product would prove a substitute.

(b) The per capita consumption among adult men and women or of the particular classes, by age, to which your product will appeal.

(c) The territorial variations in the consumption.

(*d*) The classes of dealers now handling a similar article.

(*e*) The classes of trade sold by these dealers.

(*f*) The sales and advertising policies and plans of competitors.

(*g*) The volume of business secured at the present time by various competitors, with regard especially to the kind, quality, finish, and price of the product each is marketing.

(*h*) The percentage of repeat sales competitors seem to be able to secure.

Consideration of all these factors certainly should supplement analysis of the market from the viewpoint of its economic and social levels. How far it would be possible to obtain dependable information covering all the points listed would depend on the nature of the business and the character of the products. Statistics on consumption are, in general, far from accurate; except in highly competitive fields, a special investigation, by the sampling method at least, would be necessary to secure the specific information on which sound policies are based.

It might be well to carry the inquiry beyond mere market factors. Business is a competition of individuals as well as of products. Your analysis of the market, then, is not complete unless you know all that can be learned about the major influences that affect that market. What, then, of the organizations and the men behind the products your goods must meet? What are their characters? Their attitude toward business? Their experience? The capacities of their organizations? Their capital and resources?

It is of importance to know whether your competitors are dreamers and fighters, willing to risk all they have for the sake of the business and their vision of its future, or whether they are conservatives insisting on their annual profits and grudging expenditures that are not immediately productive. You ask whether they are newcomers in the field or whether they have the background of emergency knowledge acquired only by those who have grown up in a trade. Are their making and selling forces competent and efficient and the routine of their production and distribution activities well established? Is their selling plan positive yet flexible enough to adjust itself to unusual situations? And finally, have they resources more or less ample than your own?

Abundant capital will enable them to perfect their products, to secure good men for all important positions, to install the best equipment and standardize all their factory and sales operations, to finance, build up, and train a capable sales force, to test their materials of demand creation, to buy materials in the lowest cash market, to make easier terms to dealers and consumers, to offer free trials of the product, to carry on extensive advertising campaigns to exploit their goods, their terms, and their service. Capital alone will not do all these things; it only renders them possible. But the possibilities as well as the actualities of competition are elements which the manager of a new undertaking or of an old business expanding must consider in the analysis of his market. That market, when all prior claims have been subtracted, may prove to be no market at all.

CHAPTER XV

ORGANIZATION OF DEMAND CREATION
PRICE POLICIES

SINCE gain is the immediate aim of business, it seems obvious that the price which a manufacturer obtains for his product must be based on factory cost, with sales and delivery expense and an allowance for profit added. Taking a line of trade or all articles of the same class as a whole, this is true; income must exceed outgo or a business soon exhausts its resources. But the individual manager's price problem seldom takes rise in the factory, nor is it solved by simple addition of the elements of delivered cost.

Usually the process is reversed. The established market price for the article or for substitutes having the same general function or utility is the starting point as well as the imperative factor in the solution of the problem. In fixing this market price, over short periods or single selling seasons, even a basic element like the cost of raw materials is a consideration secondary to the economic relations of supply and demand for the finished goods.[1]

---

[1] A study of the relations between quotations for raw cotton and the market price of three well-known lines of bleached muslins, Lonsdales, Hopes, and Lonsdale cambrics, from 1879 to 1914, discloses an interesting example of an economic principle at work. Despite the fact that standardization of products and processes had been carried further, perhaps, in cotton textiles than in any other important industry, a comparison of the cost of raw cotton and the prices for finished goods shows frequent and sharp divergences where, because of manufacturing conditions, close parallels might be expected. Again and again advances attended reductions in costs

234

PRICE POLICIES

There are practical grounds for this approach, though the rule of thumb enters too much into price-fixing, and too often producers launching a new commodity go on the assumption that the prevailing market price for any given grade is right. They trust to their own resourcefulness or the ingenuity of their works executives to turn out the same thing at a margin of profit. Experience has taught them, too, that the first factory output of a new article is usually at a cost higher than the level easily maintained when the operations have become familiar, when lost motion has been eliminated, and continuous production has cut down incidental wastes.

The decisive reason for considering the market quotations for competing goods as a basis in fixing prices is the necessity of making sales. But unless in the long run the price is such that the product can be moved from the warehouse floor and placed in the hands of the consumer at a profit, the whole process of its production,

of materials, and reductions were made while the market for raw cotton was rising.

Commenting on the figures, which it secured and published, "The Journal of Commerce" had this to say about how prices are controlled by the law of supply and demand:

"Many traders have come to believe that trading values are fixed by the value of the materials and production cost represented in them. Time and again this belief has been shown to be an economic fallacy. The shrewd trader in merchandise is the one who gauges his selling price by the possible demand for what he has to sell, and the supply of such merchandise is the factor that measures the success of distribution.

"These figures show that time and again cloth values have risen and been maintained without regard to the cost of the raw material values represented in the merchandise. The manufacturer naturally looks upon values from his own viewpoint, which is the one of cost of production. But the merchant must consider other factors. The potential supply in the markets, the power of the buyer to purchase and distribute, and the inherent worth of the goods in competition are powerful factors, and they are the ones that must govern the judgment of the trader."

distribution, and administration is a useless thing. The price, therefore, must be adjusted to the conditions that govern in both factory and market. It need not be the highest that can be obtained from a limited group of buyers nor the lowest that will yield a fair gain. The practical ideal is the price which will satisfy the present needs of the business yet conserve all the opportunities of profit which the future holds.

Take the manufacturer of an article competing with commodities substantially identical in kind or function; how shall he determine what the price shall be? Analyzing his problem, he finds first of all that he has choice of three general price policies: (1) selling at the market minus, (2) selling at the market par, and (3) selling at the market plus. The economist would find slightly different terms for these, describing them in turn as selling below the normal price, selling at the normal price, and selling above the normal price. For our purpose, however, the question of terminology is not significant. It is enough that there are these three distinct policies available, and that the business man may adopt any one of these to the exclusion of the others or may use two or more of them in combination to effect his purpose.

Selling at the market minus aims to increase the volume of sales by reducing the price. It is founded on the trading axiom that small profits on individual transaction mean a large turn-over. It is the business man's recognition of the truth expressed in the generalization of economic theory that lower prices will increase the amount demanded in the market. Theoretically, at least, the man who sells his product at a price below the figure established by competitors attracts the customers of other distributors. His lower price also means that they can buy more units of his commodity with the same total expenditure, thus insuring him increased volume and corresponding increase in his units of gain.

But other buyers besides those already in the market are now able to enter. Those whose unexpressed demand was not effective before, because they placed a higher value on the money in their possession or upon other commodities which could be purchased with it, now come into the market. The result is that a much larger amount of the commodity is distributed. This is true, in theory, at least, though in practice lower prices do not always over short periods attract customers from their habitual trading places. Established credit arrangements, congenial personal relations, all the forces we include under "habit" and the factors classified under "good will" work in opposition to the purely economic motive. It is only in the long run that these deterrent influences are overcome and competition works out its uniform result.

Selling at the market minus does not ordinarily involve a differentiation of the product from the stock product of like nature, though there are many exceptions to the rule. Nor are trade-marks, brands, or trade names always used. The producer depends upon the lower price to attract purchasers in numbers and looks to a larger turn-over to give a reduced proportion of overhead expense per unit sold. He also depends upon lower factory costs, made possible by the economies of larger scale production, to add further savings. These two forces together extend his area of profit, and he operates at increasing returns. Yet from the point of view of distributing policy the difference in price forms the basis of the appeal to the consumer. And the successful use of the policy in a competitive market, therefore, depends upon continued ability to undersell distributors of substantially identical products.

This policy finds illustration in the sales plans of a great many department stores. It is the basis of bargain-counter selling; and in the bargain department stores, selling at the market minus is the dominant policy. Their businesses are organized and operated with an eye single to selling under the market. They ransack the country in their search for bankrupt stocks and the excess stocks of sound wholesale and retail concerns which have overbought in certain lines or undersold because of local weather or industrial conditions. They advertise these bankrupt stocks, mill ends, and wholesale clearances as the basis of their ability to offer standard goods at cut prices. Many of them operate on a cash basis and are thus able to take advantage of the opportunity for close buying offered by the temporary difficulties of other merchants.

Many others adopt the policy of dealing in "seconds" or in sub-standard goods which resemble standard products but have been cheapened by the dropping of say ten threads to the square inch in a silk or cotton fabric or the slighting of quality or finish in wood or metal product. The enormous trade in sub-standard merchandise may be regarded as an outgrowth of the policy of selling at the market minus, though logically it is an effort to differentiate commodities from the price viewpoint and adjust them to the needs and resources of social strata less exacting than those for whom the originals were created.

But nearly all department stores at times reduce

prices upon staple commodities either to attract customers to a current sale or as a permanent store policy. Here the increased volumes, arising from trade drawn from competitors and from new consumers brought into the market, decrease the proportion of overhead expense each unit must bear and allow purchases in larger quantities. These larger quantities put the manager into a position to force the producer to share with him the economies of large-scale production. He demands and secures the jobbers' prices. Often, indeed, he is able to take over the entire output of certain factories, and in some cases he deems it advantageous to operate factories of his own, a procedure which he has had to share recently with the "chain stores" which are making advances in every part of the country and with many defensive buying associations of small retailers. In the department store, moreover, the customer attracted by the offer of a staple commodity at less than the prevailing price is likely also to purchase other commodities yielding a wider margin of profit.

This, indeed, is the motive at the back of almost every bargain sale advertised by a store selling standard merchandise; it aims to bring the customer into the store and within range of its countless selling influences, even at the sacrifice of all profit on the "leaders" advertised. The "leaders" offered by the catalogue houses are in exactly the same category. I am not criticising such bargain advertising, but only recognizing its purpose, as every business man must in considering his own price policies. The majority of producers and merchants, indeed, make use of "leaders" to exploit their regular lines, nor should such bargain events be confused with the clearing sales of overstocks of seasonal goods which merchants, wholesale and retail, find advisable at the end of each selling period. These clearing sales are not to be classed with selling under the market, because the psychic value of the merchandise to the consumer has fallen since the season was young.

To the manager putting out a new product in a competitive field, selling at the market minus is the easy method of securing distribution. If middlemen are essential to his plan, they will expect a price concession as an inducement to stock and push the article. The larger the concession the greater will be their interest in diverting demand from established lines giving them less return. It may not be necessary to cut the retail price; so great is the influence of the average retailer on the buying of his customers, outside the large cities, that he will have little trouble in substituting an honestly made product on his own assurance that it is good.

To this substitution nationally advertised brands offer serious impediment, as do also distinctive trade-marked specialties long in the market and usually asked for by name. Even against advertised articles, the dealer with an established following can make the first sale of the new product by suggesting or demonstrating its chief selling points and urging its purchase. Repeat orders then will depend on the impression the product makes on the user. Should its value seem less than that of established competing goods, the retailer's favor will not keep it moving; and the cost to the consumer of the new commodity will have to be lowered to the point where the balance favors price on the one hand as against well-known quality and service on the other.

The bulk of non-trade-marked specialties and of goods which carry dealers' brands are distributed below the normal market price. The theory of such distribution is sound enough. The middleman by undertaking all the work of demand creation relieves the producer of this effort and expense and allows him to give all his time to manufacturing operations. The margin between the open market price and the price actually charged the middleman is the latter's pay for the function he performs in demand creation. The disadvantage, from the manufacturer's standpoint, is that the origin of his product usually is not impressed on consumers in any way and he thus loses the repeat orders which its excellences should bring him. Either the wholesaler or retailer is at liberty to switch this demand to a substitute at a moment's notice.

A great many makers of trade-marked products also deliberately adopt the policy of selling under the market because of the powerful buying appeal resident in a lower price. A new concern is almost forced to offer some such inducement to purchase. It is the recognized way of entering the market, except when the product is obviously superior to the thing it would displace or when its less distinctive quality or utility is exploited by direct salesmen or consumer advertising. Like the producer himself, the middleman is in business to make all the money he can; and a new product affords opportunity for a better bargain in exchange for the outlet the manufacturer must have.

A new brand of parlor matches, for instance, may be in every way equal to the matches he has been distributing either for resale or for use; but unless there is an evident waiting market for it, there is no reason why he should invest capital, devote space and time to it, and take the risks involved unless it gives him greater returns. If he can buy the new match for ten or fifteen cents a case cheaper than competing brands, he has a motive for handling it and for trying to create demand for it.

The same market situation faces the manufacturer of any one of a thousand staples and semi-specialties distributed through trade channels. In a lesser degree it applies to highly differentiated specialties of many sorts, including those marketed through direct sales forces. Given approximately equal quality, utility, and prestige, ability to "shade the price" is often the deciding factor in a sale. Such ability, of course, may be the result of low production costs, of economies in distribution or administration, or of unusually effective organization of all the activities of the business. It illustrates again the law of interdependence which threads through all these operations. But unless the delivered cost of the goods, as compared with competing lines, is low enough to permit the necessary reductions, adoption of the policy of selling at the market minus is no more than a deferred invitation to the sheriff to take charge.

Another important consideration here is the influence of the lowered price in bringing new consumers into the market. Chart III, on the opposite page, illustrates the action of this policy.

The curve of the line L–M, of course, is hypothetical. The diagram is incomplete also, because it does not indicate the important factor that other producers are selling at a higher level and that customers are attracted from them, or that old customers are likely to increase the amount of their purchases as the price decreases. How far this is true depends upon the contour of the curve.

If L–M is nearly horizontal, that is, if the demand is elastic, a small decrease of price will bring a large number of purchasers into the market. On the other hand, as L–M turns toward the vertical, fewer purchasers will

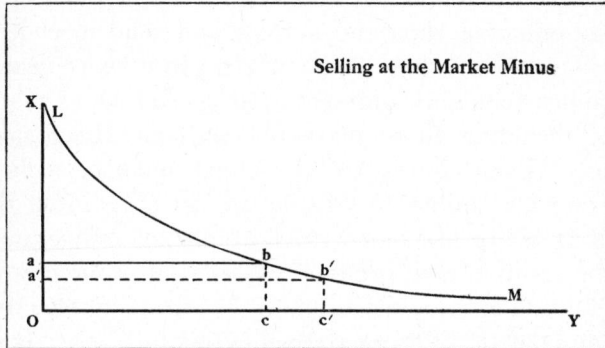

CHART III

This chart attempts to show graphically the operation on the demand side of the market of the price policy termed "selling at the market minus." On the ordinate *ox* is laid off a scale of prices for the commodity. On the abscissa *oy* are laid off the number of purchasers. The arc *LM* shows the number of purchasers at a given price, growing fewer as the price increases and greater as the price decreases.

Now if *oa* represents the prevailing market price for the commodity, and *oc* the number of purchasers at that price, it is apparent that if the price is reduced from *oa* to *oa'*, new consumers will be brought into the market and the number of purchasers at the price *oa'* will be *oc'*, a number greater than *oc*.

enter the market at any given price. Here the demand is said to be inelastic, as is the case with the necessaries of life.

A certain amount of salt will be bought, no matter what the price. A high price will check consumption to some extent, and a low price will encourage liberal, even careless use. But once the supply indispensable to the support of life is secured, the demand falls off rapidly. The business man adopting the policy of selling at the market minus, therefore, must determine whether the demand for his product is elastic or inelastic. Is he

243

selling a necessity or a luxury? The success or failure of his campaign may depend on the care with which he makes his analysis.

Selling at the market par was the distribution policy characteristic of the period during which the stress was on production. It is still a common policy in the marketing of staple goods. Briefly this policy consists in the acceptance of the market price existing for the commodity. The producer does not seek to attract purchasers by maintaining a price somewhat lower than that at which his competitors sell, nor does he attempt to establish his product, as a distinct commodity, upon a new and higher price basis. He recognizes the market price as something beyond his control and he sells his commodity at this established level.

With this price policy, the merchant-producer has two general methods of increasing his area of profit. He may devote himself to reducing his factory expense by a better organization of his plant, or he may seek to increase his sales, in order to secure the economies of large-scale production and a reduced proportion of overhead expense on each unit of product turned out.

A field in which the policy of selling at the market is general is the steel business in normal times. The small independent manufacturer accepts the market price of a given steel product as a fixed condition, sells his "share" of the total output, and depends upon holding down his plant costs to maintain his profits.

In general, if the merchant producer adopts the policy of selling at the market, he must differentiate his product from that of his competitors and then build up a particular demand for it. To do this he must employ the same means he would use to establish the product as a distinct commodity upon a higher price level. Trade-marks and trade names, coupled with added utility, niceties of finish, evenness of quality, or more convenient packages, serve at the basis for an increased demand for the commodity upon the same price level as substantially identical products. And in selling at the market, superior promptness in delivery may become a factor of great importance in increasing sales.

Recent developments in the textile industry illustrate the adoption of the policy of selling at the market, combined with an attempt to increase sales at the market price by a differentiation of the product. Apparently the textile manufacturers who are branding their goods do not seek to establish a new price level for their product. Instead they aim to increase their sales by building up a demand for their commodity in competition with the product of other manufacturers at the prevailing price level.

Chart IV is a graphic representation of one phase of this policy. It brings out the idea that new consumers may be drawn into the market at an existing price level by giving the differentiated commodity an added importance in the eyes of the consumer. To revert to the economist's terminology again, a higher subjective valuation is placed upon the commodity by the consumer. Its importance to him increases. Though at prevailing prices his subjective ratio of exchange is too low to permit purchasing the stock commodity, he may purchase the differentiated commodity at the same price because of a greater subjective valuation which he places upon it. And this greater subjective valuation may be due to the prestige of a well-known trade-mark or to the greater convenience or service of an improved pack-

age, such as the air-tight cartons in which cereal products are distributed.

Selling at the market plus is perhaps the most characteristic price policy of modern distribution. In recent

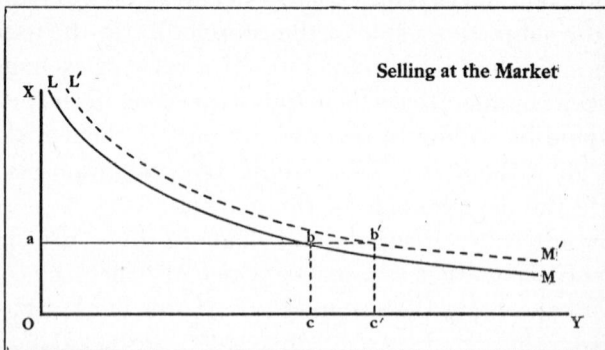

CHART IV

This is an attempt to show graphically the effect of a stimulation of increased demand for
a commodity without any increase in the price at which it is marketed.

The ordinate, ox, is a scale of increasing price. The abscissa, oy, shows the number of purchasers. The arc LM indicates the number of purchasers at any given price, growing less as
the price is increased and greater as the price is decreased.

If the established market price is represented by oa, the number of purchasers at that price
will be represented by oc. If then by stimulating an increased demand for his product, the
merchant-producer is able to increase proportionally the number of purchasers at each price
level, the demand curve LM will be replaced by L'M', and at the price, oa, a greater number
of purchasers, oc', will purchase.

This chart does not, of course, show how customers already in the market are drawn from
other merchant-producers to the purchase of a differentiated product for which a demand is
stimulated at the same price level as the products of the other merchant-producers.

years the effort among progressive manufacturers has
been not alone to anticipate unformulated human wants
and create new products to satisfy them, but to improve
staple commodities and develop new psychic values and
utilities in them. The limit set by a common market
price for commodities of the kind and class which they
manufacture has been rejected. They find opportunities of demand creation and profit in the difference between this established market price and the varying

subjective valuation placed upon their commodities by consumers of different purchasing power and different social positions and personal habits.

The economists tell us the "consumer's surplus" is the difference between the market value of a commodity and the subjective value of the commodity to the user.[1] Each individual sets up for himself a ratio of exchange between commodities which finds expression in the price he would be willing to pay for any one of them rather than go without it. These subjective valuations constitute the demand side of the market.

The interplay of supply and demand gives rise in a competitive market to a market price at which the consumer can obtain the commodity. If this market price is above that fixed by the subjective ratio of exchange of the consumer, he drops out of the market, utilizing his purchasing power to secure other commodities. But if the market price is below that which the consumer would be willing to pay to obtain the commodity, he purchases; and the difference between his subjective ratio of exchange and the objective market ratio of exchange constitutes his "consumer's surplus." The man of means, for example, who buys his morning paper for a cent, would still purchase it if the price were fixed at five cents, at ten cents, or possibly more. Somewhere in the ascending scale a point would be reached at which even the man of means would drop out of the market. But long before that point was reached, less well-to-do readers would have ceased to purchase the paper. And the difference between the price at which the well-to-do man would drop out of the market and the market price

[1] See F. W. Taussig, "Principles of Economics," Vol. I, page 128 and following.

of one cent which he actually pays represents his personal "consumer's surplus."

The more able distributors turn, though usually unconsciously, to the existence of this margin as the basis of a demand for what is to all intents and purposes a new commodity. That is, they differentiate a product from a staple commodity for which a market price has been established and establish an effective demand for the modified product upon a new price level, higher than that established for the commodity of which it is a modification.

The means used for differentiation are more numerous and more effective than those employed when the price policy adopted is selling at the market par, since the margin available for the differentiation is larger and the potential gain greater. Sometimes slight modifications are enough to render it better adapted to the use to which it is put. Sometimes niceties of trimming and equipment are sufficient. Sometimes a new and more convenient style of package is used. Sometimes the distributor builds up an atmosphere of good taste about the goods or a reputation for constant quality which insures the consumer against dissatisfaction. Sometimes the distributor depends upon "service" or special conveniences to the consumer provided as collateral to the commodity. Always, however, the aim is to isolate his product from the stock commodity of substantially like nature. And nearly always the distributor utilizes trade-marks or trade names to identify his product as a distinct commodity and to make sure of the repeat order when the purchaser enters the market again.

He must then convey knowledge of his differentiated product to those consumers whose subjective ratio of exchange would have led them to pay a higher price for the stock commodity before transferring their demand to other goods. By calling attention to the superior qualities, or convenience, or constant reliability of his

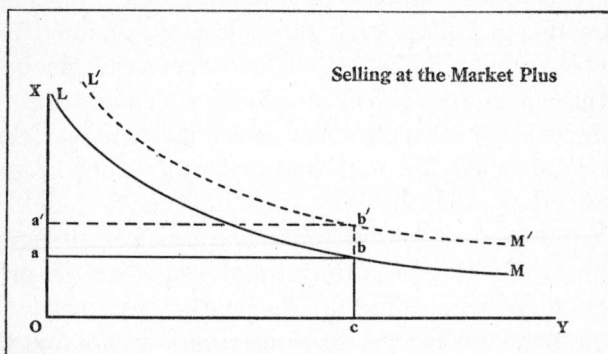

CHART V

This chart illustrates the effect of the price policy termed "selling at the market plus." On the ordinate *ox* is laid off a scale of prices for a staple commodity. The abscissa *oy* shows the number of purchasers.

The demand curve *LM* indicates the number of purchasers at a given price, growing less as the price increases and greater as the price decreases. Then if *oa* represents the market price of the staple commodity, *oc* will represent the number of purchasers. Now if the merchant-producer differentiates his product from the staple commodity, and stimulates a demand for it, the effect is to increase the number of possible purchasers at each price level. Thus the demand curve *LM* is replaced by the demand curve *L'M'*.

Obviously the merchant-producer may dispose of the differentiated product at a price *oa'*, higher than the price *oa*, without reducing the number of purchasers, *oc*. In other words, he can profit by the increased demand through raising his price rather than by increasing his sales.

differentiated product, he transfers to it a portion of the demand that formerly found expression in the purchase of the stock commodity. How this altered demand develops is indicated graphically in Chart V.

The marketing of hats furnishes an illustration of this development. If derby hats were distributed as a staple, unbranded and at a single market price for a given quality, many consumers would pay $3 for a staple hat whose individual ratio of exchange would render

249

them willing to pay more than $3 for a hat rather than go without. But certain producers have distinguished their hats from the staple kinds by their brands. By calling attention to niceties of trimming and finish and by emphasis upon the correctness of their styles some of them have built up a demand for their hats at $5.

These trade-marked hats and the staple hats selling at $3 are substantially the same commodity, but are differentiated by detail modifications. These detail differences render the well-to-do consumer willing to pay a higher price for the trade-marked hat. No doubt the demand for the more expensive hat depends in part upon the consumer's feeling of security that his hat will be of good quality and of proper shape if it bears the name of a producer who has built up this market prestige. This feeling of security forms a part of the subjective valuation placed upon the hat. No doubt, too, motives of emulation sometimes enter in, and the consumer derives part of his gratification from the mere fact that he purchases a hat which is known to sell at a higher price than those purchased by his less well-to-do neighbors.

It is of interest to note that other manufacturers of branded hats have in recent years fixed their prices at $4 and $6, appealing to consumers upon different price levels from those reached by prior distributors of trade-marked hats. Thus they reach with a $4 hat a group of consumers not available to the distributors of $5 hats because their subjective ratios of exchange did not render them willing to pay $5 for a hat. And with a $6 hat they draw from the distributors of $5 hats certain of the consumers whose subjective valuation of a hat renders them willing to pay more than $5 for one that pleases them.

The policy of selling at the market plus makes the most severe demands on the ability of the distributor. To succeed he must have an unusual equipment, including knowledge of human nature, of the psychological reactions of the individual consumer, and must be able to give proper weight to such motives as social emulation and all the varied factors that enter into the consumer's subjective ratio of exchange.

The process resulting from the increasing adoption of this price policy and the increasing differentiation of commodities at various price ranges is closely analogous to the creation of new commodities. When the hat trade splits up into a number of individual brands, practically distinct commodities at different price levels, the situation from a social point of view is little different from that arising from the creation of new commodities which are not merely modifications of existing commodities.

If the safety razor be regarded as a new commodity rather than as a modification of the old-style razor, it provides us with an opportunity to test the social justification for the creation of a new commodity. When the first widely advertised safety razor was put upon the market at $5 a considerable margin of profit was left to the producer. It was said at the time that the actual cost of manufacture was less than $1. Now this wide margin of profit made possible an extensive advertising campaign which brought the new device to the attention of the entire consuming public. Everyone, whether in the large centers or remote districts, learned of the safety razor and its uses. Great numbers purchased the razor because the subjective valuation which they placed on the new commodity exceeded the price asked. The large reward received by the distributor may properly be regarded as compensation for bringing about a better adjustment to meet human needs.

To-day the safety-razor demand is well established, and those consumers whose individual ratios of exchange do not render them willing to pay $5 for a safety razor are able to gratify their conscious need by a choice of many similar products at prices ranging as low as twenty-five cents. It is an interesting problem for the producer whether, in view of the enormous demand for blades, the initial price of $5 might not well have been reduced in later years and selling effort concentrated on the production and distribution of blades. Every extra razor sold would mean the creation of an added and more or less permanent demand for blades. This is the sales policy followed in marketing many office and factory appliances; the initial price of the device is little more than its delivered cost and the profits come from the sale of supplies necessary to its operation.

Now when the producer of a commodity already marketed by other producers sets off his commodity from others of like kind, and sometimes even by minor improvements is enabled to build up a demand for it on a higher price level than that of the stock commodity, he has made a more accurate adjustment in supplying human wants and has brought the possibility of this more accurate adjustment to the attention of consumers. The purchaser of a trade-marked hat at $5 would buy a staple hat for $3 if the $5 hat did not give him equal or greater proportional gratification, taking into account

PRICE POLICIES

the differing objective ratio of exchange. Obviously, the consumer who buys a trade-marked hat does so because he prefers to pay $5 for such a hat rather than $3 for an unbranded hat, and to criticise the payment of the additional $2 for the differentiated product because the modifications are not substantial is to attempt to substitute for the subjective valuation of the consumer as a basis of exchange an external social standard. The more highly differentiated the scale of commodities is, the more accurately will it be possible for the individual consumer to satisfy his material wants.

For true value is not objective, but subjective. The practical basis of exchange is the extent to which the article will satisfy the desire of the purchaser. The price you can secure depends on the intensity of this desire, not on the material value of the finished product, such as its calories of food value or its wearing qualities. The problem, then, is to intensify the demand for your goods, to add to the material value a psychic value in the gratification the customer experiences in its color, flavor, design, or style.

The manufacturer who is successful in establishing a differentiated product as a distinct commodity on a new price level is, for a time, in the position of having a monopoly as to the differentiated commodity. Such competition as he has is the indirect competition of the similar staple. His position often enables him to obtain temporarily a margin of profit out of all proportion to the cost of the actual improvements in the differentiated product. This, again, may be justified as a reward for turning the resources of nature to the better satisfaction of human wants. As advertising is the price we pay for instruction in better methods of satisfying our wants, so this is the price we pay for the invention of better methods. Of course, if the policy of selling at the market plus results in a higher price on a staple necessity for the marginal consumer, it goes beyond all justification. But this, I believe, will rarely if ever happen. In the main, the policy affects only the specialties. And even from these the large percentage of profit will decrease as other producers, observing the pioneer's gains and following his example, differentiate their products from the original staple in the same or in different ways. This rise of competition at the new price level and the premium put on features which make selling points will tend to force in the differentiated commodities the substantial improvements in quantity, quality, or service warranted by the higher price.

CHAPTER XVI

ORGANIZATION OF DEMAND CREATION
COMBINATION OF AGENCIES

THE fundamental purpose in demand creation is effective transmission of ideas about the goods to prospective buyers at the lowest unit cost. Analysis of the market will locate these probable customers. A wise price policy will establish a balance between the widest practicable distribution and maximum profit. Laboratory tests of the materials of demand creation will determine which selling points have strongest appeal and the quantity and sequence in which they are most convincing. Similar studies and "try-outs" will show the relative efficiency of the middleman, the direct sales force, and the various kinds of advertising in communicating ideas to possible purchasers. And a survey of the considerations involved in the location, construction, and equipment of the sales plant will show how best to turn these factors to the main purpose.

All these activities are preliminary. They produce results only when the agencies of demand creation are set in motion. Before this can be done, or at least before the forces of distribution find equilibrium of greatest profit, one further problem must be solved — what combination of agencies is to be used to reach the market and what part of the work of demand creation is to be performed by each.

There are many marketing situations, to be sure, where a single agency of demand creation is adequate.

AN APPROACH TO BUSINESS PROBLEMS

If stress is put upon the combinations of two or more, it is because relatively few business men recognize to what extent this is a possible problem for them. The majority still gamble on their business instinct and experience; and the success or failure of the campaign is the only evidence they have whether these were or were not safe guides. If their previous experience has indicated that advertising or a direct sales force is an efficient agency of demand creation, they are likely to adopt it for distributing the new product although the latter may be quite different in character. If they make any studied comparison of the various agencies, it is probably on the basis of average cost of selling, without any serious attempt to analyze the market from the viewpoint of its accessibility to each agency or to consider each agency from the angle of its ability to transmit the particular kind of ideas about the goods involved.

In fact the business man too seldom realizes how intricate is the problem of determining the agency or the combination of agencies which is exactly adapted to reach the various geographic or social and economic strata of his market. Too often he adopts one method and becomes an advocate of it, disregarding other methods entirely or taking them up in a perfunctory way. While it is true that the method adopted may be more efficient than any other single method, for his particular work of demand creation the solution of the problem by no means stops here. For the agency which is relatively efficient in reaching one geographic area may be inferior to another method in reaching another area. And a system of distribution which has proved effective in reaching buyers on one economic level may be comparatively ineffective when employed to reach another.

COMBINATION OF AGENCIES

The problem of finding the most effective combination of agencies, then, is most complicated. Each distinct area and economic and social group must be treated as a separate unit for study and analysis.

The manager selling through salesmen ordinarily finds a decreased selling cost as he increases his sales within his immediate territory. But as he widens his market, the selling cost usually increases.

Here a combination of salesmen and direct advertising may cut his cost of demand creation. He may, for instance, reduce the number of salesmen's visits by one half and either prepare the way for them or supplement their efforts by a series of "follow-up" letters or by personal correspondence. In areas more distant or with a widely scattered population, it may be profitable or even necessary to eliminate the salesmen entirely. Selling by mail through direct advertising may be the most effective method, cost considered. The important thing always is that no one agency should be adopted to the exclusion of all others merely because its use has proved profitable in previous ventures. There may be sections where it is positively unprofitable and where it can be supplemented or entirely supplanted by other methods of demand creation.

The method of sale is a factor of importance in the problem of agency selection. If sale is in bulk, the purchaser seeing the actual goods before buying, distribution through a series of middlemen is generally most feasible. In such a situation expense ordinarily prohibits direct handling. Only in exceptional cases, where, for example, small household appliances are sold by door-to-door canvass, is the handling of the product by exclusive salesmen practicable. Sale in bulk is also possible by either direct or general advertising, where the size and nature of the product permit its sale and shipment on approval or subject to trial by the purchaser.

If sale by sample is the method best adapted to the commodity in question, middlemen or direct salesmen are likely to be the most efficient agencies of demand creation. Such commodities, indeed, are distributed through both middlemen and direct salesmen, the sale at each stage being by sample until the final movement from retailer to consumer, when the sale becomes one of bulk. Direct salesmen in the majority of cases sell from sample. And even demand creation by direct advertising is in some cases practically sale by sample. For the distributor by mail of a commodity which is not bulky may send for inspection and test a sample of the commodity with his direct advertising.

Where sale by description is used exclusively, direct or general advertising is likely to be the most effective agency. Increasing knowledge and skill on the part of advertising managers, writers, and illustrators, coupled with recent advances in the mechanical processes of reproduction and printing, have enlarged the scope and effectiveness of advertisements until they seem alone an adequate and economical means of demand creation for a multitude of commodities and staple specialties. The establishment of a domestic parcel post equipped to convey twenty-pound packages to any part of the country and to make collections on delivery has added further effectiveness to advertising by providing a cheap, popular, and universal agency for the supply of goods which have been marketed by printed and written symbols.

COMBINATION OF AGENCIES

It is possible, though generally not economical, to distribute a commodity through a series of middlemen, the sale at each stage being accomplished by description. And the use of salesmen in selling by description is very common. Take the cases where furniture, heavy machinery, hardware, and like commodities are sold from photographs, from catalogs, and more recently through the use of moving pictures.

The extent to which any one agency of demand creation can be used must not be decided alone, however, on theoretical grounds. In many cases the middleman is already strongly intrenched and the whole business structure is based upon his activities. His relations with his customers are long established, his retention of many of his traditional functions, such as financing operations, sharing the risk, and even transporting the goods, clinches his hold on his trade territory and makes him a necessary factor in reaching the dealers or consumers he serves.

Choice of the agency for demand creation also reacts upon the materials of demand creation (ideas about the goods) and upon the goods themselves. Under the orthodox type of distribution, the basis of the sale to the middleman is his opportunity to dispose of the goods at a profit. Because of this emphasis on price and salability, the tendency of the orthodox system in marketing unbranded commodities is to turn the energies of the producer toward lowering the cost of production and reducing the price. The influence of satisfaction or dissatisfaction on the part of the consumer comes to him only indirectly through a chain of middlemen. Moreover where the goods are not differentiated by trademark or trade name, their identity is often completely lost in the successive stages of distribution. Even the retailer in many communities and neighborhoods concerns himself rather with salability than with ultimate satisfaction to the customer. And if the customer is not perfectly satisfied and accepts the product only because it is the best he can get, his objections must ordinarily be relayed through two or more middlemen before they can reach the producer.

Only marked defects in quality, therefore, are likely to be brought to the attention of the producer. Thus he fails to establish that touch with consumers which would guide him toward improvements in quality and service in his goods. Since his attention is not directed primarily to those elements, leakage of demand is likely to result. He is not manufacturing the precise commodity which the market desires and would buy with the least outlay of money and energy for demand creation.

The differentiated, trade-marked product, on the other hand, encounters a barrier to a wider market in the fact that it competes for the middleman's interest and selling effort directly with the latter's own "house brands" and with articles of lesser quality or prestige which allow him a greater unit margin of gain. Few wholesalers consider themselves established with their trade until they control several lines marketed under a firm name or symbol. Nor is the "house brand" any longer the exclusive possession of the jobber. The larger retail stores feature many trade-marked "staple specialties" of their own, if the phrase "staple specialties" is permissible to describe commodities only slightly differentiated from the standard market types.

The "house brand" may be regarded as a logical

outcome of current conditions in distribution, of successful attempts by manufacturers to market advertised products through the regular channels of the trade. The wholesaler, arguing that his salesmen do an indispensable part of the actual work of demand creation, carrying knowledge and samples of scores of lines into remote villages which few single manufacturers could afford to cultivate, sees no ethical or practical obstacle in the way of bringing out similar articles under his own name and pushing these instead of the manufacturer's advertised brands.

From the viewpoint of the jobber and the retailer alike, the advertised product presents an element of danger in that its sale cannot be controlled. After contributing what seems to him an important factor in the creation of demand and the securing of general distribution for such articles, the wholesaler may see his discount cut; and the retailer may be compelled either to accept an increased sales quota or to give up a line which has become identified with his store through his advertising and through selling talks with his customers. The "big stick" policy in handling the trade is so recent in the memories of many middlemen that it still colors their attitude toward those newly advertised products and advertising manufacturers whose reputations for fair treatment of their distributors have not been subjected to decisive tests.

It is only a nationally exploited line of clothing or shoes, for instance, which can secure mention of its individual trade-mark in the advertising of certain important stores necessary to its distribution scheme in the larger cities. The policy generally adopted by these stores in connection with advertised articles not exclusively controlled is to stock and supply them when called for, but to give every display advantage to their private brands and to offer these when the customer does not request a specific product. This is certainly fair merchandising — presuming that the house brands are the equals of the trade-marked specialties in quality and service. Yet the manufacturer who has blazed the way in a particular field may properly feel that such practice deprives him of some of the fruits of his campaign of demand creation.

The opposition of middlemen to any reduction of their margin is general enough to present a serious problem to the producer. Often the latter postpones taking over the function of communicating ideas about his goods directly to the user because he sees that he must continue to pay the middleman for that work, whether or not it is performed by him, or else develop independent agencies of physical supply. The latter step involves, of course, the outlay of considerable capital for the establishment of branch warehouses and organizations or of branch retail stores in such centers of population as promise sufficient volume of potential sales.

On the other hand, retailers in certain fields have been educated, through observation or demonstration of the effect of advertising on sales, to acceptance of a lowered margin or trade-marked goods in exchange for repeated campaigns of demand creation. This may be witnessed, for example, in clothing, or more recently in shoes, where national exploitation of one trade-marked line has given it an exclusive agent in almost every town of importance in which the company does not maintain a branch store. In other lines, producers have found it advantageous to undertake the wholesaler's work of physical supply rather than compensate him for a selling function no longer performed.

In directly assuming the burden of demand creation, the manufacturer has choice of two agencies, an exclusive sales force and general or direct advertising. Since their function is the same, the transmitting of ideas about the goods not only to the ultimate users but also to such middlemen as it may be advantageous to employ in distribution, the analogy between them is very close. In many fields they may be used as substitutes, one for the other; yet each retains its zones of special utility and both reach their highest efficiency, as a rule, when they supplement one another in the work of demand creation. It is a significant fact, in this connection, that some of the largest mail-order houses, committed to a policy of direct advertising, have found it profitable in certain districts to employ salesmen to take orders for their merchandise.

The combination of sales force and advertising is often advantageous because the personal equation of the individual "prospect" is an unknown quantity in demand creation. You may discover and standardize and record a thousand selling points about your product. From this material you may construct a sales argument which is logical and decisive, and then reduce it to a written or printed form which disarms criticism and defies betterment. The special and exclusive virtue of advertising, indeed, is that it allows you to transmit to the reader exactly those ideas you wish to convey in the exact form that seems best for their transmission. But unless you are intimately acquainted with every possible customer you address and are able to adapt your selling talk, your pictures, your diagrams, to his immediate state of mind, your standard argument will shoot wide much oftener than it hits the mark. If your circle of prospective users is broad enough, you can content yourself with this average result. If the range of your product is narrow, you must find some way to adapt both approach and selling talk to the attitude and situation of the individual buyer.

Adaptability is the salesman's strength, just as accuracy in the transmission of ideas is a dependable quality of advertising. The average business man, as an individual prospect, does not exist. His moods, his interest in proposals not plainly relevant to the task he happens to have in hand change with the passing hours. The approach or selling talk which would merely rouse impatience at a time when he is absorbed in a problem might secure quick recognition and interest when that problem is disposed of.

But advertising cannot choose the moment of its approach except in a very limited or a very general way. If direct or local, for example, it can avoid Monday mornings and the crest of "rush" seasons like the weeks before Christmas and Easter in retail stores. If general, it can choose its mediums with the aim of presenting ideas at the time or in the place where the prospect is most likely to entertain them and it can concentrate on the seasons when buying is general. But all advertising lacks the salesman's ability to sense immediate conditions which may be either propitious or adverse and to base action on what is thus perceived.

The same capacity in a seasoned man allows him to feel out the prospect's attitude toward the product or service he represents and to shape his talk so that he can avoid touching convictions or prejudices which might interfere with the sale. Moreover he can discover the objections which occur to the prospect as he considers purchasing. By meeting them he can turn them into buying arguments; at the least he can take them away with him for further study and future answer. Any specialty salesman of experience will agree that he cannot forecast the workings of a new prospect's mind or determine beforehand just what objections will emerge. Where advertising stakes all its chances on finding the average buyer in an average mood, the salesman can bring as much intelligence, tact, and skill as he possesses to the problem of avoiding the unfavorable occasion and inducing a receptive attitude toward what he has to offer.

Once the prospect's attention is engaged, the salesman has the appeal of personal presence to give warmth and color to his assembly of facts and figures. For personality still has much to do with the transactions of business. Few products have an actual monopoly of value or utility; the enthusiasm or tact or resource of the salesman frequently is the decisive factor in influencing the purchase. There is more than one instance on record where a sales force which had analyzed and developed to the full the consumer uses of an inferior product has held the market against a better article until the factory experimental rooms, working night and day, could match the merits of the competing product.

In the distribution of many staple specialties like furniture, shoes, dry goods, and the like, the assurance of a straightforward, competent, and likeable salesman that the "goods are right" often carries greater weight with the retailer than the guarantee of the house behind them. So true is this that within their territories many traveling men are virtually in business on their own account; by grace of long acquaintance and fair and friendly dealing they have acquired a hold on their trade which it is no easy matter to overcome. Recognition of this fact has prompted many intensive advertising campaigns to establish a direct contact with dealers or consumers and emphasize the house rather than the salesman as the responsible force behind the merchandise.

Because of his personal contact and adaptability, the salesman can also build a convincing argument from materials which advertising would present much less effectively. He can stage his sale. If a sample of the product is the key argument (it usually is in the case of a specialty), he can introduce it at the exact moment when the other man is prepared to concentrate upon it. If it is a machine of any sort, he can demonstrate those functions which would be of importance in the prospect's business. Better yet, he can lead the latter to operate the thing himself and thus come a step nearer to understanding and accepting it. If it is a new fabric, an unfamiliar food product, a differentiated garment or line of garments, he can analyze it from the standpoint of the individual he is addressing and shape his sales talk to drive home its advantages either for direct use or for resale to consumers.

More important still, when the salesman has created a demand for his goods he is at hand to close the order immediately. Experience or intuition tells him when this moment comes, and his will power goes into the balance to overcome the buyer's inertia, his tendency to put off decisions when decision means paying out money. So generally is this negative, defensive motive recognized that sales managers urge on their men at all times the supreme importance of closing the order. To overcome this inertia when advertising is the agency used, the demand created must be much more imperative. There is no salesman at hand to seize the propitious moment, and some positive action must therefore be suggested to the prospect, the signing of an inquiry card, telephoning the local agent, or telling him of a store where the goods can be secured.

The direct sales force and producer advertising, then, are different agencies for accomplishing the same end. This is to transmit, or to secure the transmission of, ideas about the goods to the prospective buyer's mind more directly and more accurately than the orthodox chain of middlemen will transmit them.

The character of his product may permit a manufacturer to send his salesman or his advertising direct to the ultimate user and to make direct deliveries by express, freight, or parcel post, or through his own branch houses or stores. Again, distribution through retailers may be the only method possible, and the nearest his salesmen can come to influencing the prospective consumer is to teach dealers and their clerks its outstanding selling points and to train them to use and demonstrate these intelligently. Here he can supplement this indirect contact with advertising aimed at the consumer, the dealer, and the clerk. Or, needing both the wholesaler and retailer for physical supply of his tooth paste, gloves, watches, breakfast food, or whatever his product is, he may put the burden of demand creation on advertising, backing it up with introductory or supplementary campaigns of sampling and demonstration to prospective users.

AN APPROACH TO BUSINESS PROBLEMS

In comparing salesmen with different forms of advertising, the business man often judges both agencies upon the direct returns over a short period. This does not take account of all three classes of demand aroused by selling effort — expressed conscious demand, unexpressed conscious demand, and subconscious demand. The direct and immediate return from selling efforts depends solely on expressed conscious demand. But the business man must consider the unexpressed conscious demand and the subconscious demand. Take the case of an advertised collar. A man notices the advertisement, reads it, and decides that at some future time he will try it. Months later perhaps he does so. His purchase is not reflected in the immediate returns, yet clearly it is a result to be reckoned with in any comparison. Or suppose the man merely notices the advertisement. At a later date, when purchasing collars, he is shown the advertised brand along with another. The brand being vaguely familiar from the advertisement, he purchases it in preference to the others. Here, too, the aroused demand is of a degree not reflected in immediate returns, yet it is of value to the distributor.

It is obvious, then, that in balancing the advantages of selling through salesmen against selling through advertising in whole or part, the business man must consider not only the demand reflected in the direct immediate returns alone but also the lesser degrees of demand which, while not immediately effective, bring later results and contribute to make demand continuous.

Thus a salesman might make fifty calls at an expense of $100, and ten sales might result from his efforts. Or for the same $100, 5,000 pieces of direct advertising could be mailed, resulting perhaps in only eight sales.

COMBINATION OF AGENCIES

Or, again, if the same $100 were used in the insertion of a page advertisement, in 100,000 of the circulation of a standard magazine, only six would result. Now it is apparent that, judging by the direct results, the salesman is the most efficient agency of distribution, the direct advertising next, and the magazine advertising least efficient. But the manager will bear in mind that, while the salesman made ten sales, he had only forty opportunities to create the lesser grades of demand. The direct advertising gave 4,992 opportunities for the creation of demand falling short of immediate expression, and the magazine advertising, perhaps, 49,994 such opportunities, assuming that one person saw the advertisement in half the copies printed — not an improbable assumption since each copy of a magazine is usually read by several persons.

Aside from furnishing a basis for laboratory tests of ideas, direct advertising, especially the written communication, has certain distinct advantages. It is possible to convey the exact shade of meaning, in detail and elaboration. The letter writer has absolute supervision over the written symbols he is using. Style, substance, manner of presentation are under his direct control. He can balance the time devoted to description and argument on the one hand against the time devoted to the anticipation of objections on the other. He can present his exact proposition, avoiding misrepresentation or misunderstanding. He can be courteous or blunt, ceremonious or informal, conservative or forcible, as the occasion may require.

The advantages and limitations of direct advertising cannot, of course, be reduced to direct measurement. Yet direct advertising, general advertising, and the use

of salesmen can be measured on the basis of a common
unit — cost, as measured in the effectiveness of calls.
Say, for example, that the cost for 100 calls by the salesman is $100, the cost for 100 letters is $3.35, and the
cost for 1,000 readers of a page advertisement in a
magazine is $1. A hundred dollars in the first case
reaches 100 prospective customers, in the second case
3,000, in the third case 100,000. Which method produces the most orders on a given expenditure? That is
the test.

A sound selling policy, then, must be built up on a
careful analysis of the market by areas and strata and
upon a detailed study of the proper agency or combination of interrelated agencies to reach each area and
stratum. The economic generalizations expressed in
the law of diminishing returns must be recognized. A
sound selling policy, furthermore, must weigh not only
the direct results obtained from the use of one or the
other agency over a short period, but also the less
measurable results represented by the unexpressed conscious demand and subconscious demand which go to
aid the selling campaign of the future. And at every
point the elusive human element is present and cannot
be left out of the account.

In any study of the agencies of demand creation the
drift toward a shortened cycle of distribution presents
one of the most interesting developments in modern
business. It is significant of broad changes and readjustment in our market machinery and it is also a factor to be carefully considered by the producer in selecting his agencies of demand creation.

Starting with the manufacturer's assumption of various functions performed by the middleman, it has

brought about a counter movement with the same end among both wholesalers and retailers. On the one side, many manufacturers of shoes, clothing, and silverware (to mention only the most typical lines) have virtually eliminated the wholesaler, selling direct to the retailer. Many others have dropped all middlemen and deal with the consumer in person, either by the mail-order route, by exclusive stores, or by special salesmen.

To compensate for this loss in potential volume, the natural growth of the country keeping up his accustomed average of sales, the wholesaler in his turn has developed his super-profitable "house brands" and reduced the chain by one member, turning manufacturer himself. And even here there is divergence in method. Of two great merchandising houses in Chicago, one has adopted the policy of ownership of many important sources of supply, while the other follows the radically different course of control of many small producers by furnishing them with working capital, patterns or style suggestions, and a market for their total output, thus allowing them to go back to the original function of the manufacturer and concentrate on production problems alone. The large retailer, therefore, has short-cut distribution as effectively as the advertising manufacturer, by owning or controlling sources for several of his principal lines. The sum of these parallel movements has been in the direction of simplification and economy for a relatively small but significant section of business.

Out of the antagonistic yet concurrent efforts of the producer, the wholesaler, and the retailer to simplify distribution by elimination will probably come a class of efficient, broad-gauged middlemen (already indicated by the rise of such individuals in every field) who will recognize that each function in distribution is best performed by its appropriate agency and will coöperate with the producer in getting rid of duplicate effort and in securing the greatest number of turn-overs per dollar of capital and expense. The integration of trade and of industry can be effected by the coördination of functions and individual efforts. It is not dependent on the concentration of ownership and control.

AN APPROACH TO THE SALES PROBLEM

SECTION II

PHYSICAL SUPPLY

CHAPTER XVII

PLANT AND OPERATION POLICIES

PHYSICAL supply of the goods is the final step in distribution, supplementing the work of demand creation and making it effective by putting the product in the consumer's hands. Through the various agencies developed for the purpose, it applies further motion to the material already changed in form by the activities of production. In this application of motion to change the place of the transformed material, demand creation may seem to have the more important part. But both are necessary to bring about the new place and ownership utilities which are the essence of selling; and both are so interdependent in their relations that policies and methods cannot be fixed for one without keeping in mind their influence on the operations of the other.

The problem of physical supply can be simply stated. How shall the maximum of aroused demand be satisfied, with minimum demand leakage and least expense, present and future sales both being considered? Time, convenience, and service are the three things the prospective buyer looks to; the producer's task is to provide the goods when they are wanted, where they are wanted, and in the condition and volume which the market at the moment requires.

Minimum leakage of demand is one of the main considerations. Aroused demand is not only a useless thing,

275

but is actually detrimental unless the product can be delivered before the edge of curiosity and desire is dulled. The woman who asks her grocer for a new naphtha soap, whose lasting qualities she has seen advertised weekly or monthly, will soon lose patience and interest in the quest if the grocer assures her that he cannot find it in the market. If she trusts her grocer — and no manufacturer can ignore the fact that customer confidence is the solid basis of retail trading — she will accept his statement and dismiss the claims of the new soap, particularly if inquiries at other stores show that they also have not stocked it. From expressed conscious demand, she drops down the scale of interest to the zero level; and disappointment induces a negative attitude which must be overcome before the process of demand creation can be begun again.

If the product is sufficiently differentiated from the staple offerings, like, for example, a naphtha soap which will not dissolve too rapidly in hot water, appeals to the economy motive may renew her desire to make a trial purchase. But for a commodity only slightly differentiated from the standard, an initial breakdown in physical supply like this forms a serious hindrance to distribution. There is lost ground to be regained; the materials of demand creation lack their first fresh appeal; and the prospect's experience has made her skeptical of the manufacturer's promises of service.

It is true that consumers' requests are the best evidence of aroused demand, and that middlemen generally require some such evidence before they will purchase a specialty competing with an item already in stock. Hence a delay, and thus a dilemma for the producer. It is, indeed, a serious problem so to coördinate the demand-creation campaign and the plan for putting the goods within reach of prospective buyers that the interval between the expression of aroused demand and the delivery of the product shall be as short as possible. The ideal, of course, is immediate delivery; and there are practicable ways of attaining this ideal or of discounting the effect of the delay on the prospective buyer. We shall say more about them a little later.

The point to be emphasized at the outset is that the leakage of demand due to defective physical supply puts a heavy tax on the operations of distribution. How great this waste is cannot be estimated with any degree of accuracy; but it is fair to say that a large proportion of unsuccessful advertising campaigns have failed because provision was not made for physical supply of the goods on a scale as broad as the advertising plan. Leakage of demand resulted because the vital principle of balance was not observed.

While sales were made in bulk, and in the many cases where they are still made in bulk, the problem of physical supply, as distinct from demand creation, cannot arise. Delivery is made at the time of purchase; demand creation and physical supply are coincident. But where sale by description or sale by sample is employed, a demand is created which is effective only if the goods can be made readily available to the prospect. If a considerable expenditure of energy is required of the customer or if there is a considerable lapse in time before the demand created is satisfied, a large share of the aroused demand will be lost. Time and convenience are thus essential elements. If any rule is to be formulated it is that there must be the least possible interval between exciting demand and satisfying it. Demand creation without effective physical distribution represents pure waste.

Approaching his problem of physical supply, the manufacturer finds that its activities break up, as in production and demand creation, into two main groups. There are plant policies, having to do with the location, construction, and equipment of his warehouses and their attendant shipping facilities; and there are operating policies which govern the problems of materials, agencies, and organization. The classification is indeed more obvious here than in demand creation for the reason that the factors dealt with once more are tangible and measurable things.

The materials, for example, are the goods themselves. The agencies are either: (1) functional middlemen in the transportation field, railroads, express companies, and the parcel post; (2) areal middlemen, wholesalers and retailers; or (3) agencies of direct supply, branch houses, and exclusive agents or retail stores. Supplementing the agency of transportation are the producer's own delivery facilities for transportation of the goods for part or all of the way from the main plant or branch house to the place where the consumer comes in contact with them. To the traditional groups of areal middlemen also might be added the special types more recently evolved, such as wholesale and retail catalog houses, buying associations of dealers and consumers, chain stores, and warehousing and delivery concerns.

It appears at a glance that here are three distinct economic functions: (1) transporting the goods to create place utility, (2) storing the goods to create time utility, and (3) physical transfer of the goods to create ownership or possession utility. The problem of physical supply is complex because the agencies which the manufacturer must use are not aligned according to these economic functions but have developed along trade and sectional lines as well as those of convenience and individual initiative.

To get relatively wide distribution at minimum cost he may require only the middlemen of the orthodox system. To supply the largest possible percentage of aroused demand without leakage and with reasonable expense, however, he may be obliged to use several agencies to reach different economic or geographic groups of consumers. The sacrifice of an economical method of demand creation may be necessary in order to insure thorough physical distribution of the product. Or, on the other hand, the upbuilding of an exclusive organization of supply agencies may be required to take advantage of the demand-creation plan on which the success of the business depends.

It is the existence of these problems, the difficulty of establishing a balance between the opposing requirements of demand creation and physical supply and of maintaining this balance in the face of changing conditions, that give the business man his function and opportunity and justify his, at times, exaggerated gains. In my view of things, the man who effects a new and more economical combination of forces in production or distribution is entitled to the savings he effects until such time, at least, as competition has learned to utilize or match his discovery.

Society must pay for its short cuts, either in market rewards to individual innovators or in public appropriations for the study and recommendation of the most efficient processes by which it is fed and clothed and housed. The latter would be the simplest, most direct, and most economical method of arriving at results which thousands of business men are attempting to approach by roundabout, detail ways. This would not involve the quenching of individual incentive and the initiative which springs from it, by the socializing of our machinery of production and distribution. Instead, by more speedily standardizing the conditions, methods, materials, and processes on which all business men must concentrate until they have been standardized, organized national investigation of these common factors of business would so much the sooner release for creative purposes the enormous funds of capital and human energy now dissipated in unproductive motions.

From the consumer's standpoint, service is the key to physical supply. A commodity is of dominant value to him only when and where it will satisfy some material or psychic want. Its appeal decreases in proportion to its lack of time and place utility. The problem of the producer is to anticipate the consumer's need, to bring the product within easy reach at the moment the demand develops and to keep on bringing fresh units to the point of contact as long as the demand continues. The location, construction, and equipment of the supply plant, therefore, are essential considerations, governed in the main by policies analogous to those which apply to similar problems in production and demand creation. In discussing the other policies, indeed, many of the factors which count in physical supply were anticipated, by reason of the mutual interdependence of the three groups of activities.

It is enough, then, to suggest the main elements in location. Accessibility to the market is obviously the first of these, with emphasis on transportation facilities and charges. If sale is by sample or by description, the warehouses may be placed with an eye single to service, remote from both sales offices and factory if speed in delivery is thereby increased. This is one of the two motives for branch warehouses at strategic points, the other being the savings made in freights on carloads to these market centers and package shipments in the tributary zone. The advertising value of stock rooms adjacent to the sales department is a negligible quantity, now that the motor car has put the downtown office within easy reach of the warehouse district.

Except in the case of machinery and other heavy products where the customer may wish to inspect the actual unit to be delivered, bulk sales by the manufacturer involve no special plant problems in physical supply. The retail store in fact remains the one agency in distribution where sales in bulk retain their importance. Even here, in the larger cities, the desire to secure a selling location in the high-rent zone has separated the salesroom from the stock room and made selling by sample common in furniture, grocery, and department stores. In groceries, perhaps, this advance is most typical of the new viewpoint and new spirit of analysis that are making themselves felt in business.

Speed and economy of handling likewise dictate the policies of construction and equipment. The character of the goods, the building standards, the material resources of the locality, and the amount of capital available are the factors which the manager has to consider. In a business of any size, he has the technical knowledge of his works executives to draw upon and can safely leave to them the detail execution of the policies determined with their aid. Lacking such counsel, the head of a small business is still able to secure specific information on every phase of construction and equipment from outside specialists or from authoritative books and articles in trade and technical periodicals.

The small business has its compensations in that it is usually compact, and handling operations can be kept under the personal control of the manager. Its internal transportation and storage problems are too simple to require elaborate mechanical conveyors, tiering machines, electric "mules," overhead trolleys, and other labor-saving devices to keep costs on a reasonable plane. Its outside transportation is an equally simple matter. If the product is bulky, a switch track serving both the receiving and dispatching platforms and connecting with the local railroads is the sum of requirements. For valuable small products, goods made of delicate materials, or articles shipped in small lots, the advantages of a switch track would be next to nothing. The problem of outside transportation was considered at some length, however, in an earlier section of this volume in the chapter on factory location. It will suffice here to repeat that the character and speed of the service required to insure deliveries on the customer's terms is the main factor, though the cost of providing for such service balanced against the financial situation of the business may postpone adoption of the most desirable policy.

In his choice of agencies for physical distribution, the manufacturer encounters certain limitations. The nature of the product, its unit price, and the buying habits of consumers may indicate the middleman as the most effective and economical means of supply. For staples, this is a matter of course, since the work of demand creation is largely in his hands; but this agent serves also for branded foods and trade-marked specialties in dry goods, women's wear, notions, hardware, furniture, toilet and medicinal preparations, men's clothing and furnishings, and many other lines of semi-staple necessities and luxuries which lend themselves to this method of physical supply, even when the middleman is not the chief agent of demand creation.

At the same time, every one of these lines furnishes numerous instances of physical distribution without the aid of the middleman, the producer assuming all the work of supply save actual transportation. The retail catalog houses have blazed many trails in this particular field, but their experience would be an unsafe guide to the manufacturer of a single product or a limited line. Despite their control of production sources, the mail-order concerns must rank as middlemen, their exercise of the important middleman function of assembling, storing, and assorting many kinds of commodities being an essential element in their success.

In analyzing his supply problem, the manager looks first to the buying habits of his prospective customers and the incentive he can offer them to change, if a change be necessary to give him maximum distribution at minimum expense. Does his product fall within the wide range where the consumer puts convenience first, either because the amount of money involved is small and values are standardized or because the nature of the product puts a premium on frequent small purchases close at home?

It would be a doubtful experiment, for example, to attempt to distribute a new brand of flaked cereal otherwise than through retail stores. The custom of the average housewife is to order factory-cooked breakfast foods from her grocer in small quantities to insure freshness and original flavor. To overcome this fixed habit and the belief that cooked breakfast foods deteriorate with age would probably be a much more difficult task than to divert a good share of existing demand to a new brand marketed through orthodox channels. The money incentive that could be offered for the direct purchase of a dozen packages at one time, too, would be lessened by transportation charges out of all proportion to the value of the shipment.

Admitting that this is an extreme example of "convenience goods," there is nevertheless a great number of commodities either low in price or of only occasional use which must be placed within easy reach of the consumer at the moment his demand takes form in order to achieve adequate sales. The stock of any neighborhood dry goods, hardware, drug, or grocery store will furnish hundreds of such articles, many of them trade-marked and highly differentiated from competing products. Differentiation, trade-marking, and vigorous campaigns of demand creation are responsible, indeed, for this wide physical distribution and for the consumer's recollection of the trade name or brand when subconscious demand for the article is turned into conscious demand by his need of it or sight of it displayed in a store.

Accentuate this differentiation by closer adaptation to the consumer's wants and keep up or increase the selling campaign, and the subconscious demand for time and convenience goods can be transformed into conscious or expressed demand to satisfy future wants or wants suggested by the advertising as immediate or impending.

For products put forward in this manner, the retailer

and jobber with their waiting stocks are not necessary agencies of physical supply; the parcel post or a railroad or express company will furnish the single missing element of transportation. It is primarily a question of demand creation. If your ideas about the goods have sufficient force and appeal to dominant buying motives, you can make your sale entirely by description and pay a transportation middleman for delivering the product.

This is the method of the catalog houses, whether they specialize in one line like women's garments or attempt to cover all lines of merchandise. Price is the basis of their differentiation of products, the aim being to offer each customer the kitchen apron or winter hat which comes nearest to her notion of what she wants to pay. Lowered prices and large assortments are, indeed, their chief materials of demand creation. Adopting the policy of selling at the market minus, they adjust their production policies to their price scale, ownership or control of sources making them in this respect manufacturers rather than merchants, and thus observe the principle of balance and the principle of interdependence which should govern in all the activities of production and distribution.

An interesting sidelight on the changes taking place in distribution is the successful effort of many manufacturers seeking maximum distribution in the larger cities to convert their trade-marked specialties into "convenience goods." Limited in their downtown sales by the tendency of the big stores to push house brands or competing products with wider profit margins, they have turned to the neighborhood stores as supplementary outlets. Kayser gloves, Arrow collars,

Community silverware, and a long array of advertised products are recognized by consumers as the same, no matter where they are purchased. Buying them close at hand when they are needed is so much easier than having to foresee and provide for future wants that the time and place utilities thus created are superior to the attraction of the larger assortments downtown. Not always, to be sure, but often enough to make the neighborhood store an increasingly important factor in supplying urban demand. The tendency is accentuated by the local retailer, who exploits the articles in the neighborhood to prove that his stock is composed of standard merchandise.

The producer who is tempted to break away from orthodox channels of distribution must bear in mind also that any scheme of direct supply involves problems of financing, handling, and shipping of which the middleman system would practically relieve him. The elimination of the wholesaler alone, though it has been effected in nearly every line of business by individuals who deal direct with their retailers, causes a transfer of capital burden which might neutralize in a specific case all the advantages of direct supply. The conditions and problems set up in the packing and shipping rooms, in the credit, collection, and accounting departments are vastly more complex, of course, in a business having one or two or three thousand dealer accounts than in one which seeks its market through fifteen or thirty or fifty wholesalers.

The manufacturer who deals direct usually is able to place his line with one of the best retailers in each locality and to establish close relations with him. If his product appeals to all classes, however, this sacrifices not a little aroused demand which might be supplied by dealers of lesser standing to whom the jobber, by reason of his nearness, can safely extend credit and dispatch orders, in combination shipments, which would not repay the producer's handling and administration costs.

In seasonal trades, again, manufacturing policies are greatly simplified by distributing through the middleman. Instead of driving machines and men at excessive speeds during the actual selling period, advance sales to jobbers can be used to equalize production, thus increasing efficiency and reducing unit costs. When the wholesaler is not able to finance the advance deliveries himself, these can be made the basis of banking credit, whereas the piling up of large quantities of unsold stock at the factory would be counted by bankers a somewhat speculative undertaking for any business not long established and without abundant working capital.

One of the factors not to be overlooked is that the middleman in a great many lines seems solidly established. His adherents claim with considerable show of authority that nearly ninety per cent of the output of our small factories is distributed through the jobber and that eighty per cent of the products turned out by our larger concerns seek consumers through his hands. Despite the success of the innovators and their short cuts to the consumer, therefore, the individual manager's supply problem does not hang solely on the elimination of the wholesaler or of all middlemen. The profitable approach is just as likely to be that of utilizing the middleman for physical distribution and coöperating with him in the performance of his other function of demand creation. It is not safe to ignore his control of the immediate market for a multitude of commodities, or to overlook the fact that, if he is not already distributing a passable substitute for your product, development of demand for it will surely bring about the addition of such a substitute to his lines. By trying to eliminate him, you divide your market and make necessary a more intensive campaign of demand creation to overcome his competition.

The direct agencies of physical supply hardly require definition; their special fields and functions are obvious. The branch house, the exclusive agent, and the manufacturer's chain store are all instruments to the same end; they aim to control the supply function at every stage and insure delivery of the goods to the ultimate user in perfect condition and with the least possible loss of time and convenience utility. The net result is minimum leakage of aroused demand.

Branch houses and chain stores are the concomitants of sales volume. Either the aroused demand is so great that the facilities of local middlemen are inadequate to supply it; or the demand is of such character that it may easily be diverted to other products by the middleman; or the volume of sales makes it profitable to take over the supply function as an auxiliary business. Whatever his motive, the manufacturer establishing branch houses or chain stores must realize that in the first case he is multiplying his administration problems and in the latter is assuming the risks and attacking the problems of a new and radically different range of business activities.

The exclusive agent has more the character of partner-middleman operating in a special territory, furnishing part or all of the necessary working capital, and bound up in his interests with the interests of the parent concern. The warehousing concern, on the other hand, usually limits itself to the function of receiving and storing goods at some strategic market center, and of assorting, packing, and shipping orders in accordance with instructions from the producers or merchandisers it serves.

As in demand creation, the producer's subtler and more important problems have to do with the organization of his supply system — the choice of the agencies to be used, assignment of the work to be done by each, and coördination of their activities to cut out duplicate efforts and to promote economy of stocks, reduce handling and transportation expense, and yet provide such service as will conserve the maximum of aroused demand. In our earlier discussions of the middleman's part in demand creation, enough was said about his function as a supply agency to indicate his capacities in this direction and the situations and lines in which he can be employed.

The average manufacturer takes the line of least resistance or solves all his problem of supply at a stroke. He chooses the middleman and accepts as necessary the limitations which the choice puts on his business. Or he swings to the other extreme and decides to market his product by mail and make deliveries through the parcel post or some other functional middleman of transportation. But the constructive business man breaks up his supply problem into several unit problems and proceeds to solve each on its merits, keeping an eye meanwhile on the effect of the solution on his other activities. Knowing the capacities of the middleman and the advantages and disadvantages of direct systems of supply, he analyzes his market and chooses the agency which will best serve each physical area and economic level without incurring undue expense or interfering with demand creation.

One well-known maker of men's and women's shoes, for instance, distributes the bulk of his output through a chain of retail stores maintained in the larger cities. In lesser places, he avoids the internal competition between lines in the usual shoe store by giving the agency to a high-grade clothier who is willing to put in a shoe department, stocking full lines of the advertised men's lines and taking special orders for women's shoes until demand has developed. Local conditions may sometimes point to a department store as the most promising distributor; or a shoe dealer's control of the town's best trade and his desire to identify his store with a line so well advertised may dictate his selection as the advantageous agency. In territory served by neither chain stores nor retail agents, mail orders are accepted and the shoes are delivered by parcel post. Provision for supplying aroused demand is thus made wherever the manufacturer's advertising penetrates, the combination of agencies depending on an analysis of local requirements or opportunities instead of a hard-and-fast policy of dealer representation alone or of direct supply.

This typical case suggests the flexibility of plan essential to effective distribution. Neither in demand creation nor in physical supply does the wise manager attempt to solve his problem as a whole and evolve a standard policy applicable to all the economic and geographic divisions of his market. Instead, he recognizes each group as a unit requiring individual analysis, calling, perhaps, for a special combination of supply agencies, if leakage of demand is to be avoided. In serving

PLANT AND OPERATION POLICIES

a field relatively small as compared with the national market, he will encounter widely varying conditions in the larger centers and their suburbs, in cities having a preponderant industry or class of industries, and in towns and villages on which agricultural populations depend for their merchandise needs. And even when he has classified and grouped these district and local markets, he will find case after case where the personality, imagination, or selling ability of a single merchant has upset all the conventions of trade and brought under his control lines usually considered as having no affinity.

Initiative of this sort, based on searching analysis, is responsible for the intensive distribution of to-day which has multiplied supply sources in an effort to turn highly developed specialties into convenience goods. Putting dollar watches into hardware stores to reach classes of prospects who never enter a jeweler's illustrates this tendency. Pickles, preserves, and marmalades are now displayed in the long unused windows of butcher shops. Household remedies and disinfectants can be had in many groceries. "Side lines" of specialties for the use of men are found in cigar stores, pool rooms, and other places where they resort. The corner drug store becomes a neighborhood trading center because it is open evenings, Sundays, and holidays, has made convenience goods of a multitude of commodities which appear also in the stocks of its hardware, dry goods, candy, stationery, jewelry, and haberdashery neighbors.

Up and down and across, the whole fabric of distribution has been searched for points of approach to groups of prospects inaccessible by traditional methods and for new and more effective contacts with prospects

291

still unsold. Demand creation is transformed into a problem of physical supply. The problem of offering the commodity to the consumers at the time and in the place where it is needed or is able to suggest its need influences all the prior activities of the business. The safety razor, for example, becomes a gold-plated birthday or Christmas gift and thus breaks into the jewelry store where such gifts are bought.

PART III
THE PROBLEMS OF ADMINISTRATION

CHAPTER XVIII

PLANT AND OPERATION POLICIES

GOING back to our fundamental classification of business activities, it will be recalled that these activities divide into three main groups according to their purposes. In production the object is to change the form of the materials, in distribution to change their place, and in administration to facilitate these other changes. Despite the sharp cleavage of functions, it is only in exceptional cases that a clean-cut division of activities into three coördinate groups is found in actual practice.

The "general" departments which concern themselves severally with finance, purchasing, employment, credits, collections, accounting and auditing are frequently recognized as a separate administrative group. Seldom, however, is it realized that their distinctive function of facilitating operations demands unit handling under a common executive, with authority corresponding to that of the factory superintendent and sales manager in their respective fields. Instead, the departments report individually to the head of the business; more often than not the work of one or more of them is under his immediate supervision.

This retention of control is a survival from the time when small-scale production allowed the manager to guide all the operations of his business. The man who owns and runs a neighborhood saw mill, for example, performs all important functions himself, except perhaps actual direction of the sawing. He buys and measures his logs himself or takes orders for sawing on commission. Daily he indicates what timber is to be converted into lumber and what sizes are to be produced. He "waits" on customers and receives their cash in payment or agrees to give them credit until they market their wheat or corn or hay. He makes a memorandum of the sale, carries a ledger account with the purchaser, and either sends him statements until the bill is paid or goes out collecting when he needs funds to meet his pay roll or some other necessity. He "hires and fires" helpers as occasion may demand. He secures personal loans from the bank to tide over his busy season or makes shift to worry through on his own capital. If he has a problem in office management, it is only to decide whether or not he needs a girl to answer the telephone and keep his few accounts.

As a business develops from this simple type, the problems of administration, of facilitating and keeping control of all important operations, grow in number and significance. Because head sawyers and mill foremen are relatively easy to find, the lumberman whose business is expanding surrenders first his supervision of manufacturing activities. Next, if the growth continues, he finds himself so occupied with buying, financing, credits, and the like that he turns the marketing over to a sales manager. But even when his undertaking has grown to the point where individual executives look after most of the administrative functions, the owner will probably continue personal buying of stumpage and financing of new operations without considering how concentration on these activities forces him to neglect others equally essential.

In a word, as the division of labor is carried further and further in the activities of production and of distribution, the control of operations becomes increasingly complex. The pieces on the chessboard of business are multiplied and the final result depends more and more on the way in which each piece is manipulated to further the general plan. The necessity of coördinating and supervising the countless resulting details compels the management to deal with paper representations of the materials, motions, and relations involved instead of directly with the things themselves.

The possibility of thus keeping in touch with the significant activities of a business has the further effect of enlarging organizations and the scale of operations. And finally, the scope and complex character of business and the distance of the controlling executives from the things controlled put such a premium on efficiency in all these facilitating activities, that the principle of the division of labor is extended and the classification and organization of functions follow as a matter of course.

The introduction of machinery for compiling and assorting statistics, for writing reports, tabulating information, and checking mental calculations indicates how great is this increase in administrative activities. The need, therefore, is imperative for an organized method of bringing them all together, of establishing their relations, and of holding them at such distance from the executive that no one of them will exercise undue influence on his decisions, — in short, a method of keeping them in balance with all the other activities of the business.

AN APPROACH TO BUSINESS PROBLEMS

The tardy discovery of a common purpose in their functions is probably due to belated analysis. It is only within the last twenty years, indeed, that they have begun to take on real importance and acquire a separate entity. In the small or medium-sized business the usual practice is to associate some of them with the factory or sales organization and to retain others under the eye of the executive. Only the larger concerns, facing the urgent problem of keeping them all effective and under control, have set them apart as a group of auxiliary functions directly related with but impossible to classify as activities of either production or distribution. The Taylor system puts extraordinary emphasis on facilitating activities, particularly those which directly affect production. In the average factory, however, a sharp line is drawn between "productive" and "nonproductive" labor and effort is made to keep the latter at a minimum.

Confronted with this multiplicity of motions and operations, the manager, as well as the student of business, finds that some scheme of classification is necessary to make their relations clear. When we inquire their purpose, their common character as the facilitating activities of business comes out immediately. Pursuing the analysis along the lines already made familiar, we find that they break up into two groups concerned with plant and operating functions. As before, the first group subdivides according as the functions relate to location, construction, or equipment of what might be called the "office plant."

Adopting again the method of approach used in analyzing the activities of production and distribution, the manager finds that many of the policies governing this first group of activities were solved when the corresponding policies for the factory and sales units were determined, because the mutual relations of administration and the other two groups are even closer than those between production and distribution. In plant location, for instance, we saw in an earlier chapter that nearness to sources of materials and supplies was a positive requisite in a great many industries. Automatically, then, the location of the purchasing department would be fixed by the same considerations. In no other way can such effective coördination between manufacturing and purchasing policies be secured as when the production heads and the buyer are in daily and friendly contact.

Even when the important markets for materials are distant, the sales departments of the supply concerns are alert to anticipate the wants of customers and prospects and to keep them informed of all changes in prices and conditions. The isolated purchasing agent, it is true, misses his full share of the occasional bargains in staples which the emergency needs of supply houses provide for the man at the central market. He loses also the benefit of contact and exchange of ideas with other buyers both in trade gatherings and in the functional associations which are doing so much to standardize everyday practice.

By proper organization, however, he can unload the purchase of all but his most important lines on assistants and hold himself free for buying trips to the sources of these latter before he makes his seasonal or annual contracts. Meanwhile his presence at the factory allows him to draw on the counsel and information of the entire organization, from the manager's newest interpretation of a general buying policy to the gossip picked up by some department head whose knowledge of the market is too slight for him to give it relevance and value.

But the purpose of this chapter is no more than to analyze broadly the activities of administration and illustrate the manner in which the suggested approach can be applied to their solution. It is enough therefore to point out that the essential factors in facilitation — speed, accuracy, and minimum expense — are at their best when the administrative departments are physically near to the making or selling departments which they check and serve. Ability to have orders approved by the credit department with the least possible delay is an important aid to the sales force. Collection policies are likewise inseparable from future sales and from the present finances of the business. Employment activities must be responsive to the daily, almost hourly, requirements of both factory and sales divisions. Accounting, auditing, and statistical departments, by the character of their functions, must keep close on the track of all the other units in the three major divisions. In all these cases distance and elapsed time reduce efficiency and increase costs. Finance is the single exception to the rule of advantageous nearness, and this only when the amounts involved are too large to be handled safely and legally by any but metropolitan bankers or commercial-paper houses.

Sound business policy envisages many compromises, however. When conditions prescribe a separation of the manufacturing and marketing units, a corresponding grouping of the administrative departments according to the special affinity of each may be necessary, or frank division of each into local organizations for purchasing, employment, and those recording functions common to both production and distribution activities. Where branch houses are maintained, this division is carried even further, though the "home office" usually retains control over the district organization.

Construction and equipment policies in administration may be dismissed with a line. In the main, they parallel those of distribution so closely that there is no need of repeating that analysis here.

When we turn to the operating activities of administration, we see that they also split up in the accustomed way and range themselves under materials, labor, and organization. But there is this important difference: the materials of administration or facilitation — that to which motion is applied — are the paper representations of the functions which are performed. These paper representations are either *causal* (purchase or employment requisitions or shipping requisitions) or *resultant* (outgoing invoices, vouchers, and general and department records).

How this classification squares itself with current business practice may be easily tested. Purchase requisitions refer to plant and equipment or to materials and supplies, while employment requisitions have to do with labor. They originate in either the manufacturing, the distributing, or the facilitating activities of the business. The first group of functions centers in the purchasing agent, and labor brings us back to the employment bureau or to the officials who do the hiring for the production, sales, and office divisions. Besides the factory or finished stock departments which supply the products required to fill customers' orders, the shipping requisitions directly involve the credit man, who must approve the order before it is filled. On the resultant side, the outgoing invoices are the affair of the credit and collections departments. The vouchers represent the responsibilities of the financial end of the business, while the accounting, auditing, and statistical departments occupy themselves with the house records.

These various departments, or the executives and employees who perform the facilitating functions with which each is charged, are the agencies of administration. They correspond to labor in production, and to middlemen, direct salesmen, and advertising in demand creation. In considering their activities, the manager finds himself engaged with three different sets of problems.

The first group has to do with the broad policies involved in determining the "what" and "how" of facilitation. These are his affair, since he alone is able to decide what shall be the relations between the administrative department and the two other great divisions of the business. Nor can anyone else establish the proper balance between the speed, accuracy, and cost of the facilitation service. The object, of course, is to coördinate the work of each department with all the remaining activities of the business and to direct its internal activities only so far as is necessary to effect this coördination.

These internal departmental activities constitute the second group of administrative problems. They are detail in character and grow out of the need of expressing the manager's broad policies in the facilitating functions performed by each department and in its external contacts with all other departments. They are of lesser import to the manager for the reason that a competent department head usually assumes all responsibility for them. Once the main policies to be observed are laid down, he will be able, as a rule, to accommodate his internal policies to the same purposes.

The third class of problems is concerned with organization of the mechanics of administrative effort, with the smooth and effective working of the routine by which the general policies of the manager and the detail policies of the department heads are carried out. Perhaps because so many of the operations involved are the same or nearly the same in all the departments, the value of organization and standardization, with a common executive to look after the routine, has been generally recognized and an office manager given supervision over all but the special facilitating function of each department. This not only secures efficiency of operation, but also relieves the manager of the burden of settling minor disputes between executives reporting directly to him.

The manager's chief problem, of course, is to reconcile the frequently conflicting purposes of the administrative departments and of his factory and sales divisions. This is a task closely paralleling that of maintaining a uniform standard of cost, quality, and service in the activities of production and distribution when opposition of interests occurs.

By way of illustration, the purchasing agent, to whom price is a primary consideration, may insist on substituting for some specified material, tool, or supply requisitioned by the factory another which the state of the market allows him to buy at a bargain. Here either executive may be right. The cheaper material may not be fit for the use to which it will be subjected or the processes which it must undergo in manufacture, yet the production head may not be capable of demonstrating this fact to the buyer. On the other hand, the latter, through wider acquaintance with market resources, is often able to provide a better machine or material at the same price or one of equal quality at a lower price, but cannot persuade the factory executive to accept his judgment.

Both are specialists, concentrating on their characteristic functions, and with the specialist's inclination to see the transaction from no other viewpoint than his own. Friction naturally ensues unless the manager steps in and fixes a policy that overlooks no buying advantages which can be conserved without sacrificing factory efficiency or quality in the product. The recurrence of such situations and the consequent necessity of interpreting the same basic policies in terms of each fresh dispute constitute strong reasons for the organization of the facilitating departments into a separate division under its own executive, with authority coequal with that of the sales manager and the factory head.

This, of course, is one solution of the manager's problem of organization, of keeping control of the operations of administration without undertaking a load of detail or abandoning his strategic position apart. Though the general problem parallels that of organization in distribution, the nature of the primary departmental functions makes the matter of control more complicated. In distribution — and in production, too, for that matter — each activity leads up to the next in order, and all focus on the final transfer of the goods to the consumer. In administration each department is an independent unit dealing direct, so far as its main function goes, with the making or selling group.

Within the department the technique of this function is generally well understood. It remains for the manager to define the policies which shall govern its application, to determine how the department shall divide or concentrate its operation, and to lay down rules which will insure coöperation with all the other units of the organization.

The character and scale of the business help to define the scope and function of each department. As the organization increases in size, these activities take on added importance both because of the volume involved and because there is less of personal contact between department heads. Hence it is that many concerns have taken the initial step toward the ideal here suggested and have transferred the departments handling them from production or distribution to an administration division.

Nothing more than a glance at these functions and the policies which guide them is possible. The purchasing department, for instance, has as its chief responsibility to keep available at all times a sufficient supply of the materials and equipment required by production. The kind of materials, the qualities, the quantities to be kept on hand, even the terms on which they may be bought are all dictated, wholly or in part, by the management's policies in production, distribution, and finance.

Absolute standards may be set not only for the kind and quantity of materials but for all classes of equipment and supplies. Or within the limits fixed by the general policies of the management on cost, quality, and service to the customer, the buyer may exercise wide discretionary power in his choice of materials or his substitution of one machine or supply for another. He may be a mere clearing house for quotations or he may be a powerful factor in production costs.

Sometimes this depends on the latitude allowed by the manager, but oftener on the buyer's own departmental policies, on the adequacy or inadequacy of his records, on his knowledge of market shifts and of the basic conditions behind them, on his acquaintance with technical processes, his progressiveness in adapting new materials to the uses of his plant, his information about the individual situations of his suppliers, his ability to keep his stocks in balance and to secure the low market price without overbuying. The human factor also counts. His attitude toward salesmen is reflected in their formal dealings with him or in "good buys" and friendly "leads" on sources in non-competing lines. His tact and skill is shown in reconciling the standards fixed by "the front office" with the demands of department heads. All these are matters of internal, departmental policy, it is true, but none the less they are expressions of the wise manager's buying policies.

So, also, with the employment head. Like the purchasing agent, his first function is supply, to establish and maintain touch with sources from which he can draw all the various classes of labor required by the production, sales, and administrative divisions, in both executive and in clerical or workman types. Besides this initial contact, he has in many organizations a continuous contact with such of the rank and file as are susceptible of development through training courses and through shifting to more responsible positions as their capacities increase. In the average organization, he surrenders the function of development to the department executives, retaining only authority to transfer men who are obviously misplaced and to find other positions for men with whom departments are dissatisfied.

It is not within his province to designate how men shall be managed or made more efficient or paid. These are policies which the manager of the business determines, as a rule, in direct consultation with the production, distribution, and administration executives. It is the practice in a great many organizations, however, to give the employment head a degree of negative control over these relations between bosses and men. No workman, for instance, can be discharged without a review of the case and the reasons for his discharge by the employment head. If injustice has been done him, the fault is remedied, whether the routine or the individual boss was to blame. Labor "turn-over" is recognized as having a significant relation to production efficiency; one of the functions of the employment department is to hold it down and make the most of available labor by transfers and "lay-offs" instead of dismissals for extra hands.

As to the qualifications of the men to be hired, the manager may well set up standards to be observed, physical, mental, and moral. Quality men make for quality products and satisfactory relations with customers. Here, again, the character of the business and the kind of work to be done are imperative factors in the choice. Above all, the wise manager will insist that the men to be hired must harmonize with the prevailing type already in the business; otherwise friction is sure to arise.

Many organizations, indeed, make it a rule to fill all positions of even minor responsibility by promotion from within, sacrificing the occasional advantage to be had by hiring competent executives or specialists from outside in order to secure harmony in operation, observance of house policies, and the incentive to self-development which a policy of promotion always supplies. It is interesting to note, also, that in a business where everybody is congenial and intensely interested in his work, the outside man of different character or standards who will not fall into line and adopt the organization spirit is in many cases indirectly "fired" by the other employees.

It is difficult, in considering the various agencies of administration, to indicate even the outstanding problems and policies, without exceeding the bounds set for a single chapter in the book. The functions of the credit department, in fact, alone would furnish material for a chapter, so many and intimate are its relations with the activities of distribution and so important its influence on finance. It is the primary office of the credit man not only to keep selling safe, but to hold the number of rejected accounts at a minimum consistent with an average loss from bad debts agreed upon with the management as a standard allowance. His function is, indeed, not negative, but positive and causal, since favorable action in every possible case is the aim and favorable action results in the exchange of goods in the finished stock room for the customer's promise to pay. This promise becomes an asset in the business, its value depending, first, on the customer's ability to pay, and second, on the customer's willingness to pay promptly when the obligation falls due.

PLANT AND OPERATION POLICIES

Now the same customer's ability to pay and willingness to pay promptly may vary widely on different credit bases. Here the general policy of the manager comes in as a defining element. This may be one of great liberality, with terms and payments so arranged that the chief concern of the credit man is with the honesty and business ability of the buyer rather than with his immediate assets. On the other hand, caution and exact adherence to trade usages may be the rule. Between these extremes, any one of many combinations of strict dealing and consideration for the customer may be required by the nature of the product, the character of customers, general or seasonal market conditions, and the internal situation of the business itself.

To make the first policy practicable, for instance, ample working capital, a wide margin of profit, a strongly competitive selling situation, a limited number of prospects, and salability or earning power on the part of the product might all be necessary. A steam shovel or motor truck might be sold to a young contractor on terms which would allow earnings to take care of all payments after the initial deposit, if the buyer's character were above question and his record indicated experience in excavation or transportation work. The product in this case would not be consumed and might be reclaimed on default of payments. An inflexible credit policy might be required when the profit margin is small, the unit price low, a great number of customers involved, and capital none too abundant; or, again, when consumer advertising has created such demand for the product that dealer-customers have little choice but to stock it and pay for it on the manufacturer's terms.

Departmental policies likewise reflect the ideals or decisions of the manager. A friendly attitude toward customers and prospects, for instance, tact in making inquiries, in explaining the conditions on which credit can be granted or the reasons why it must be refused, or advice to buyers on the conduct of their businesses and the elimination of practices and risks which limit their buying power. Again, speed in passing on orders to expedite service and aid the sales department, maintenance of competent records and use of every available source of information to determine the exact status of each proffered account, including, perhaps, interchange of ledger records with other firms, either direct or through trade or local associations. And, finally, co-ordination of credit policies with those of the sales department, to the end that no order shall be refused when a plan can be devised for making its acceptance safe, and no prospect or salesman shall be antagonized through his failure to understand the reason for the refusal of an order when such a course is necessary.

Between credits and collections the relations are so close and the interdependence so absolute that both functions are usually handled by a single department until the volume of transactions makes their separation advisable. When a credit account passes maturity, it becomes a collection; but the policies which direct its subsequent handling are much the same as in credits. There is, however, this important difference: consideration for the past-due customer stops short of that shown the prospect seeking credit. In the latter case only potential profits, balanced by an element of risk, are involved; in the former, the assets of the seller are directly at stake and his right to recover them is recognized as paramount even by the debtor. The process of "gentling" ceases, therefore, as soon as it becomes evident that some unexpected cause, like a crop failure, an industrial disturbance, or some personal misfortune is not to blame for the delinquency. Recourse is had to sterner methods, ending with an appeal to the law, if the amount involved is large enough and the debtor is possessed of assets sufficient to satisfy the expected judgment and costs.

The handling of past-due accounts, indeed, puts forward problems as difficult and important as the granting of credits. To help the debtor to pay, rather than to exact his pound of flesh, is the policy of the forward-looking manager. At no stage of the negotiations, short of the appeal to the courts, does he leave action to the discretion of any outside agency; or, indeed, entirely to the decision of his own collections head.

Of all the activities of administration, control of finance is the last which the average manager surrenders. The money end of the business has long been recognized as his peculiar province, and it is only in very advanced organizations that he has the courage and wisdom to put it in its proper departmental place. His policies, of course, must guide the treasurer or whatever official assumes the function of providing and protecting the necessary capital at the lowest possible cost and the corollary function of maintaining the right balance between too much capital in dull periods and too little in rush seasons.

The financial needs of a business are twofold: (1) plant or fixed capital, which usually goes into the land, buildings, machinery, and other fixed assets necessary to the business; and (2) operating capital, need for which grows out of the activities of other administrative divisions, purchasing, employment, and credits. Fixed capital obviously is invested money; operating capital is usually composed of invested money, loans made from banks or private persons, and frequently also undivided earnings.

After the first capital needs of his business are satisfied, the problem of the manager is to establish the most efficient balance between the invested and borrowed portions of his working capital. The latter must vary with the seasonal rise and fall of sales and changing general conditions which may require long credits to customers one year and allow them to discount their bills the next. It is recognized as safe and profitable policy to let borrowed capital carry the peak loads provided by the seasonal and extraordinary demands and to maintain the invested portion at the point where it will take care of ordinary needs and permit of at least an annual "cleaning up" of loans. Banks usually require this, indeed, except in the case of rapidly expanding undertakings or concerns with an overwhelming preponderance of security in the way of fixed assets and raw or finished stock. Not a few businesses, with reserves large enough alone to carry the peak loads, keep these invested in marketable securities as an emergency fund and make short-time loans to satisfy temporary extra requirements. The larger the element of risk involved, the higher the rate of interest this temporary capital will command.

All this assumes, of course, adequate initial capital for the undertaking. It is not too much to say that four in every five American industries are launched on the basis of hopeful selling possibilities rather than on that of employing capital seeking an outlet. The manager's big financial problem for many years is to secure money to meet immediate requirements and to care for necessary extensions at the factory and in the field.

It is not uncommon to find all the other activities of the business subordinated to this one problem of keeping a working balance in the treasury. The plant is rented, power is taken from a service company, equipment and materials are bought on terms rather than price, castings are purchased outside to avoid investment in a foundry, the economies of lot production are sacrificed to a made-to-order schedule, the products turned out are those which can be sold in the shortest time, heavy discounts are given for cash, all except the indispensable functions of distribution and administration are eliminated or performed in some fashion by the manager himself. The average small venture, indeed, offers a striking demonstration of the interdependence of all the activities of business and the influence of that which seems most remote on the problem immediately in hand.

Besides the function of securing capital, the manager must lay down broad policies for the protection of that which he is using. His long look ahead must include the future needs of the business. Funds must be provided beforehand to meet contemplated expenditures for extensions in production or sales, else working capital will suffer. Insurance must cover factors of risk such as fires, accidents, and customer failures, in order to safeguard capital and command the lowest market rates on loans.

For the same reason, such a balance must be maintained between liabilities and quick assets as will satisfy the banks that their loans are safe and a low rate of interest justified. That other important element in finance, credit with supply sources of materials, equipment, and service must also be protected by prompt payment of all accounts, since the resources thus made available more than compensate for the obligations involved. The governing policies of the manager necessarily include the coördination of activities in credits, purchasing, employment, and all other departments whose conduct affects finance. The routine by which these guiding policies are carried out may be left to the treasurer or other official responsible for them.

It is hardly possible to speak definitely of managerial policies toward the records of a business. These fall into four groups each having a common function or purpose. (1) Accounting has for its objects the more or less mechanical recording of the operations of a business in terms of a common unit and the matching of expenditures for motions and materials with the results of those motions and materials in their converted form. (2) Auditing provides a system of checks and queries on expenditures to make sure that they have been properly recorded and charged to the department benefiting by them and to guarantee that a fair equivalent has been received for each dollar paid out, whether for materials or the motions applied to them. (3) Cost-keeping involves a classified analysis of expenditures for unit operations and groups of operations and a comparison of such expenditures with the returns therefrom. The form of this comparison shall emphasize variations from the normal standard, since these demand the attention of the manager. Occasional "sample" analyses may suffice for minor processes; daily costs on the major or governing operations are necessary to keep the manager informed of significant changes. (4) Statistics consider the records, cost of operations, and the commercial returns from a prophetic rather than a historical point of view. Their purpose is to forecast the future in the light of the past, to trace the relation of past costs to possible future costs and attainable results, and to fix standards and quotas for unit and grouped operations, expenditures, and incomes.

As constructive factors in administration, all these records are developments of the last twenty years or less. Even in the late '90s, it was the exception rather than the rule to find a cost-keeping system which was more than a collection of accurate figures on materials and arbitrary guesses at the value of the labor and "overhead" expense involved. Accounting had hardly been carried past the stage where its records meant anything but a stupid history of purchases and sales, of outgo and income. I recall examining one set of purchase books in which every item bought for nearly fifteen years had been entered in chronological order: item, one Remington typewriter; item, one car load of pig's stomachs; item, one hundred pounds of Babbitt metal. But no attempt had ever been made to classify purchases or to bring together materials or supplies of the same character in order that the management might know the relations between total purchases of any kind and the total product resulting from them.

Even to-day it is common practice to maintain accounting, cost, and statistical records which have no logical place or purpose in the controlling scheme of the business. Yet purpose here is the decisive test, as it is in determining the value or worthlessness of any other motion or operation in business. With such a test, "What is the purpose of this record?" it is possible to classify and to coördinate or combine all useful records, and to eliminate those which have no practical value.

Nine years ago, when cost accounting was on the first crest of its vogue, the president of a large mid-western company reduced his cost department from twenty-five to five men by proposing this test of purpose for every record that was being kept. Instead of a separate cost ticket on each standard machine made, for instance, sample costs were run on only one job in every fifty to check and insure manufacturing efficiency, since no other reason existed for cost-keeping in this particular case. And so on through the whole top-heavy structure, conceived in a specialist's enthusiasm for recording every detail, whether it was useful or merely curious.

The most important thing in any system of records, then, is that it should be a means, not an end. The purpose being facilitation, no method or record should be employed which does not actually forward the activities of the business. The records should fit the business, not the business the records. They should grow out of its operations and necessities rather than be superimposed from the top. At the same time, it must be borne in mind that the scope and functions of records increase so rapidly as a business expands that sooner or later the point is reached where the recording functions must be organized and coördinated if the manager is to retain control of operations.

The strategic position for the manager, as we have already seen, is one free from the routine of any department yet in touch with the significant details of all. From no other viewpoint can he secure a clear vision of his business, protect himself from department bias, and overcome a tendency to lay too much stress on the activities which are most familiar or most interesting to him. I do not mean that the head of a business must withdraw himself from contact with all details in order to keep his perspective. In innumerable small businesses the owner-manager is of necessity the sales manager or factory superintendent, the advertising manager or the purchasing agent, to say nothing of his handling the finance and perhaps of credits and collections.

It is to just such a man that the classification of business activities here proposed should be most suggestive, since it emphasizes as of equal importance with the organization of production and distribution the coördination of those facilitating activities which are frequently administered haphazard because the consequences of neglect are slower to appear. In the large business also the management deals with details, but only with symptomatic details. The popular conception of the head of a big enterprise is of a man engaged in transactions involving millions of dollars. Yet in a business of great size it may be a mere matter of routine to put a note for one hundred thousand dollars in the bank, while the question of making a change in the product which would add or subtract only a fraction of a cent in cost may be a significant detail which the head himself must handle because it might affect some function of the product or some quality which commends it to its public. The big business man, therefore, is constantly concerned not with routine trifles but with symptomatic details.

Acceptance and use of this classification does not

necessarily mean the formal partition of an organization into production, distribution, and administration divisions, though such a plan of organization in effect is successfully employed by leading American industries. The purchasing agent may remain a factory official; the experimental department may continue to work under the sales manager; and so on. The important thing is that the manager himself should recognize that these activities are of interest not only to the factory and the sales department but to the entire organization.

Viewed thus, their oversight and direction are as essentially the manager's concern as supervision of making and selling operations. By *placing* them, as facilitating activities related to the whole business, on a par with the activities of production and distribution, the scheme of classification set forth in this volume gives the manager the correct focus and a rational approach to the problems arising from them. The first service of any good classification, indeed, is to allow the man using it to back away from the things with which he is immediately occupied and to see all the activities involved in their true relations and proportions. This strategic position, aloof from details (or at least recognizing them as details), leaves him free to sense the broader problems which changing conditions and increasing social control of private enterprises are proposing for his solution.

CONCLUSION

CHAPTER XIX

THE EXTERNAL PROBLEMS OF BUSINESS

IF the vital relations of any business were charted, its internal and external activities might be represented as two circles impinging upon one another, with the management on the alert at the point of contact. The internal problems would arise out of the interrelations of the activities of production and distribution and of what we have been calling administration, for lack of a better name. The external problems would have to do, first, with the special public the business is concerned with, its customers and prospective customers, its direct and potential competitors, and the general body of labor from which it draws its workers, executives, salesmen, clerks, and factory operatives. And outside this circle, another much larger might be traced to indicate the relations of the business with the general public. Included in this larger group also would be the individuals making up the special public of the business and the members of its organization. For the attitude even of employees is affected by their social judgment of the business, its methods, and its aims.

Unless he is blind or obstinate, the business man of to-day must realize that he is no longer autocrat of a private undertaking, able to base his policies on personal whim or desire or an entirely selfish conception of business. Just as society is asking of its college men what return in community service they are making for the exceptional training advantages accorded them, public opinion is beginning to put the same query to business men in sharper and more specific fashion.

"Here," society says, "you have been given opportunities and advantages in your business such as no body of men at any other stage of the world's progress ever enjoyed. You have raw materials, fuel, and supplies that are cheap, abundant, and of excellent quality. You have machinery of surpassing ingenuity and capacity, able to perform almost any task you set for it at a cost amazingly slight. You have labor of exceptional intelligence to direct and supplement the functions of these machines. You have a comprehensive transportation system which allows you to locate where land is low in price and buildings can be cheaply constructed, yet makes a great continent available as a market for your product and a source for your supplies of labor, materials, and equipment.

"Almost every necessary element and favorable condition you could ask are provided for you. You have only to supply the organizing ability which will pick out the right product to make or sell, and choose the right materials, the right equipment, the right location, the right method of marketing. Over against your organizing ability and capital, I set these contributions of mine. What, besides the market minimum of value and service at the price, are you going to supply as *my* profit on my investment of community machinery and opportunity?"

Without formulating its approach to the problem, the public has been applying more and more inclusively the basic test of purpose to the activities of business men. It has come to feel that the large margin of profit hitherto allowed permits them to practice many of the mere "arts of commerce." It has sensed the existence of useless motions, observed the needless duplication of essential functions, and in some cases, as, for example, the establishment of a 'government parcel post to carry package freight in competition with the express companies, it has sought a drastic short cut to a fairer balance between service and cost.

In other instances it has adopted milder measures of regulation and adjustment, as in the work of the Interstate Commerce Commission, the Federal Trade Commission, the Federal Reserve Board, and the activities of state and local boards for the supervision of trade and industry. It is from this attitude of society, crystallizing after long agitation into definite policies of regulation, that arise what may be termed the external problems of business. They are of growing importance, of immediate importance, indeed; and no discussion of business policies would be complete without some effort to analyze them and suggest how their solution may be approached.

In dealing with both the general public and his special public, the manager is not so much concerned with the immediate activities observed as with the actuating motives which they express. When he begins studying the public and its relations with his own undertaking, he finds that he must first take account of the motives likely to influence the various social groups or strata to action favorable or unfavorable to his purposes. The comfort his employees enjoy in pleasant, well-lighted, and well-ventilated work rooms, for instance, is likely to reflect itself in a community esteem which will have a favorable influence on local sales and on the attitude of that section of the public from which he must draw his workers. A practical classification of the public, then, might be based, first, on the relations of the business with the various strata, and next on the common motives which will permit group handling and group control.

All this has to do with the business as an individual enterprise, apart from all other concerns and responsible only for its own actions. But the manufacturer or merchant must reckon now with the public's changing attitude toward all business, toward the particular industrial or trade group to which his concern belongs, toward the special form of organization which he has adopted. For a long time the fullest measure of competitive freedom for the individual was the rule, on the theory that society was best served when every man's initiative was given full play. As the possibilities of organization, coördination, and integration in the industries and trades became clear, the wisdom of an extreme *laissez faire* policy began to be questioned. As a consequence, the management to-day faces a whole series of external problems which did not exist until these new social forces were set in motion.

To solve the problems he must understand the motives which control them and must be able to establish their specific relations with his undertaking. The function of the classification proposed in this volume, indeed, is not only to allow him to see all the activities of his business in proper perspective and to allocate his internal problems as they arise, but also to enable him to value the external conditions affecting them and to adjust his internal policies before the possibility of reconciling them has passed by.

THE EXTERNAL PROBLEMS OF BUSINESS

In determining the policies which shall govern his relations with the general public, the business man will recognize three modifying influences — or three phases of the same powerful influence — to which he must accommodate his activities. Of these, the hardest to understand, yet the real force to reckon with, is *public opinion*, the reaction of contemporary thought or emotion or ethical sense upon the activities of business and the conditions under which they are carried on.

The *law* is the second influence. But law is simply the crystallization of public opinion into a definite enactment; while the *government*, the third influence, is no more than an administrative agency for putting this formulated public opinion into effect.

The wise man is the man who keeps abreast of public opinion, who detects the changing viewpoint of the country or the community and so modifies his individual business practice that he later coöperates with rather than opposes the operations of the law or the machinery of the government. The average business man, however, is so submerged in the details of his undertaking that he either fails to catch the drift of public opinion or does not realize its vital bearing on his business. Not until the law formulating this public opinion is enacted or is about to be enacted does he awake to its purport. Then he discovers that the people, through various civic organizations, have been studying the underlying question much longer than he had suspected.

Public opinion is the fundamental force, yet even now business men are more intent apparently upon the interpretation of the law and the attitude of the government than upon developments in the public mind. Watching all the legislative, judicial, and administrative machinery in motion, the manager of a business may too readily conclude that his important external problems are concerned chiefly with it, not with smoking car debates, the gossip of a switch shanty or the discussion of a woman's club. But it is this talk and the convictions which emerge from it that are the things he must consider.

The passage of the Interstate Commerce Act in 1887, for instance, was the first positive break in a long-continued policy of federal encouragement of private enterprise, particularly evident in the subsidies and land grants to railroads and the protective tariff for the fostering of industries. The Sherman Anti-Trust Law followed in 1890, but a dozen years were to elapse before court decisions, defining the jurisdiction of the Interstate Commerce Commission and the inclusive scope of the Sherman law, emphasized the principle of control underlying both enactments.

No better illustration could be cited of the power of public opinion to modify the established law as interpreted by the courts and administered by the government. The Commerce Act as adopted expressed the current feeling that discriminations in railroad rates for or against individual shippers or communities constituted a menace to the business of the country. The Sherman law was quite as definite in its attack on contracts and combinations in restraint of trade. But neither effected any radical change in the practices they were aimed at until the courts and the national government began to feel the pressure of a more thoroughly aroused public sentiment a full decade later. Had the railroads taken cognizance of this public opinion and reshaped their rate and traffic policies in accord with it, they might have been spared some of their troubles in the last seven or eight years.

This pressure has continued and grown stronger. Witness, among other effects, the decisions of the United States Supreme Court dissolving the Northern Securities Company and the oil and tobacco combinations, canceling the exclusive anthracitic coal contracts, affirming the right of the Interstate Commerce Commission to fix general or zone rates on its own initiative, and declaring the constitutionality of the long and short-haul clause of the Commerce act. On the administrative side, also, there are the defensive suit pending against the International Harvester Company, which hinges on the ability of that concern to throttle competition rather than on any actual efforts to that end, the inquiry into the internal efficiency and policies as well as the trade conduct of the United States Steel Corporation, the successful attacks on the methods of discouraging competition employed by the "bathtub trust," and other virtual monopolies maintained through control of basic patents.

And, finally, the legislative program of the Sixty-third Congress included the Clayton law, defining unfair trading practices, and the act establishing the Federal Trade Commission, the latter standing toward business in general in much the same relation as the Interstate Commerce Commission stands toward the railroads and the shippers of the country. As this chapter is written (November, 1915), the first important suit to enforce the Clayton law has been begun at St. Louis, the sales contracts and price-fixing methods of the United Shoe Machinery Company being under fire as unlawful practices that lessen competition and promote monopoly.

AN APPROACH TO BUSINESS PROBLEMS

This increasing concern of the federal and state governments with business practices opens up a new vista of external problems to the manager. They have to do with four general groups of business relations now under scrutiny or already under control: (1) the form and size of organizations and their relations with other organizations, outside the buying and selling of products or services; (2) the relations of a business with its employees; (3) its relation with customers; and (4) the responsibility of individual officers for corporation acts.

Under the first heading come the suits for the dissolution of combinations like the American Tobacco, Standard Oil, and Northern Securities companies, the prohibition of interlocking directorates and of ownership through single stock control of competing business, the forbidding of pooling and price-fixing agreements between normally competing concerns, and the limitation of new security issues in the public utilities field by the various state boards for the regulation of such companies.

Government control of the relations of a business with its employees has taken shape largely in welfare legislation, like the workmen's liability and compensation laws now in force in a majority of the states, in the child-labor laws, in the laws limiting the hours of labor for women, and in the fire and sanitary building codes of the states and cities. The agitation for a minimum wage law based not on the ability of the worker to produce but on his living needs is evidence of a radical trend in public opinion which will have to be taken into account. Really an economic question, involving the elimination of the unfit worker "at the margin," it is so confused with human values that, as with so many other business problems, it may have to be decided on other than economic grounds.

The pure food law and the rate-making provisions of the Interstate Commerce Act are typical of the statutes directly affecting the relations of a business with its customers. The supervision of price-fixing, which is one of the main issues involved in the St. Louis federal suit against the United Shoe Machinery Company, the right of manufacturer to fix the resale price of his product, and the direct regulation of prices of products or services where the monopoly factor or a question of public policy enters in, are all questions still in process of settlement but offering serious external problems for the consideration of the business man.

How far the last function may go is illustrated by the recent Oklahoma law empowering the state Corporation Commission to regulate the price of petroleum and the volume of its production within the state. The Commission is directed to fix the actual value of crude oil by comparing the market prices of products with the cost of refining plus a fair profit, to limit production whenever the market price of crude oil fails to yield a profit on this basic figure, and to allot to each well owner his share of the current production allowed. In a word, the coöperative action forbidden to the well owners by the federal anti-trust laws is here assumed outright by the state and the control of his production and distribution activities is taken from the individual producer. That the intention is to aid him and prevent the demoralization of an industry does not decrease the significance of the act.

In the same category of undefined hazards is also the final attitude of the government and the law as to the responsibility of individual officials for the acts of the corporations which they control. On this point the law certainly lags behind public opinion; in time it is likely more closely to reflect public sentiment.

This trend toward government regulation of economic activities is a matter of growing concern to every manager. In the past, the average man has left the threshing out of proposed restrictive legislation or administrative orders to the larger commercial and industrial units, on the theory that their interests in the matter were so great that they could be trusted to represent his interests also, or for the more specific reason that usually he did not realize the importance of the question until it was brought to his attention by the action of these larger concerns. In the future, however, the attitudes of the national and state governments toward business are bound to have an increasing influence on the conduct of every factory and store.

No longer can the head of a small business leave the adjustment of his relations with the law, the government, and public opinion to the grace of his big neighbors or competitors or the zeal of the men who run his trade association. He must coöperate with his trade rivals and associates in conveying to the public in general and to the men who make and execute the laws an understanding of the activities, the relations, and the necessities of business. Otherwise ill-conceived or doctrinaire legislation will hamper the operations of trade and industry to such a degree that the burden of added expense, under the law of competitive business, will have to be passed along to the consumer.

Regulation must be intelligent; it must be at the hands of men who know the technique of business, who can distinguish between essential and non-essential activities, and can further the first while they are eliminating the latter. In self-defense, therefore, as well as for the sake of progress, every business man must begin to consider the shaping of legislation and the choice of administrative officials as external problems of his business.

The slogan "good enough is the enemy of the best" is written large upon the wall of one great American factory. It expresses the idea that must be carried, sooner or later, into every activity of business. Individual initiative will effect this standardization, just as it has accomplished the cheap refining of petroleum and steel. But society through its legislative and administrative machinery could provide wholesale short cuts to efficiency by organizing this questioning of methods, materials, and results, by directing and financing an unending search for the useless motion and extending it to all the operations of business.

There has been no lack of public inquiries, recently directed at various phases of trade and industry. They effected little, however, because they dealt only with phases, as in the recent government investigation of price maintenance, for instance, and failed to consider the problem in its broad relations with other problems. This because the investigators lacked an approach to the problems they were trying to solve, such a classification, perhaps, as we have been using here to determine the relations of business activities and to make our problems understandable.

We have seen, too, how this classification embodied the germ of efficiency by providing a test which will differentiate necessary from useless motions. It might

AN APPROACH TO BUSINESS PROBLEMS

also be employed in the government's analysis of trade
and industry as a whole, in order to determine for its
own use and for the individual business man's use what
motions are essential and what ones may be spared.
This, I think, is the big, undefined purpose behind our
unrelated public inquiries into business operations.
There is the feeling that waste and useless motions hold
the cost of doing business above the rightful level;
and investigation after investigation is launched in
response to public pressure to discover and remove the
cause.

Society, indeed, needs to know more about the activities of business, to realize their relations and inter-
dependences. Individually its members must understand that if useless motions are to be tracked down
and eliminated in order to reduce costs, consumers must
coöperate. Frequently they demand so much service
that the business man, forced to comply, is obliged to
increase his mark-up on delivered cost to keep his margin
safe. Such service means extra motions, extra equipment, extra labor. If a community or a class insists on
this extra service, it should understand that it must pay
for it.

When it exercises its collective function of law-
making, too, society must consider lest it lay on business
a burden of costly reports, unnecessary building or labor
restrictions, inequitable taxes and the like which business in turn must pass back to its members in their rôles
of individual consumers. When a satisfactory level of
efficient operations is worked out for trade and industry,
it will come through the common effort of business and
society to eliminate the countless useless motions that
exist to-day.

THE EXTERNAL PROBLEMS OF BUSINESS

Summed up, then, the business man has two distinct groups of problems to consider. In approaching and solving them he must keep always in mind the universal application of the principles of balance and of interdependence. He must remember that no question can be dealt with in the light of departmental requirements alone, or even as one affecting only production or distribution or administration policies. Instead, it must be handled as a matter involving many, perhaps all, of the other activities of his business. But more is necessary. He must not only perceive these contacts and establish right relations between activities within his organization and within the circle of his special public; he must also accommodate his policies and his practice with the convictions, and at times the sentiments, of the general public as finally expressed by the law and the administrative acts of the government. In a word, the external problems of business thus become internal problems in the sense that no intra-organization policy can safely be determined without taking into account the attitude of society toward the activities involved.